CW00832544

Child Law in Ireland

CHILD LAW IN IRELAND

By

Dr LYDIA BRACKEN

Published by
Clarus Press Ltd,
Griffith Campus,
South Circular Road,
Dublin 8.
www.claruspress.ie

Typeset by
Gough Typesetting Services,
Dublin

Printed by
SprintPrint
Dublin

ISBN
978-1-911611-09-7

A catalogue record for this book is available from the British Library

All rights reserved. No part of this publication may be reproduced,
or transmitted in any form or by any means, including recording and
photocopying, without the written permission of the copyright holder,
application for which should be addressed to the publisher. Written permission
should also be obtained before any part of the publication is stored in a
retrieval system of any nature.

Disclaimer
Whilst every effort has been made to ensure that the contents of this book
are accurate, neither the publisher and/or author can accept responsibility for
any errors or omissions or loss occasioned to any person acting or refraining
from acting as result of any material in this publication.

Copyright © Lydia Bracken 2018

FOREWORD

The vigorous growth of reforming legislation in the area of what can loosely be described as "family law" has mushroomed in recent years. In this book, *"Child Law in Ireland"*, Dr Lydia Bracken approaches the topic from the perspective of the child and provides the reader with an up-to-date and a concise analysis of the Irish child law system. The book addresses a wide range of child law topics including children's rights; parentage; donor-assisted human reproduction and surrogacy; guardianship, custody and access; an overview of child protection legislation and case law; representation and participation of children in proceedings which affect them; and education. Richard A Posner said that the best books for practicing lawyers, law students, and academic lawyers are books that judges should also read. This book is one of those books that we will all benefit from reading because it provides a very accessible overview of the many developments in both public and private child law issues in the last number of years including: the General Scheme of the Assisted Reproduction Bill 2017; the Children and Family Relationships Act 2015; the Adoption (Amendment) Act 2017; the Adoption (Information and Tracing) Bill 2016; the Children First Act 2015; and the Education (Admission to Schools) Bill 2016, among others. The author treats these topics comprehensively and cuts cleanly to the core of the issues involved.

Lydia is a lecturer and Director of Clinical Legal Education at the School of Law, UL. She is a graduate of UCC (BCL, 2010; LLM, 2011; PhD, 2015) and is also a barrister. Her PhD thesis examined the implications of "the best interests' principle" in the context of same-sex parenting in Ireland and she has a particular interest in "non-traditional" families and contemporary issues in family formation including surrogacy. Lydia combines both academic excellence and legal practice, yet has a very down to earth practical approach typified by her management and supervision of students involved in the Street Law project run by University of Limerick. This project is an innovative approach to legal education where law students teach law at grassroots level to allow them an opportunity to apply their "learned" black letter legal knowledge at university to raise awareness and educate secondary school pupils about the law, rights and legal system. This is not a "one way" exchange however as university law students develop clinical legal skills and ability to distil legal principles and put them into plain English in a clear and concise manner. This "win win" concept has been utilised by FLAC since the late 1960's and has enabled many, many newly qualified solicitors and barristers to develop these skills in the same way and the Street Law project takes this approach deeper providing undergraduates with opportunities for acquiring valuable transferrable skills.

In the same practical way, *Child Law in Ireland* provides the reader with knowledge and information in a well laid out and accessible manner. This book will serve as a welcome addition for both students and members of the different branches of the legal profession.

Judge Rosemary Horgan
President of the District Court
August 2018

PREFACE

Child law addresses the law as it relates to children and young people. It encompasses aspects of international human rights law, constitutional law, criminal law, the law of torts, medical law and equality law to name but a few. It engages various actors: the child, parents (both legal and social), members of the extended family, teachers, health care professionals, administrators, government officials and others. It also impacts on wider society as we all play an important role in the protection of children and in creating a social environment that embraces different family forms, respects personal choices, and values the voices of children within that society.

This book is written for those working within or studying the operation of Ireland's child law system. In each chapter, the book incorporates an examination of Ireland's international obligations under the United Nations Convention on the Rights of the Child (UNCRC) and the European Convention on Human Rights (ECHR), as well as examination of the Irish Constitution and the domestic legislative framework. This book addresses a wide range of child law topics including children's rights; parentage; donor-assisted human reproduction and surrogacy; guardianship, custody and access; child protection; representation and participation; and education. This book does not address all child law topics, for example child abduction or youth justice. Although both topics undoubtedly form part of Ireland's child law system, they are vast topics that raise issues concerning international law and the criminal process. As such, this concise book simply could not do justice to the myriad of issues arising in those areas. Experts in those fields have comprehensively addressed both topics elsewhere.

A number of changes have occurred in Irish child law in recent years. These changes are documented in each chapter of this book. The reform process makes child law a very interesting and dynamic area of practice and study, but equally, the absence of consolidated legislation in Ireland makes it difficult to keep up-to-date with the most recent developments. While every effort has been made to ensure that this book reflects the most recent developments in Irish child law, the law stated in this book is as it stood in April 2018. It has been possible to incorporate some changes that occurred after this date.

I would like to thank everyone who has supported the writing of this book. I am particularly grateful to David McCartney of Clarus Press for his advice and enthusiasm throughout the writing and publication process. I am also grateful to my colleagues at the School of Law, University of Limerick, for their collegiality and for fostering a wonderful working environment. I have had the benefit of working with, and learning from, many inspirational mentors and friends over the years and so I thank all of those who have shaped my understanding and knowledge of child law to date. Finally, I thank Gill, Caroline, Tim, Patrick and John for their unwavering support and encouragement, not only in the writing of this book, but in every endeavour that I take on.

Dr Lydia Bracken
July 2018

TABLE OF CONTENTS

TABLES OF CASES

TABLES OF LEGISLATION

TABLE OF CONVENTIONS

CHAPTER 1

INTRODUCTION

Child law addresses the law as it relates to children and young people. It entails both private and public dimensions creating a complex tapestry of laws that encompass children, families, society and the State. Children's rights are a fundamental part of this body of law. The United Nations Convention on the Rights of the Child (UNCRC) provides a comprehensive international framework for children's rights and sets important (albeit minimum) standards for the treatment of children. In this book, the provisions of the UNCRC that concern the areas of: parentage; guardianship; custody and access; adoption; child protection; representation and participation; and education, are considered alongside the Irish legal provisions in these areas to examine whether the rights of the child are fully vindicated under Irish law.

Although Ireland ratified the UNCRC in 1992, Ireland's "Children's Referendum" in 2012 brought the concept of children's rights to wider public attention throughout the country. The "Children's Referendum" was held with the aim of inserting a new Art 42A into the Irish Constitution to expressly recognise and protect the rights of the child. The referendum was passed and the amendment was signed into law in 2015.[1] Many assumed that the success of the referendum would herald a sea change for child law in Ireland, prompting greater scrutiny of legal provisions and, where necessary, impetus for reform of laws across the child law system. As this book will demonstrate, positive change has occurred in many areas since 2012. However, in some areas, reform has been slow and, arguably, not always designed in a manner that fully vindicates the rights of the child.

Among the positive changes in Irish child law, policy and practice prompted by the Children's Referendum was the establishment of the Child and Family Agency (Tusla).[2] Tusla is a "dedicated State agency responsible for improving wellbeing and outcomes for children."[3] It is responsible for many important services relating to children in areas including child protection, family support and education services. Article 42A has also been credited with instigating changes in policy, such as the introduction of *Better Outcomes, Brighter Futures: The National Policy Framework for Children & Young People 2014–2020*. This is an all-Government policy framework that establishes a shared set of outcomes for children and young people, towards which all government departments

---

[1] The result of the referendum campaign was subsequently challenged before the Irish courts which delayed the insertion of Art 42A into the Constitution.
[2] Tusla was established by the Child and Family Agency Act 2013.
[3] See: <http://www.tusla.ie/about>.

and agencies must work, to ensure a coherent response for children and young people. The policy identifies five national outcomes for children and young people, towards which efforts should be directed. The five outcomes for children are that they are:

1. Active and healthy, with positive physical and mental wellbeing;
2. Achieving their full potential in all areas of learning and development;
3. Safe and protected from harm;
4. Have economic security and opportunity;
5. Connected, respected and contributing to their world.[4]

Numerous legislative developments have also occurred since the referendum and proposals for law reform in a number of areas of child law have been put forward over the past number of years. These developments are discussed throughout each of the chapters in this book. For example, among other things, proposals to regulate assisted human reproduction and surrogacy in the Assisted Reproduction Bill 2017 are discussed in Chapter 3; reforms in the area of parentage and parental responsibility under the Children and Family Relationships Act 2015 are discussed in Chapters 3 and 4; changes to Ireland's adoption laws introduced by the Adoption (Amendment) Act 2017 are examined in Chapter 5; the Children First Act 2015 is discussed in Chapter 6; and proposals to amend the system of school admissions set out in the Education (Admission to Schools) Bill 2016 are considered in Chapter 8. In each chapter, Irish law and policy are benchmarked against international standards contained in the United Nations Convention on the Rights of the Child (UNCRC) and the European Convention on Human Rights (ECHR) and the existing law and proposals for reform are assessed against the obligations created by Art 42A of the Constitution.

Chapter 2 of the book addresses the topic of children's rights. In Ireland, children's rights are protected by a number of sources, including the UNCRC, the ECHR and the Irish Constitution (Bunreacht na hÉireann). These sources are outlined and discussed in Chapter 2. This discussion provides the basis for the evaluation of laws in later chapters.

The changing nature of parentage is examined in Chapter 3. This chapter outlines the legal provisions that apply in Ireland to determine who is regarded as a legal parent. The development of

---

[4] *Better Outcomes, Brighter Futures: The National Policy Framework for Children & Young People 2014–2020*, (Stationery Office 2014) p xiv.

assisted reproductive technologies has meant that, nowadays, a number of persons may be involved in the conception of the child. As such, it is argued that the traditional rules of parentage must be altered to accommodate these new family forms. The Children and Family Relationships Act 2015 recognises this by setting down specific rules of parentage that will apply where a child is conceived through donor-assisted human reproduction (DAHR). There is currently no specific legislation in place to regulate surrogacy in Ireland but the Assisted Reproduction Bill 2017 proposes to address this area. These developments are also considered.

Chapter 4 examines the law relating to guardianship, custody and access. It details changes introduced by the Children and Family Relationships Act 2015 and explains how the separate statuses or concepts operate within the Irish child law system. Article 42A.4.1° of the Irish Constitution requires that provision shall be made by law that in proceedings concerning the adoption, guardianship or custody of, or access to, any child, "the best interests of the child shall be the paramount consideration."[5] This provision is given legislative effect by s 3 of the Guardianship of Infants Act 1964, as amended by s 45 of the Children and Family Relationships Act 2015 (the "2015 Act").[6] Chapter 4 also examines the "best interests checklist" introduced by the 2015 Act to guide the determination of the best interests of the child as well as legislative provisions enacted to vindicate the right of the child to express his or her views in guardianship, custody and access proceedings.

Ireland's adoption laws are considered in Chapter 5. This chapter outlines the law as it applies to domestic adoption and intercountry adoption and examines the changing nature of adoption in Ireland. Although adoption continues to be a process that transfers parental responsibilities and rights from the birth parents to the adoptive family, there has been a move towards more "open" arrangements where the child can maintain some element of contact with the birth parents. However, the legacy of the traditional closed system of adoption is still felt in Ireland as adopted persons do not have any specific right of access to their birth records. The Adoption (Information and Tracing) Bill 2016 proposes to provide for a scheme whereby adoption information, including the information required to obtain a birth certificate, may be provided to an adopted person in certain circumstances and subject to conditions. The

---

[5] Bunreacht na hÉireann, Art 42A.4.1°.
[6] Guardianship of Infants Act 1964, s 3, amended by Children and Family Relationships Act 2015, s 45.

provisions of the Bill are assessed in Chapter 5, along with the recent changes introduced by the Adoption (Amendment) Act 2017.

Chapter 6 examines Ireland's system of child protection. This chapter includes an examination and critique of the use of the Child Care Acts 1991 to 2015, under which children may be taken into State care. Unfortunately, there are shortcomings in Ireland's child protection system which mean that vulnerable children do not always receive adequate alternative care in a timely manner. The main problems within the current system are addressed along with suggestions for reform where relevant. The guidance contained in *Children First: National Guidance for the Protection and Welfare of Children*[7] and the statutory obligations created under the Children First Act 2015 are also discussed as are the provisions of the National Vetting Bureau (Children and Vulnerable Persons) Act 2012. The chapter also examines the issue of corporal punishment as an aspect of violence against children.

The representation and participation of children in legal proceedings are discussed in Chapter 7. This chapter outlines the requirements of Art 12 UNCRC in respect of hearing the voice of the child and it examines the provisions that exist in Irish law to facilitate the representation and participation of children in public law proceedings. It is argued that child-friendly procedures, that is, procedures that allow the child to express his or her views, are vital but should not be adopted in isolation. Where legal proceedings are taken concerning a child, it is submitted that the judgment itself must be child-friendly. As such, this chapter also outlines the requirements and characteristics of a child-friendly judgment in order to illustrate the benefits of this form of decision-making.

Chapter 8 addresses the topic of education. Education is a broad topic that touches upon many different areas of child law. The issues that arise in education encompass aspects of constitutional law, the law of torts, employment law and criminal law among others. Ireland's education system has a strong constitutional dimension. This is because Art 42 of the Constitution establishes that parents are the primary and natural educators of their children, while the role of the State is established as a subsidiary one. Religion also plays a major role in the education system due to the fact that around 96 per cent of primary schools in the State are denominational schools. As such, issues arise concerning the role of religion in school admissions policies and in respect of the

---

[7]	Department of Children and Youth Affairs, *Children First: National Guidance for the Protection and Welfare of Children* (2017).

constitutional right of children to opt-out of religious education under Art 44.2.4° of the Constitution. These and other issues are discussed in Chapter 8.

Finally, Chapter 9 offers some considerations for the future of Ireland's child law system and revisits some of the most pressing issues requiring future reform to ensure that the child law system fully vindicates all of the rights of Irish children.

Taken together, each chapter in this book provides a broad and accessible analysis of the Irish child law system. Each of the Chapters demonstrate the developments that have taken place in the child law system in recent years and include analysis of the most recent reforms and proposals for reform in the area under discussion. However, it is clear that in each of the areas under discussion some element of future reform is required. The need for future reform is underlined by the recommendations of the Committee on the Rights of the Child in its concluding observations on Ireland's combined third and fourth periodic reports, discussed in Chapter 2. Among other things, the Committee has made recommendations to the Irish State in respect of: the implementation of the right of the child to have his or her best interests taken as a primary consideration; assisted reproduction and surrogacy; promoting respect for the views of the child; information disclosure and family tracing in adoption; social work emergency services; and the role of religion in the education system.[8] These issues are addressed throughout this book as areas for potential future reform. The aim of each discussion is to identify ways to achieve a child law system that fully vindicates all of the rights of the child and, ultimately, lives up to the aspirations of the Children's Referendum.

---

[8] Committee on the Rights of the Child, *Concluding observations on the combined third and fourth periodic reports of Ireland* (March 2016).

INTERNATIONAL AND NATIONAL PROTECTION OF CHILDREN'S RIGHTS

Introduction

Children are rights-holders. They enjoy rights in a variety of contexts, such as in matters of health, education, family life, play and recreation, and protection from abuse and harm. Child-specific rights allow children to grow and develop in a safe and age-appropriate manner through all stages of life. The value in recognising that children have independent rights lies in the fact that where there are rights, there are corresponding duties. As Raz has proposed, "a law creates a right if it is based on and expresses the view that someone has an interest which is sufficient ground for holding another to be subject to a duty."[1] The recognition of children's rights acknowledges the interests of children and places corresponding duties on others to fulfil them. It is much harder for children to assert their interests than it is for adults and so it is important for their rights to be expressly set out to ensure that they are not overlooked.

The recognition of children as rights-holders is a central tenet of child law and of the arguments that will be raised in each chapter of this book. In Ireland, children's rights are protected by a number of sources, most notably under the United Nations Convention on the Rights of the Child (UNCRC), the European Convention on Human Rights (ECHR) and the Irish Constitution (Bunreacht na hÉireann). Each of these sources will be discussed in this chapter. It is important to note, however, that there is some resistance to the recognition of children as independent rights-holders. As such, it is first necessary to consider those arguments before turning to examine the sources of children's rights.

Should Children Have Rights?

Some commentators argue that children do not need specific rights of their own. This contention is premised on the fact that children are human beings and therefore they benefit from all of the same rights that are bestowed upon adults and do not require their own specific rights. In addition, there is sometimes a fear that, in giving rights to children, we dilute the rights of adults and so children's rights should not be recognised so as to maintain parental authority.[2] In Ireland, for example, the "Children's Referendum"

---

[1] Joseph Raz, "Multiculturalism: A liberal perspective" (1994) *Dissent* 67.
[2] For discussion of some of these arguments see: Martin Guggenheim, *What's Wrong with Children's Rights* (Harvard University Press, Cambridge, Mass., 2005); and Michael Freeman, "What's Right with Rights for Children" (2006) 2 *International Journal of Law in Context* 89.

(which resulted in the insertion of a new Art 42A into the Irish Constitution to expressly recognise the rights of the child) was opposed by some voters as it was seen "as a threat to the rights of parents, specifically the right of parents to interpret what is best for their children."[3]

Children are in a position of vulnerability and this point is often used to argue that they require specific rights to protect them from harm. Indeed, a desire to protect children from harm was the driving force behind the earliest children's rights instruments, discussed later in the chapter. This protectionist stance is, of course, a rather paternalistic view of the child, and it should be noted that children's rights are not limited to protection, health, education and non-discrimination, but include the whole range of civil, political, social, economic and cultural rights.[4] These rights include those that protect children but also those that empower children and give them agency, such as rights to participation and self-determination.[5] Typically, it is these latter rights that give rise to concern by those who are opposed to the idea of children as rights-holders, as they are seen to involve the emancipation of children from adults and to weaken the position of the family. That said, Fox Harding notes that the first laws to restrict child labour and those providing for compulsory education were themselves initially resisted on the basis that they constituted an interference with family autonomy and decision-making.[6]

Children's rights do not, however, exist in a vacuum and do not require that that the rights of adults are abandoned. Further, given that in most cases children's rights can only realistically be enforced by adults, it could be argued that children's rights actually *strengthen* the adults' position. As Hardiman J noted in *N v Health Service Executive*

> "A right conferred on or deemed to inhere in a very young child will in practice fall to be exercised by another on his or her behalf. In practice, therefore, though such a right may be

---

[3]   Child Law Clinic (UCC) and Centre for Children's Rights (QUB), *Case Study: The 'Children's Referendum' 2012* (Child Law Clinic and Centre for Children's Rights, 2015).

[4]   Michael Freeman, "What's Right with Rights for Children" (2006) 2 *International Journal of Law in Context* 89, p 89.

[5]   Bevan classifies the latter rights as "self-assertive" in nature: Hugh Bevan, *Child Law* (Butterworths, London 1989).

[6]   Lorraine Fox Harding, *Perspectives on Child Care Policy* (Longman, London, 1997), referenced in Jane Fortin, *Children's Rights and the Developing Law* (3rd edn, Cambridge University Press, Cambridge, 2009), p 8.

ascribed to a child, it will actually empower whoever is in a position to assert it, and not the child himself or herself."[7]

It should also be noted that the United Nations Convention on the Rights of the Child (UNCRC), discussed further below, contains numerous references to the rights and responsibilities of parents. The UNCRC recognises that parents are the primary caregivers for their children and it places obligations on States Parties to support parents. For example, in Art 5 UNCRC, States are required to respect the responsibilities, rights and duties of parents to provide direction to their children. A similar requirement is imposed on the State in Art 14(2). In Art 7, children have the right to be cared for by their parents, while Art 9 provides that the State must ensure that the child is not separated from his or her parents against their will unless it is in the child's best interests. In addition, Art 18 requires the State to provide appropriate assistance to parents in the performance of their child-rearing responsibilities. There are many other references to the role of parents throughout the Convention. In this light, it is clear that the recognition of children's rights does not abolish or devalue the role of parents.

Of course, in any judgment concerning a child, the best interests of the child must be central to the decision-making process,[8] and sometimes those interests will outweigh those of adults.[9] The priority given to the best interests of the child is justified on the basis of the vulnerability of children. As Freeman notes

> "children are especially vulnerable: they have fewer resources—material, psychological, relational—to rely on in adversity; they are usually blameless and certainly did not ask to come into the world; for too long children have been treated as objects of concern (or worse objects) rather than as persons; and even today they remain voiceless, even invisible, when disputes are fought over them."[10]

---

[7] *N v Health Service Executive* [2006] 4 IR 374 at 503.

[8] The weight afforded to the best interests of the child will depend on the applicable legal provision. For example, under Art 3 UNCRC, the best interests of the child are expressed as "a primary" consideration, whereas under Art 21 UNCRC, the best interests of the child are "the paramount" consideration.

[9] The Irish case law discussed later in this chapter does, however, arguably paint a different picture. Similarly, in England and Wales, Jonathan Herring has noted that "we do not at present have a problem with the interests of children being given excessive weight at the expense of the interests of adults.": Jonathan Herring, "The Welfare Principle and Parents' Rights" in Andrew Bainham, Shelley Day Sclater and Martin Richards, *What is a Parent? A Socio-Legal Analysis* (Hart Publishing, Oxford, 1999), p 100.

[10] Michael Freeman, "What's Right with Rights for Children" (2006) 2 *International*

One of the first documents to address children's rights was the Geneva Declaration on the Rights of the Child, which was adopted by the League of Nations in 1924. This declaration emphasised that "men and women of all nations, recognizing that mankind owes to the Child the best that it has to give, declare and accept it as their duty that, beyond and above all considerations of race, nationality or creed", certain rights are owed to children.[11] The Declaration went on to set out five specific obligations on State parties and it laid the foundations for a number of other international children's rights treaties that followed.

On 10 December 1959, the United Nations adopted the Declaration of the Rights of the Child 1959. This was a more detailed instrument which set out ten specific rights of the child, including the right to non-discrimination, the right to special protection from harm, the right to a name and nationality, the right to education, and the right to be protected against all forms of neglect, cruelty and exploitation. The Declaration of the Rights of the Child 1959 formed the basis for the United Nations Convention of the Rights of the Child (UNCRC), which was adopted by the UN General Assembly 30 years later on 20 November 1989. The Declaration of the Rights of the Child 1959 was not binding on UN States and so it was thought necessary to create a convention that would set out the specific obligations on States to protect the rights of the child in a single instrument. The idea of creating a specific convention to address the rights of the child in this way was first proposed by the Polish Government in 1979, the International Year of the Child, and was followed by a 10-year drafting process. The length of the drafting process underlines the fact that it was sometimes a difficult process, in particular as the nations had to reconcile their differing national and cultural beliefs and traditions to reach a compromise on the content of the rights that should be protected by the Convention. The UNCRC was finally adopted in 1989 and entered into force on 2 September 1990. Whereas the Geneva Declaration on the Rights of the Child 1924 and the Declaration of the Rights of the Child 1959 were largely confined to matters of care and protection, the UNCRC establishes that children are themselves rights-holders and recognises a broader catalogue of children's rights. To date, 196 countries have ratified the Convention (the United States of America is the only country which has not ratified the Convention), making it the most widely ratified human rights treaty in history. As such, the UNCRC is now the fundamental international legal

---

Journal of Law in Context 89 at 95.
[11] Geneva Declaration of the Rights of the Child 1924.

instrument for the protection of children. Ireland ratified the UNCRC on 21 September 1992.

In the European context, the European Convention on Human Rights (ECHR) provides protection of the rights of children. Although the ECHR does not contain any specific reference to the rights of children, children as individuals are entitled to protection under the ECHR, in the same way that adults are. In addition, the European Court of Human Rights (ECtHR) is permitted to make reference to the UNCRC when considering cases that affect children and it has done so on a number of occasions. Indeed, the UNCRC has been ratified by all Member States of the ECHR which arguably gives it a higher status than other international treaties in the jurisprudence of the ECtHR.[12]

At domestic level, children's rights are specifically protected under Art 42A of the Irish Constitution. Following the successful "Children's Referendum" in 2012, the Thirty-First Amendment of the Constitution was signed into law on 28 April 2015.[13] The new Art 42A now provides for express constitutional recognition of the rights of the child.

This Chapter will outline the protection of children's rights in Ireland under the UNCRC, the ECHR, and the Irish Constitution.

United Nations Convention on the Rights of the Child (UNCRC)

The UN Convention on the Rights of the Child (UNCRC) is a comprehensive, international agreement on the rights of children, adopted by the United Nations General Assembly in 1989. The status of the UNCRC as a fundamental children's rights instrument is reflected in the fact that it is the most widely ratified human rights treaty in history. Ireland ratified the UNCRC on 21 September 1992. Through ratifying the UNCRC, the Irish State committed itself to ensuring the practical realisation of all rights in the Convention for all Irish children. It should be noted that the UNCRC sets *minimum* standards for the protection of children's rights. States Parties can (and often should) go beyond these minimum standards

---

[12] Ursula Kilkelly, "The Best of Both Worlds for Children's Rights? Interpreting the European Convention on Human Rights in the Light of the UN Convention on the Rights of the Child" (2001) 23 *Human Rights Quarterly* 308.

[13] The result of the referendum campaign was subsequently challenged before the High Court and Supreme Court which delayed the insertion of the amendment.

when introducing domestic regulations to protect the rights of all children.

Article 1 of the UNCRC defines a child as "every human being below the age of eighteen years unless under the law applicable to the child, majority is attained earlier." Articles 2 to 41 subsequently set out the rights that are protected by the Convention. These rights are comprehensive and address all areas of relevance to the child. The rights are often divided and grouped according to the three P's of protection, participation, and provision.[14] Among the protection rights set out in the UNCRC are the right to protection from abuse and neglect (Art 19), the right to special protection for a child deprived of his or her family environment (Art 20), and protection from sexual and other forms of exploitation (Arts 34 and 36). The participation provisions include, among others, the right of the child to express his or her views (Art 12), the right to freedom of expression (Art 13), and the right of access to information (Art 17). Examples of the provision rights include the child's right to health and access to health services (Art 24), the right to an adequate standard of living (Art 27), and the right to education (Art 28).

Article 4 UNCRC provides for the implementation of these rights. It provides that

> "States Parties shall undertake all appropriate legislative, administrative, and other measures for the implementation of the rights recognized in the present Convention. With regard to economic, social and cultural rights, States Parties shall undertake such measures to the maximum extent of their available resources and, where needed, within the framework of international co-operation.[15]

Article 4 places a positive obligation on States Parties to implement the civil and political rights of the child protected under the UNCRC, while at the same time recognising that implementation of the child's economic, social and cultural rights may be limited by available resources. This does not mean that a lack of resources will absolve the State Party of its obligations under the UNCRC. Instead, the Committee on the Rights of the Child, the body that monitors States Parties compliance with the UNCRC, has explained that Art 4 requires the "progressive realisation" of rights, such that "States need to be able to demonstrate that they have implemented

---

[14] Thomas Hammarberg, "The UN Convention on the Rights of the Child — And How to Make it Work" (1990) 12 *Human Rights Quarterly* 97.
[15] United Nations Convention on the Rights of the Child, Art 4.

'to the maximum extent of their available resources' and, where necessary, have sought international cooperation."[16] This provision ensures that States Parties introduce legislation and other measures to give practical effect to the rights set out in the Convention.

1. General Principles

All of the rights set out in the UNCRC are guided by four "general" or "guiding" principles. These principles are regarded as the fundamental values of the Convention, which are to be applied in order to interpret and implement all of the rights of the child contained in the Convention. Each right protected under the UNCRC must applied in light of, and in accordance with, the general principles. The general principles are also free-standing rights in and of themselves which may be applied to a particular situation.

The four general principles are:

- Article 2, which requires that the child is protected against all forms of discrimination;
- Article 3, which provides that in all actions concerning children, the best interests of the child shall be a primary consideration;
- Article 6, which protects the right to life, survival and development of the child; and
- Article 12, which protects the right of the child, who is capable of forming his or her own views, to express those views freely in all matters affecting the child and that those views are given due weight in accordance with the age and maturity of the child.

(a) Article 2: Non-Discrimination

Article 2 UNCRC provides that

"1. States Parties shall respect and ensure the rights set forth in the present Convention to each child within their jurisdiction without discrimination of any kind, irrespective of the child's or his or her parent's or legal guardian's race, colour, sex, language, religion, political or other opinion, national, ethnic or social origin, property, disability, birth or other status.

---

[16] Committee on the Rights of the Child, *General Comment No. 5 (2003) General measures of implementation of the Convention on the Rights of the Child (arts. 4, 42 and 44, para. 6)* CRC/GC/2003/5, para 7.

2. States Parties shall take all appropriate measures to ensure that the child is protected against all forms of discrimination or punishment on the basis of the status, activities, expressed opinions, or beliefs of the child's parents, legal guardians, or family members."[17]

This article requires that States Parties take appropriate measures to prevent all forms of discrimination against children. This includes an obligation to actively identify individual children and groups of children who may require special measures to protect them from discrimination, such as children from ethnic or cultural minorities who may be more likely to experience discrimination. Legislation may be required to address discrimination, but the Committee on the Rights of the Child has noted that educational measures may also be required to change attitudes and thereby prevent discrimination in the first place.[18] Thus, Art 2 is not confined to legal protections but it also has a role in shaping social attitudes and directing normative behaviour.

(b) Article 3: The Best Interests Principle

Article 3 UNCRC provides that

"1. In all actions concerning children, whether undertaken by public or private social welfare institutions, courts of law, administrative authorities or legislative bodies, the best interests of the child shall be a primary consideration.

2. States Parties undertake to ensure the child such protection and care as is necessary for his or her well-being, taking into account the rights and duties of his or her parents, legal guardians, or other individuals legally responsible for him or her, and, to this end, shall take all appropriate legislative and administrative measures.

3. States Parties shall ensure that the institutions, services and facilities responsible for the care or protection of children shall conform with the standards established by competent authorities, particularly in the areas of safety, health, in the number and suitability of their staff, as well as competent supervision."[19]

---

[17] United Nations Convention on the Rights of the Child, Art 2.
[18] Committee on Rights of the Child, *General Comment No 9 (2006) The rights of children with disabilities* (CRC/C/GC/9), para 9.
[19] United Nations Convention on the Rights of the Child, Art 3.

The Committee on the Rights of the Child has explained that the best interests principle is a threefold concept: it is a substantive right; a fundamental interpretative legal principle; and a rule of procedure.[20] Furthermore, the Committee has set out that "there is no hierarchy of rights in the Convention; all the rights provided for therein are in the 'child's best interests' and no right could be compromised by a negative interpretation of the child's best interests."[21] Therefore, all of the other rights contained in the UNCRC must be applied to guide the best interests principle. The principle must also be flexible and adaptable so that the best individual solution can be found for each child or group of children.

There are references to the child's best interests in many other articles of the UNCRC, for example in Art 9 (separation from parents); Art 18 (parental responsibilities); Art 20 (deprivation of family environment and alternative care); Art 21 (adoption); Art 37(c) (separation from adults in detention); and Art 40 (juvenile justice). The Committee on the Rights of the Child has explained that where the best interests of the child are expressed as "a primary consideration" under the UNCRC, this means that those interests "may not be considered on the same level as all other considerations" and "a larger weight must be attached to what serves the child best."[22] Where the best interests are described as "the paramount consideration", they are to be the "the determining factor when taking a decision."[23]

As will be seen in later chapters, the concept of the best interests of the child is inherently vague and subjective. Nonetheless, the best interests principle is deeply ingrained in child law. There are ways to reduce the discretion that the principle affords to the decision-maker but, in the end, a value judgment will be required to resolve the dispute and to determine the best course of action for a particular child or group of children. The measure of discretion afforded to the decision-maker in this regard underlines the importance of the UNCRC and its general principles; these

---

[20] Committee on the Rights of the Child, *General comment No. 14 (2013) on the right of the child to have his or her best interests taken as a primary consideration (art. 3, para. 1)* CRC/C/GC/14, para 6.
[21] Committee on the Rights of the Child, *General comment No. 14 (2013) on the right of the child to have his or her best interests taken as a primary consideration (art. 3, para. 1)* CRC/C/GC/14, para 4.
[22] Committee on the Rights of the Child, *General comment No. 14 (2013) on the right of the child to have his or her best interests taken as a primary consideration (art. 3, para. 1)* CRC/C/GC/14, paras 37 and 39.
[23] Committee on the Rights of the Child, *General comment No. 14 (2013) on the right of the child to have his or her best interests taken as a primary consideration (art. 3, para. 1)* CRC/C/GC/14, para 38.

rights should be used to guide the application of the best interests principle and therefore reduce the subjectivity of decision-making.

Although the best interests principle is a vague concept, it must be acknowledged that this is not an unknown feature in the Irish legal system. Value judgments and discretion are common in many areas of law, such as in determining the "reasonable man" standard in the law of tort. The best interests principle is simply another element of a flexible and adaptable body of law. The best interests principle recognises that it is more difficult for children to assert their rights than it is for adults. The principle ensures that the decision-maker will consider the position of the child and choose the result that best promotes that child's interests. The indeterminate nature of best interests allows that decision to accommodate the child's developing interests and needs.

(c) Article 6: The right to life, survival and development

Article 6 UNCRC provides that:

> "1. States Parties recognize that every child has the inherent right to life.
>
> 2. States Parties shall ensure to the maximum extent possible the survival and development of the child."[24]

Under Art 6, States must interpret "development" in its broadest sense to encompass the child's physical, mental, spiritual, moral, psychological and social development. The State must aim to achieve the optimal development for all children through the enactment of legislation and other measures. In the context of the right to health, the Committee on the Rights of the Child has said that States must identify risks and protective factors that underlie the life, survival, growth and development of children so as to design and implement evidence-informed interventions.[25] The Committee has also considered Art 6 as part of the right of the child to freedom from all forms of violence and has emphasised that violence should not only be considered in terms of "life" and "survival", but also as part of the "development" aspect. The State must provide comprehensive protection from violence and

---

[24] United Nations Convention on the Rights of the Child, Art 6.
[25] Committee on the Rights of the Child, *General comment No 15 (2013) on the right of the child to the enjoyment of the highest attainable standard of health (art. 24)* CRC/C/GC/15, para 16.

exploitation in order to protect the child's right to life, survival and development.[26]

(d) Article 12: The right of the child to express his or her views

Article 12 UNCRC provides that

> "1. States Parties shall assure to the child who is capable of forming his or her own views the right to express those views freely in all matters affecting the child, the views of the child being given due weight in accordance with the age and maturity of the child.
>
> 2. For this purpose, the child shall in particular be provided the opportunity to be heard in any judicial and administrative proceedings affecting the child, either directly, or through a representative or an appropriate body, in a manner consistent with the procedural rules of national law."[27]

Article 12 imposes a clear legal obligation on States parties to recognise the right of the child to freely express his or her views and to accord those views due weight, according to the child's age and maturity. States are required to ascertain the child's views and to consider them in accordance with age and maturity. Article 12 also ensures the procedural implementation of this right by providing the child with a mechanism for those views to be heard. The exercise of the child's right to be heard is a vital aspect of decision-making and the creation of law and policy as the child is the individual most affected by these decisions and should therefore be able to participate. Equally, however, the child has the right *not* to express his or her views if he or she so wishes. As the Committee on the Rights of the Child explains, "[e]xpressing views is a choice for the child, not an obligation."[28]

Article 12 applies to "the child who is capable of forming his or her own views." As such, there is an obligation on States to assess the capacity of the child in this regard, but States should start with a presumption in favour of the child having such capacity. There is no age limit set by the Convention in respect of capacity and States are not encouraged to set their own. This is because a child is capable of forming a view at any time; the Convention does not

---

[26] Committee on the Rights of the Child, *General comment No 13 (2011) – The right of the child to freedom from all forms of violence* CRC/C/GC/13, para 62.

[27] United Nations Convention on the Rights of the Child, Art 12

[28] Committee on the Rights of the Child, *General Comment No. 12 (2009) The right of the child to be heard* CRC/C/GC/12, para 16.

require that the view is an intelligible one or that it is expressed in words. Rather, it is recognised that views can be expressed through non-verbal forms of communication including play, body language, facial expressions, and drawing and painting. In this way, even very young children are deemed capable of forming their own views.[29]

Once the child's views have been expressed, they must be adequately considered and "given due weight in accordance with the age and maturity of the child."[30] Again, it is not recommended that States set a minimum age in this regard because "[c]hildren's levels of understanding are not uniformly linked to their biological age."[31] Maturity refers to the ability to understand and assess the implications of a particular matter, and must be assessed on a case-by-case basis when considering the individual capacity of a child. Thus, the child's views will not be determinative of the matter but will be taken into account in accordance with his or her age and maturity.

2. Optional Protocols

As noted above, the UNCRC provides for minimum standards to protect children. States parties are encouraged to go beyond these minimum standards in their domestic legal systems where possible. In addition, there are three Optional Protocols which complement and add to the obligations contained in the Convention. The Protocols are "optional" in that States parties are not required to ratify them, although they are encouraged to do so. The Optional Protocols supplement and strengthen the minimum standards set out in the UNCRC. The three Optional Protocols are:

- the Optional Protocol to the Convention on the Rights of the Child on the involvement of children in armed conflict (OPAC);
- the Optional Protocol to the Convention on the Rights of the Child on the sale of children, child prostitution and child pornography (OPSC); and
- the Optional Protocol to the Convention on the Rights of the Child on a communications procedure.

The Optional Protocol to the Convention on the Rights of the Child

---

[29] Committee on the Rights of the Child, *General Comment No. 12 (2009) The right of the child to be heard* CRC/C/GC/12, para 21.
[30] United Nations Convention on the Rights of the Child, Art 12(1).
[31] Committee on the Rights of the Child, *General Comment No 12 (2009) The right of the child to be heard* CRC/C/GC/12, para 29.

on the involvement of children in armed conflict (OPAC) was adopted and opened for signature, ratification and accession on 25 May 2000 and it entered into force on 12 February 2002. To date, 167 States parties have ratified this Optional Protocol. This Optional Protocol requires that States Parties take all feasible measures to ensure that members of their armed forces who have not attained the age of 18 years do not take a direct part in hostilities and it prohibits the compulsory recruitment of children under the age of 18 years into the armed forces. Voluntary recruitment of children under the age of 18 years is permitted but States are required to undertake certain minimum safeguards in conducting such recruitment. For example, States must ensure that this recruitment is genuinely voluntary and that informed consent has been acquired from the child's parents or legal guardians. Ireland ratified this Optional Protocol on 18 November 2002.

The Optional Protocol to the Convention on the Rights of the Child on the sale of children, child prostitution and child pornography (OPSC) was adopted and opened for signature on 25 May 2000 and entered into force on 18 January 2002. To date, 174 States parties have ratified this Optional Protocol. This Optional Protocol prohibits the sale of children, child prostitution and child pornography, which are defined as follows:

"(a) Sale of children means any act or transaction whereby a child is transferred by any person or group of persons to another for remuneration or any other consideration;

(b) Child prostitution means the use of a child in sexual activities for remuneration or any other form of consideration;

(c) Child pornography means any representation, by whatever means, of a child engaged in real or simulated explicit sexual activities or any representation of the sexual parts of a child for primarily sexual purposes."[32]

This Optional Protocol requires that States Parties designate a specified list of acts and activities in these areas as criminal offences in their legal systems and it requires that States adopt appropriate measures to protect the rights and interests of child victims. Ireland signed this Optional Protocol on 7 September 2000 but to date has not ratified it. A number of legislative changes are required to ensure full compliance with OPSC which explains why the Optional Protocol has not been ratified thus far. In Ireland's consolidated

---

[32] Optional Protocol to the Convention on the Rights of the Child on the sale of children, child prostitution and child pornography, Art 2.

third and fourth Reports to the Committee on the Rights of the Child in 2013, the Minister for Children and Youth Affairs indicated that ratification of OPSC would be prioritised and that legislation would be introduced to ensure full compliance with OPSC.[33] The enactment of the Criminal Justice (Victims of Crime) Act 2017 and the Criminal Law (Sexual Offences) Act 2017 has brought Irish law broadly into compliance with OPSC. It is to be hoped, therefore, that ratification will occur as a matter of priority.

The Third Optional Protocol to the Convention on the Rights of the Child on a communications procedure was adopted and opened for signature, ratification and accession on 19 December 2011 and entered into force on 14 April 2014. This Optional Protocol provides for an international complaints procedure for child rights violations. It allows children from States that have ratified the Protocol to submit a complaint to the UN Committee on the Rights of the Child regarding specific violations of their rights under the UNCRC and its first two Optional Protocols, if ratified. To date, 37 States Parties have ratified this Optional Protocol. Ireland ratified the Third Optional Protocol on 24 September 2014.

Three types of complaints are provided for in the Optional Protocol:

- Individual Communications: Individual children, groups of children and their representatives may submit complaints in respect of violations of their rights under the UNCRC and the first two Optional Protocols, if ratified[34];
- Inter-State Communications: A State may submit a complaint against another State that is not fulfilling its obligations under the UNCRC. In order for this procedure to apply, both States must have ratified the Optional Protocol[35];
- Inquiry Procedure: If the Committee receives reliable information indicating grave or systematic violations by a State party of rights set out in the UNCRC or Optional Protocols, it may initiate an inquiry into the alleged violation.[36]

---

[33] Department of Children and Youth Affairs, *Ireland's Consolidated Third and Fourth Reports to the UN Committee on the Rights of the Child* (July 2013).

[34] Third Optional Protocol to the Convention on the Rights of the Child on a communications procedure, Art 5.

[35] Third Optional Protocol to the Convention on the Rights of the Child on a communications procedure, Art 12.

[36] Third Optional Protocol to the Convention on the Rights of the Child on a communications procedure, Art 13.

Article 7 of the Third Optional Protocol sets out a list of admissibility criteria which must be met in order for a complaint to be heard by the Committee on the Rights of the Child. For example, a complaint can only be made where domestic remedies have been exhausted and a complaint will be inadmissible where the facts occurred prior to the entry into force of the Third Optional Protocol for the State party concerned, unless the violation continued after that date. As such, not every complaint will be considered by the Committee. Where a complaint is admissible, it will be examined by the Committee and thereafter the Committee shall, without delay, transmit its views on the communication, together with its recommendations, if any, to the parties concerned. The Committee's recommendations are not binding on States but the State party remains answerable to the United Nations for its implementation of the Convention.

3. Monitoring Implementation of the UNCRC

The Committee on the Rights of the Child is a United Nations (UN) body of 18 independent experts that monitors implementation of the UNCRC by the countries that are party to it. It also monitors implementation of the three Optional Protocols.

All States Parties are obliged to submit regular reports to the Committee on how the UNCRC rights are being implemented in their domestic systems. States must submit an initial report two years after acceding to the Convention and must then submit periodic reports every five years. The Committee examines each report and addresses its concerns and recommendations to the State party in the form of "concluding observations".

Ireland ratified the UNCRC in 1992 and submitted its first report to the Committee in 1996. Ireland's second report was submitted 10 years later in 2006 and our consolidated third and fourth reports were submitted in 2013[37] and were considered by the Committee in 2016.[38]

In its concluding observations on Ireland's combined third and fourth periodic reports, the Committee commended Ireland for various measures adopted to improve the implementation of the rights of the child in recent years, such as the Thirty-First

---

[37] Department of Children and Youth Affairs, *Ireland's Consolidated Third and Fourth Reports to the UN Committee on the Rights of the Child* (July 2013).

[38] Committee on the Rights of the Child, *Concluding observations on the combined third and fourth periodic reports of Ireland* (March 2016).

Amendment of the Constitution (Children) Act 2012 (signed into law in 2015) to expressly recognise children as rights holders under the Irish Constitution; the enactment of the Children First Act 2015 to improve child protection measures; the enactment of the Children and Family Relationships Act 2015 to legally recognise a wide range of family relationships; and the enactment of the Gender Recognition Act 2015 to provide that a child over the age of 16 years can have their preferred gender legally recognised by the State for all purposes.[39] However, the Committee also highlighted a number of areas that need to be addressed by the Irish State. Among the recommendations of the Committee were that the State should:

- fully incorporate the UNCRC into domestic law and ratify OPSC;
- consider carrying out a national referendum on lowering the voting age to 16 years in accordance with the State's previous commitment to do so;
- ensure that children born through assisted reproduction, particularly those born through surrogacy, have their best interests taken as a primary consideration and have access to information about their origins; and consider providing surrogate mothers and prospective parents with appropriate counselling and support;
- ensure that children can opt out of religious classes and access appropriate alternatives to such classes should they wish to do so, and undertake measures to increase the availability of non-denominational or multidenominational schools in the State;
- ensure that 24-hour social work emergency services are available to children and families at risk;
- encourage and provide sufficient resources for the training of judges in family law cases involving children;
- consider incorporating provisions on information disclosure, family tracing and post-adoption support measures in adoption legislation;
- undertake measures to increase the availability of social housing and emergency housing support to protect families affected by homelessness;
- adopt a comprehensive legal framework which is in

---

[39] It should be noted that since these Concluding Observations, the Gender Recognition (Amendment) Bill 2017 has been introduced and, if passed, it will allow for children under the age of 16 to have their preferred gender recognised with parental consent.

accordance with international human rights standards for addressing the needs of migrant children.[40]

These recommendations are not legally binding on the Irish State but they do provide a powerful impetus for change which is not easily ignored. As Emily Logan, Chief Commissioner of the Irish Human Rights and Equality Commission (IHREC) has stated, the Concluding Observations "form a clear 'to do' list for the State to bring its law, policy and practice in line with international standards on the human rights of children."[41] Over the years, the UNCRC has provoked a number of changes in Irish law. For example, in response to the Concluding Observations issued by the Committee in respect of Ireland's first report, the Office of the Ombudsman for Children was established along with the Office of the Minister for Children. These developments demonstrate that the UNCRC and the monitoring process have been influential in advancing children's rights in Ireland. Ireland is required to submit its combined fifth and sixth periodic reports to the Committee by 27 October 2021. Those reports will set out how the recommendations in the current concluding observations have been addressed in the intervening period.

4. Days of General Discussion and General Comments

The Committee on the Rights of the Child also organises Days of General Discussion that bring together expert groups, NGOs, national human rights institutions and individual experts to develop a deeper understanding of the contents and implications of the UNCRC as they relate to specific articles or topics. These discussions often lead to the publication of General Comments which contain general guidance on the interpretation of the content of the UNCRC. The Committee has published General Comments on a range of provisions, including General Comment No 14 (2013) on the right of the child to have his or her best interests taken as a primary consideration; General Comment No 12 (2009) on the right of the child to be heard; and General Comment No 5 (2003) on General Measures of Implementation of the Convention on the Rights of the Child. The General Comments are not binding on States parties *per se* but the General Comments represent the Committee on the Rights of the Child's expert interpretation of

---

[40] Committee on the Rights of the Child, *Concluding observations on the combined third and fourth periodic reports of Ireland* (March 2016).

[41] "UN Committee publishes 'detailed and wide-ranging' report on Ireland's child rights record" Irish Human Rights and Equality Commission, 4 February 2016 <(https://www.ihrec.ie/un-committee-publishes-detailed-and-wide-ranging-report-on-irelands-child-rights-record/)>.

particular provisions and so the Comments are highly authoritative and carry significant weight.

The European Convention on Human Rights (ECHR)

The European Convention on Human Rights (ECHR) is a treaty of the Council of Europe established after the Second World War with the aim of re-establishing democratic government in Europe. All 47 Council of Europe member states are parties to the ECHR. The ECHR was adopted on 4 November 1950 and entered into force on 3 September 1953 after it had been ratified by 10 States. Ireland was one of the first States to ratify the ECHR in 1953.

The ECHR protects a range of civil and political rights, including the right to life (Art 2), the prohibition of torture and degrading treatment (Art 3), the right to respect for private and family life (Art 8), freedom of expression (Art 10), the right to marry and found a family (Art 12), and the prohibition of discrimination (Art 14). These rights are supplemented by a number of Protocols which have added additional rights and responsibilities since the Convention was first enacted.

The implementation of the ECHR is overseen by the European Court of Human Rights (ECtHR), which sits in Strasbourg. The ECtHR is comprised of 47 judges—one from each Member State. The Court may sit as a single judge; as a Committee of 3 judges; as a Chamber of 7 judges; or as a Grand Chamber of 17 judges. The ECtHR hears both individual petitions and inter-state petitions concerning alleged violations of the rights contained in the ECHR. There are a number of admissibility criteria that must be met before a case can be heard by the ECtHR. For example, the ECtHR may only deal with a case after all domestic remedies have been exhausted, and within a six month period from the date of the final decision at national level.[42] The judgments of the Court are legally binding on the State parties to whom they are addressed and require the State to take measures to rectify the problem.

The margin of appreciation and principle of subsidiarity place limits on the authority of the ECtHR. The role of the ECtHR is a supervisory one whereby the Member States have the primary responsibility to secure the rights and freedoms contained in the ECHR, while the ECtHR simply reviews the compatibility of

---

[42] European Convention on Human Rights, Arts 34 and 35.

domestic measures with the ECHR.[43] The ECtHR is not a court of "fourth instance". This means that the Court does not address errors of fact or law alleged to have been made by a national court, unless that error infringes the rights protected by the ECHR. The margin of appreciation gives Member States a degree of discretion in their implementation of ECHR rights. The scope of the margin of appreciation will depend on a number of factors. Where there is no European consensus in a certain area, the State will have a wide margin of appreciation and the ECtHR will not usually interfere with the decision of the national authority; in this case the national authority is seen as being "better placed" to make the determination. However, where there is a consensus on a particular matter or where a particularly important facet of an individual's existence or identity is at stake, the margin of appreciation allowed to the State will normally be restricted.[44] In certain cases concerning children, it is arguable that deference to the margin of appreciation has resulted in some decisions that did not promote their best interests.[45]

There is a lack of express provision for children's rights in the ECHR. Nonetheless, given that Art 1 of the Convention secures rights to "everyone", children can obviously benefit from the entire Convention. Many cases concerning children are taken under Art 8 ECHR which secures the right to respect for private and family life. In cases concerning Art 8, the ECtHR is required to adopt a three-stage process in determining the matter:

1. Is Art 8 applicable?
2. Has there been an interference with the rights protected under Art 8?
3. Does that interference pursue a legitimate aim and was it proportionate to that aim?

The principle of proportionality under the third limb of the test requires the Court to consider whether a fair balance has been struck between the interference in the child's Convention right on the one hand and the legitimate aim pursed by the State on the other.

The case law on Art 8 ECHR shows that the ECtHR takes a broad

---

[43] George Letsas, "Two concepts of the margin of appreciation" (2006) 26(4) *Oxford Journal of Legal Studies* 705.

[44] See, for example, *Evans v United Kingdom*, App no 6339/05 (ECtHR,10 April 2007).

[45] Lydia Bracken, "Strasbourg's Response to Gay and Lesbian Parenting: Progress, then Plateau?" (2016) 24 *International Journal of Children's Rights* 358.

view as to what constitutes "family life" for the purpose of the article. The ECtHR has emphasised that the notion of "family life" under this article is not confined to families based on marriage. Instead, it encompasses relationships where the parties, whether of the same or opposite sex, married or unmarried, are living together in a committed relationship. Children born to such relationships are recognised as part of the family unit from the moment of birth.[46] The ECtHR focuses on the quality of the relationships between the parties to determine whether or not family life exists in a particular case. As will be seen later in this chapter, the concept of the family under Art 8 ECHR is very different to the definition of the family under the Irish Constitution. However, this does not mean that Irish law is in breach of the ECHR; States are afforded a wide margin of appreciation to determine the legal recognition of different family types within their jurisdiction.

In addition to preventing an interference with the right to respect for private and family life, there may also be positive obligations arising from Art 8 ECHR that require States to take positive action to secure the right guaranteed. For example, in *Marckx v Belgium*,[47] the ECtHR found that measures that discriminated against a child born out of wedlock were contrary to the ECHR. The Court found that a child has the right to be legally integrated into his or her family and that "respect for family life implies in particular, in the Court's view, the existence in domestic law of legal safeguards that render possible as from the moment of birth the child's integration in his family."[48] This finding does not mandate any particular form of legal integration; it simply requires that legal safeguards are put in place that allow for the child to be integrated into his or her family. Similarly, in *Johnston v Ireland*,[49] respect for the child's family life placed a positive obligation on the State to improve her legal position. In this case, the child had suffered a number of legal disadvantages by virtue of the fact that her parents were not married. This, the Court found, violated the child's rights under Art 8 ECHR and it held that the State had a duty to improve her legal situation.

The ECtHR is also permitted to have regard to international agreements and conventions in its judgments. When considering cases that affect children, the ECtHR often refers to the UNCRC.

---

[46] See, for example: *Schalk and Kopf v Austria*, App no 30141/04 (ECtHR, 24 June 2010); *X, Y and Z v UK*, App no 21830/93 (ECtHR, 22 April 1997); *Gas and Dubois v France*, App no 25951/07 (ECtHR, 15 March 2012).

[47] *Marckx v Belgium*, App no 6833/74 (ECtHR, 13 June 1979).

[48] *Marckx v Belgium*, App no 6833/74 (ECtHR, 13 June 1979), para 31.

[49] *Johnston v Ireland*, App no 9697/92 (ECtHR, 18 December 1986).

In many cases, the ECtHR has relied upon Art 3 UNCRC (the best interests principle) to ensure that the rights of children were properly considered.[50]

As noted above, Ireland ratified the ECHR in 1953. However, because Ireland is a dualist State, the ECHR did not form part of Irish law until it was specifically incorporated into domestic law by the European Convention on Human Rights Act 2003 (the "2003 Act"). This Act incorporated the ECHR into Irish law at a sub-constitutional level. The 2003 Act contains four main provisions that give effect to the ECHR in Irish case law:

- Section 2 of the 2003 Act requires the Irish courts to interpret and apply laws in a manner compatible with the ECHR;
- Section 3 provides that every organ of the State shall perform its functions in a manner compatible with the State's obligations under the ECHR;
- Section 4 requires the Irish courts to take judicial notice and due account of the ECHR and the Strasbourg judgments and opinions when interpreting and applying the Convention; and
- Section 5 allows the courts to make a "declaration of incompatibility" where a statutory provision or rule of law is incompatible with the State's obligations under the ECHR.

Before incorporation of the ECHR by the 2003 Act, the ECHR still gave rise to obligations in Ireland and cases to which Ireland was a party were directly binding on the State. In fact, Ireland was party to the very first case considered by the ECtHR.[51] Since then, Ireland has been party to many more cases and the Strasbourg judgments have resulted in a number of changes to Irish law.

For example, as noted above, in *Johnston v Ireland*,[52] the ECtHR held that measures that discriminated against children born out of wedlock were contrary to Art 8. In that case, the child in question had been disadvantaged in relation to her succession rights by virtue of the fact that her parents were not married. At the time of her birth, the child's father was married to another woman

---

[50] Lydia Bracken, "Assessing the Best Interests of the Child in Cases of Cross-Border Surrogacy: Inconsistency in the Strasbourg Approach?" (2017) 39 *Journal of Social Welfare and Family Law* 368.

[51] *Lawless v Ireland*, App no 332/57 (ECtHR,14 November 1960).

[52] *Johnston v Ireland*, App no 9697/92 (ECtHR, 18 December 1986).

and, because divorce was not available in Ireland at the time,[53] he could not obtain a dissolution of that marriage. As such, the child's parents were prevented from marrying in Ireland at the time. This meant that there were no means available to the child's parents to alleviate her disadvantage. The Court concluded that, while the ban on divorce was not itself a breach of Art 8, the State had breached the article through its failure to protect children born out of wedlock. This case paved the way for the Status of Children Act 1987, which improved the legal position of non-marital children in a number of respects.

In *Keegan v Ireland*,[54] the mother of a child had placed the child for adoption after birth without father's knowledge or consent. The father applied for guardianship but his application was unsuccessful before the Irish courts and the adoption was allowed to proceed. The father subsequently brought a case to the ECtHR claiming that his right to respect for his family life with his daughter under Art 8 ECHR had been breached by the making of the adoption order. The ECtHR found that the placement of the child for adoption without the father's knowledge not only jeopardised his relationship with the child, but also set in motion a process which was likely to prove irreversible, thereby putting the father at a significant disadvantage in his contest with the prospective adopters for the custody of the child. The ECtHR held that the Irish law that allowed for the child to be placed for adoption without the father's knowledge amounted to a violation of Art 8 ECHR. This case subsequently led to a change in Irish adoption law. Now, a father who does not have guardianship of his child must be consulted in relation to the adoption before any order can be made.[55]

These cases show that, even before the incorporation of the ECHR into Irish law, the Convention provided a springboard for reform in different areas of child law and acted as a mechanism for social and legal change.

---

[53] Art 41.3.2° of Bunreacht na hÉireann previously set out that "[n]o law shall be enacted providing for the grant of a dissolution of marriage" which meant that divorce was unavailable in Ireland. That provision was subsequently repealed by the Fifteenth Amendment of the Constitution and a new Art 41.3.2° was inserted which expressly allows for a marriage to be dissolved where certain criteria are met.

[54] *Keegan v Ireland* App no 16969/90 (ECtHR, 26 May 1994).

[55] Adoption Act 2010, s 30, substituted by Adoption (Amendment) Act 2017, s 13.

Bunreacht na hÉireann

In 2012, the Irish public voted in favour of the Thirty-First Amendment of the Constitution which proposed to insert a new Art 42A into the Irish Constitution. This amendment was signed into law on 28 April 2015 and the new Art 42A now provides for express constitutional recognition of the rights of the child. Through this article, the State "recognises and affirms the natural and imprescriptible rights of all children and shall, as far as practicable, by its laws protect and vindicate those rights."[56] In addition, the amendment acknowledges the best interests principle and the child's right to be heard. Article 42A.4.1° provides that provision shall be made by law that in all proceedings brought by the State for the purpose of preventing the safety and welfare of any child from being prejudicially affected, or concerning the adoption, guardianship or custody of, or access to, any child "the best interests of the child shall be the paramount consideration."[57] Article 42A.4.2° provides that provision shall be made by law that in any of the same proceedings, as far as practicable,

> "in respect of any child who is capable of forming his or her own views, the views of the child shall be ascertained and given due weight having regard to the age and maturity of the child."[58]

Before the so-called "Children's Referendum", which led to the insertion of Art 42A into the Constitution, children's rights were not absent from the Irish Constitution, but they were largely superseded by the rights of the family. Children were entitled to protection under all of the rights contained in the Constitution, but there was no specific provision that recognised the rights of the child. Children's rights were seen to flow from, and depend on, those of the parents. Children born to married parents benefitted from the robust family protections set out in Arts 41 and 42 of the Constitution, but their rights were subsumed within the rights of the family. Thus, the major advantage of Art 42A is that it recognises that children have rights independent of the family unit.

1. The Natural and Imprescriptible Rights of the Child

Prior to the Children's Referendum, the only constitutional provision that expressly referred to the rights of the child was

---

[56] Bunreacht na hÉireann, Art 42A.1.
[57] Bunreacht na hÉireann, Art 42A.4.1°.
[58] Bunreacht na hÉireann, Art 42A.4.2°.

Art 42.5 (which was deleted upon the insertion of Art 42A). This provided that

> "In exceptional cases, where the parents for physical or moral reasons fail in their duty towards their children, the State as guardian of the common good, by appropriate means shall endeavour to supply the place of the parents, but always with due regard for the natural and imprescriptible rights of the child."

This article recognised the natural and imprescriptible rights of the child, but it did so indirectly, and due regard for these rights was only required in the most serious of cases when the State was called upon to supply the place of the parents. Article 42.5 contained the only express reference to the rights of the child in the text of the Constitution, but the child also benefitted from certain unenumerated (unwritten) personal rights flowing from Art 40.3 of the Constitution. These rights are not written in the text of the Constitution but were "discovered" by the courts over the years. In *G v An Bord Uchtála*, for example, Finlay P in the High Court held that the child "has a constitutional right to bodily integrity and has an unenumerated right to an opportunity to be reared with due regard to her religious, moral, intellectual, physical and social welfare."[59] In the Supreme Court, O'Higgins CJ found that

> "[t]he child also has natural rights … [he or she] has the right to be fed and to live, to be reared and educated, to have the opportunity of working and of realising his or her full personality and dignity as a human being. These rights of the child (and others which I have not enumerated) must equally be protected and vindicated by the State."[60]

Walsh J, in the same case, opined that

> "[t]he child's natural rights spring primarily from the natural right of every individual to life, to be reared and educated, to liberty, to work, to rest and recreation, to the practice of religion, and to follow his or her conscience."[61]

Walsh J further noted that "[t]he child's natural right to life and

---

[59] *G v An Bord Uchtála* [1980] IR 32 at 44.
[60] *G v An Bord Uchtála* [1980] IR 32 at 55.
[61] *G v An Bord Uchtála* [1980] IR 32 at 69.

all that flows from that right are independent of any right of the parent as such."[62]

Similarly, in *DG v Eastern Health Board*, Denham J stated that the child has

> "the right to be reared with due regard to his religious, moral, intellectual, physical and social welfare; to be fed, accommodated and educated; to suitable care and treatment; to have the opportunity of working, and of realising his personality and dignity as a human being."[63]

Denham J added to this list of rights in *North Western Health Board v HW*, holding that the child's rights include the right to life and to bodily integrity.[64]

Therefore, even before the insertion of Art 42A into the Constitution, the courts had found that children had various rights not expressly set out in the Constitution. The difficulty, however, was that these rights were typically subsumed within the rights of the family which, at times, impeded the full realisation of the rights of the child, as is discussed below.

2. Articles 41 and 42: The Marital Family

Where a child is born to married parents, he or she benefits from rights as part of a constitutionally recognised family under Arts 41 and 42 of the Constitution. Article 41.1.1° recognises the Family as "the natural primary and fundamental unit group of Society, and as a moral institution possessing inalienable and imprescriptible rights, antecedent and superior to all positive law", while Art 41.1.2° guarantees "to protect the Family in its constitution and authority, as the necessary basis of social order and as indispensable to the welfare of the Nation and the State."[65] Article 41.3.1° subsequently clarifies that the family referred to in the article is that based on marriage: "[t]he State pledges itself to guard with special care the institution of Marriage, on which the Family is founded, and to protect it against attack."[66] Thus, "the family" referred to in Art 41 is that which is based on marriage. This means that families where the parents are not married to each other do not come within the constitutional definition. This was affirmed most recently by the

---

[62] *G v An Bord Uchtála* [1980] IR 32 at 69.
[63] *DG v Eastern Health Board* [1997] 3 IR 511 at 537.
[64] *North Western Health Board v HW* [2001] 3 IR 622 at 727.
[65] Bunreacht na hÉireann, Arts 41.1.1° and 41.1.2°.
[66] Bunreacht na hÉireann, Art 41.3.1°.

Supreme Court in the case of *M (Immigration-Rights of Unborn) v Minister for Justice and Equality.*[67]

Article 42 of the Constitution is titled "Education." In this Article, the State

> "acknowledges that the primary and natural educator of the child is the Family and guarantees to respect the inalienable right and duty of parents to provide, according to their means, for the religious and moral, intellectual, physical and social education of their children."[68]

Under Arts 41 and 42, the child's rights are subsumed within those of the family: the child has the right to be educated by the family and to be provided by his or her parents with religious, moral, intellectual, physical and social education.[69] These articles also give rise to a constitutional presumption that the welfare of the child is to be found with the marital family. The courts have established that the welfare of the child is presumed to be found within the marital family unless there are compelling reasons as to why this cannot be achieved, or the case is an exceptional one where the parents are found to have failed in their moral duty towards their child or children.[70] In some cases, it could be argued that the application of this presumption has led to decisions that did not in fact best serve the child's welfare. The difficulty that arises in this context is not so much the presumption itself, but the high threshold required to rebut it.

The presumption in favour of the married family was first recognised in *Re JH*[71] where an unmarried mother had placed her child for adoption but later married the child's father and withdrew her consent to the adoption. The prospective adoptive parents issued proceedings under the Adoption Act 1974 to dispense with the mother's consent. In a series of separate judgments, the High Court refused to dispense with the natural mother's consent to the adoption but did award custody of the child to the adoptive parents. The court was satisfied on the evidence presented to it that, in light of the bond which had developed between the child and the prospective adopters, there was a risk that she would suffer long-term psychological harm if custody was awarded to the birth

---

67 *M (Immigration–Rights of Unborn) v Minister for Justice and Equality* [2018] IESC 14 at para 12.9.
68 Bunreacht na hÉireann, Art 42.1.
69 *N v Health Service Executive* [2006] 4 IR 374 at 454.
70 *Re JH* [1985] IR 375.
71 *Re JH* [1985] IR 375.

parents. This risk was said to be "sufficiently proximate to outweigh the contrary factors such as the anomalous legal position of the infant as the legitimised child of the natural parents."[72]

In the Supreme Court, Finlay CJ held that there is

> "a constitutional presumption that the welfare of the child ... is to be found within the family, unless the Court is satisfied on the evidence that there are compelling reasons why this cannot be achieved, or unless the Court is satisfied that the evidence establishes an exceptional case where the parents have failed to provide education for the child and continue to fail to provide education for the child for moral or physical reasons."[73]

At the time of the proceedings, s 3 of the Guardianship of Infants Act 1964 set out that in any proceedings concerning the custody, guardianship or upbringing of a child, the court, in deciding that question, had to "regard the welfare of the infant as the first and paramount consideration."[74] According to Finlay CJ, s 3 had had to be read in line with the constitutional presumption set out above. As such, he was satisfied that in the case of a contest between the natural parents of a marital child and non-parents, as arose in the instant case, the welfare of the child could *not* be regarded as the sole criterion for the court as to the question of custody.[75] The Chief Justice did not believe that the instant case was one "where the Court could or should determine the matter upon the basis of the preferred custody, having regard to the welfare of the child."[76]

The Supreme Court remitted the case to the High Court for reconsideration in light of the principles set out in its judgment. Although Lynch J remained concerned as to the potential psychological damage to the child which could occur due to a change in custody, he did not believe that such a risk was sufficient to rebut the constitutional presumption that the welfare of the child is to be found within the marital family nor to amount

---

[72] *Re JH* [1985] IR 375 at 376.
[73] *Re JH* [1985] IR 375 at 395.
[74] s 3 has since been amended by s 45 of the Children and Family Relationships Act 2015 to now provide that, in proceedings concerning the guardianship, custody, upbringing of, or access to, a child, or concerning the administration of a child's property, "the court ... shall regard the best interests of the child as the paramount consideration."
[75] *Re JH* [1985] IR 375 at 394.
[76] *Re JH* [1985] IR 375 at 394.

to a "compelling reason" why this could not be achieved.[77] Consequently, custody was awarded to the birth parents.

Another case where the constitutional presumption as to welfare arose was *North Western Health Board v HW*,[78] where the married parents of a child had refused to give their consent to allow a PKU heel prick test to be administered upon him.[79] The Health Board applied for an order allowing it to take the child temporarily into care so that the procedure could be performed. This request was denied by the Supreme Court on the basis that there was a constitutional presumption that the welfare of the child was to be found within the marital family and, as such, parents had the primary responsibility for the upbringing and welfare of their children.[80]

In this case, the Supreme Court noted that Art 42.5 of the Constitution (since removed) set out the test for State intervention in matters of family life. In light of this article, the Supreme Court found that it could not intervene in family decision making unless there were "exceptional circumstances" such as "an immediate threat to the health or life of the child."[81] This case was not regarded as an exceptional one and so the court could not override the parents' decision.[82] As Hardiman J noted, the Constitution accords a primacy to the parents, which gives rise to a presumption that the welfare of the child is to be found in the family exercising its authority freely.[83] The case could not be classified as an exceptional one so as to justify and compel intervention by the State. The test may have been advantageous for the child but it was not vital nor was it a compulsory test. Therefore, any decision to enforce the test would have effectively made the non-compulsory test compulsory.

Although this was not an exceptional case so as to warrant State intervention, it is notable that the rights of the child were largely overlooked in the judgment. As Kilkelly and O'Mahony have noted

> "[t]he extremely high threshold required to rebut [the presumption that the welfare of the child is best served by

---

[77] *Re JH* [1985] IR 375 at 400.
[78] *North Western Health Board v HW* [2001] 3 IR 622.
[79] The Phenylketonuria (PKU) test is used to check for a range of inherited conditions and is usually carried out 3–5 days after birth when a small blood sample is taken via a needle prick to the baby's heel.
[80] *North Western Health Board v HW* [2001] 3 IR 622 at 623.
[81] *North Western Health Board v HW* [2001] 3 IR 622 at 725.
[82] *North Western Health Board v HW* [2001] 3 IR 622 at 728.
[83] *North Western Health Board v HW* [2001] 3 IR 622 at 764.

the marital family] thus led to the court attaching no weight to the autonomous right of the child to have his health, life and welfare protected."[84]

This was such despite an acknowledgement by some of the judges that the test would indeed have been in the child's best interests.[85]

The constitutional presumption as to welfare also arose in *N v Health Service Executive*,[86] otherwise known as the "Baby Ann" case. Here, the unmarried parents of Baby Ann placed her for adoption. They later married and sought to have Baby Ann returned to them. This request was refused by the High Court, on the basis that Baby Ann's best interests would be served by her remaining with the prospective adoptive parents. The Supreme Court, however, ordered that Baby Ann be returned to her birth parents. The Supreme Court restated that there is a constitutional presumption that it is in the best interests of the child to be with the married birth parents and that this presumption could only be rebutted where the parents are found to have failed for physical or moral reasons in their duty towards the child as per Art 42.5 of the Constitution. The Court was satisfied that placing the child for adoption did not amount to such a failure of duty and ordered that the child be returned to the birth parents.

Kilkelly and O'Mahony have noted that

> "[t]he striking feature of this case was not just its outcome, but rather the fact that the terms of reference available to the court to make its decision did not include what was in the interests of Baby Ann or what would best protect or promote her rights."[87]

This point was highlighted by McGuinness J in the course of her judgment. The judge noted that, before the applicants married, "the central issue before the court to which all evidence would be directed would be the best interests of Ann."[88] However, once the marriage took place, "[t]he central issue to be considered by the

---

[84] Ursula Kilkelly and Conor O'Mahony, "The Proposed Children's Rights Amendment: Running to Stand Still?" (2007) 10(2) *Irish Journal of Family Law* 19 at 20.

[85] *North Western Health Board v HW* [2001] 3 IR 622 at 729 (per Murphy J).

[86] *N v Health Service Executive* [2006] 4 IR 374.

[87] Ursula Kilkelly and Conor O'Mahony, "The Proposed Children's Rights Amendment: Running to Stand Still?" (2007) 10(2) *Irish Journal of Family Law* 19 at 20.

[88] *N v Health Service Executive* [2006] 4 IR 374 at 497.

court underwent a metamorphosis; *it was no longer the best interests of the child* but the lawfulness or otherwise of the second and third respondents' custody of her."[89]

It is arguable that, in the cases considered above, the constitutional preference for the marital family and the high threshold required to rebut the presumption that the welfare of the child will be secured by that family obscured individualised consideration of the child's best interests and independent rights. In contrast to the above, the threshold for State intervention is much lower in relation to non-marital children and the constitutional presumption as to welfare does not apply to such children. Thus, as Shannon has explained, in relation to non-marital children, "the courts can ensure that the welfare of the child is the paramount consideration as there is no automatic presumption that such welfare will be found with the parents."[90]

The newly-inserted Art 42A.2.1° of the Irish Constitution establishes a different standard for State intervention in family life, but it is unlikely that different conclusions would have been reached in the above cases had the new standard applied. The previous Art 42.5 (which was removed upon the insertion of Art 42A) provided that "where the parents for physical or moral reasons fail in their duty towards their children", the State would endeavour to supply the place of the parents. Article 42A.2.1° now provides that:

> "In exceptional cases, where the parents, regardless of their marital status, fail in their duty towards their children to such extent that the safety or welfare of any of their children is likely to be prejudicially affected, the State as guardian of the common good shall, by proportionate means as provided by law, endeavour to supply the place of the parents, but always with due regard for the natural and imprescriptible rights of the child."[91]

The new article allows for State intervention in the marital family where the parents fail in their duty such that the safety or welfare of the child is "likely" to be prejudicially affected. However, the State can only intervene in "exceptional" cases. Therefore, under the new Art 42A.2.1°, cases such as *North Western Health Board v HW* would probably have the same outcome because a refusal to consent

[89] *N v Health Service Executive* [2006] 4 IR 374 at 497 [emphasis added].
[90] Geoffrey Shannon, *Child Law* (2nd edn, Thomson Reuters, Dublin, 2010), p 14.
[91] Bunreacht na hÉireann, Art 42A.2.1°.

to a PKU test arguably does not amount to an "exceptional" case nor one that is "likely" to prejudicially affect the child's welfare.

3. Article 42A – The Children's Amendment

Article 42A provides:

> "1 The State recognises and affirms the natural and imprescriptible rights of all children and shall, as far as practicable, by its laws protect and vindicate those rights.
>
> 2 1° In exceptional cases, where the parents, regardless of their marital status, fail in their duty towards their children to such extent that the safety or welfare of any of their children is likely to be prejudicially affected, the State as guardian of the common good shall, by proportionate means as provided by law, endeavour to supply the place of the parents, but always with due regard for the natural and imprescriptible rights of the child.
>
> 2° Provision shall be made by law for the adoption of any child where the parents have failed for such a period of time as may be prescribed by law in their duty towards the child and where the best interests of the child so require.
>
> 3 Provision shall be made by law for the voluntary placement for adoption and the adoption of any child.
>
> 4 1° Provision shall be made by law that in the resolution of all proceedings—
> > i   brought by the State, as guardian of the common good, for the purpose of preventing the safety and welfare of any child from being prejudicially affected, or
> > ii   concerning the adoption, guardianship or custody of, or access to, any child,
> the best interests of the child shall be the paramount consideration.
>
> 2° Provision shall be made by law for securing, as far as practicable, that in all proceedings referred to in subsection 1° of this section in respect of any child who is capable of forming his or her own views, the views of the child shall be ascertained and given due weight having regard to the age and maturity of the child."[92]

---

[92]   Bunreacht na hÉireann, Art 42A.

Under Art 42A, children's rights are expressly and independently recognised for the first time in the Irish Constitution. The obligation to protect these rights applies in all contexts, not simply where the parents have failed in their duty towards the children. In addition, Art 42A.4.1° recognises that the best interests of the child shall be the paramount consideration in certain proceedings and places an obligation on the State to introduce legislation to give effect to this principle, while Art 42A.4.2° requires that legislation be introduced to secure the views of the child. Nevertheless, although the rights of the child are now independently recognised, it should be noted that the harmonious interpretation of constitutional provisions means that Art 42A must be read in line with the existing Arts 41 and 42. This harmonious interpretation includes the constitutional presumption that the welfare of the child is to be found with the marital family, as set out above. Thus, the rights of the child referred to in Art 42A will continue to be interpreted within this framework.

Furthermore, although it is encouraging that the best interests principle and the voice of the child are recognised in Art 42A, these are not enshrined as constitutional rights. Article 42A simply requires that legislation is enacted so as to give effect to the provisions in certain limited proceedings. As will be seen in later chapters, pre-existing legislation already requires the courts to regard the "welfare" of children in guardianship, custody and access proceedings as the first and paramount consideration[93] and various legislative provisions provide for the voice of the child to be heard.[94] Therefore, although there are echoes of Arts 3 and 12 UNCRC in Art 42A, the Irish provisions are substantially weaker than their UNCRC counterparts.

The most significant changes to Irish law are brought about by the new Arts 42A.2.2° and 42A.3, which relate to adoption. Article 42A.2.2° provides that

> "Provision shall be made by law for the adoption of any child where the parents have failed for such a period of time as may be prescribed by law in their duty towards the child and where the best interests of the child so require."

Article 42A.3 provides that

---

[93] For example: Guardianship of Infants Act 1964, s 3; Adoption Act 2010, s 19; Child Care Act 1991, s 24.
[94] For example: Guardianship of Infants Act 1964, s 25; Adoption Act 2010, s 24(2) and s 54(3); Child Care Act 1991, s 24.

> "Provision shall be made by law for the voluntary placement for adoption and the adoption of any child."

These provisions allow for marital children to be adopted for the first time in Ireland. Previously, Art 42 of the Constitution created a barrier to the adoption of marital children as it provides that the parental rights and duties of married parents are "inalienable."[95] The existence of this article meant that a very strict test was required to determine whether a child born to married parents could be adopted: it had to be established that the parents had abandoned the child for a period of at least 12 months and that this abandonment would last until the child was 18 years old.[96] Thus, where a child was born during the course of a marriage, he or she could not subsequently be adopted except in the most serious of cases. Marital children can now be adopted and one consequence is that many children in long-term foster care are eligible for adoption. In addition, it is possible for married parents to voluntarily place their child for adoption. As will be seen in Chapter 5, the Adoption (Amendment) Act 2017 gives legislative effect to the new constitutional provisions concerning adoption.

Overview

This Chapter has shown that children's rights are afforded strong protection in Ireland under international conventions and national provisions. The UNCRC provides a comprehensive international framework for the protection of children's rights. In later chapters, it will be shown that the UNCRC has had a major impact on Irish legislation in different areas of child law. Later chapters will also consider the impact of Art 42A of the Irish Constitution in discrete areas. Unfortunately, many of the new constitutional provisions relating to children are largely cosmetic and do not significantly enhance the rights and interests of children. The exception to this is, of course, the provisions allowing for the adoption of marital children which are long overdue. It is disappointing, however, that UNCRC principles do not feature more prominently in the new Art 42A. It may be that the new provisions will increase the visibility of children within the Irish legal system and encourage the courts to find innovative ways to apply the new provisions so

---

[95] Art 42.1 of Bunreacht na hÉireann provides that "[t]he State acknowledges that the primary and natural educator of the child is the Family and guarantees to respect the inalienable right and duty of parents to provide, according to their means, for the religious and moral, intellectual, physical and social education of their children."

[96] Adoption Act 2010, s 54.

as to strengthen the scope of children's rights in Ireland, but only time will tell whether this actually occurs.

PARENTAGE

Introduction

Traditionally, identifying the parents of a child was a relatively straightforward task: the legal mother was the woman who gave birth to the child, based on the presumption of *mater semper certa est* ("motherhood is always certain") and the genetic father was regarded as the legal father. Where the father was married to the mother, the presumption of *pater est quem nuptiae demonstrant* ("the father is he whom the marriage points out") established that he was the legal father based on his presumed genetic contribution to the child's conception.

In most cases, these traditional rules operate satisfactorily to allocate parentage to the adults who will raise and care for a child. However, the emergence of assisted reproductive technologies, such as surrogacy and donor insemination, has required a re-examination of the traditional rules of parentage. Where assisted reproductive technologies are used, a number of persons may be involved in the child's conception. In surrogacy, for example, the creation of a child will involve the intended parent(s) and the surrogate as well as, in many cases, either a sperm donor or an egg donor (or in some cases, both). In the absence of specific laws addressing their position, each of these persons could potentially have a competing claim to parentage.[1] The question therefore arises as to how parentage should be determined in light of these competing claims.

This chapter will examine the legal provisions that apply in Ireland to determine who is regarded as a legal parent. This examination will include consideration of situations where a child is born following donor-assisted human reproduction (DAHR) and surrogacy. In this regard, the provisions of the Children and Family Relationships Act 2015 that relate to DAHR will be examined, as will the proposals to regulate surrogacy that are put forward in the Assisted Reproduction Bill 2017.

Presumptions of Maternity and Paternity

1. Maternity

In Roman law, the presumption of *mater semper certa est* ("the mother is always certain") set out that the woman who gives birth to a child is to be regarded as the legal mother. This presumption,

---

[1]   Angela Campbell, "Conceiving Parents Through Law" (2007) 21 *International Journal of Law, Policy and the Family* 242 at 246.

and its application in Ireland, was comprehensively evaluated by the Supreme Court in the case of *MR v An tArd Chláraitheoir*.[2] In this case, the intended parents in a surrogacy arrangement had supplied their gametes to create an embryo which was subsequently transferred to the surrogate mother. As such, the intended parents were also the genetic parents of the children. When the children were born, the surrogate mother was registered as the children's legal parent alongside the genetic father in accordance with the usual procedures, but the parties subsequently sought to remove the surrogate's name as the legal mother and to register the genetic mother as such. This application was refused by the Registrar for Births and so the parties sought a declaration from the High Court stating that the genetic mother was entitled to be registered as the legal mother.

The High Court began by noting that, prior to the emergence of *in vitro* fertilisation (IVF) and assisted human reproduction (AHR), the "possibility of the rebuttal of *mater semper certa est* did not arise."[3] This was because, traditionally, the woman who gave birth would always be the genetic mother; there was no means available for the birth mother and the genetic mother to be separate persons. The court noted, however, that the presumption of *mater semper certa est* "did not survive the enactment of the Constitution insofar as it applies to the situation post IVF."[4] Abbott J further noted that paternity is established or disputed on the basis of genetics. As such, he concluded that

> "To achieve fairness and constitutional and natural justice, for both the paternal and maternal genetic parents, the feasible inquiry in relation to maternity ought to be made on a genetic basis and on being proven, the genetic mother should be registered as the mother."[5]

The State subsequently appealed the ruling to the Supreme Court. Upon appeal, the Supreme Court emphasised that the task of legislating for surrogacy was "quintessentially a matter for the Oireachtas."[6] The Supreme Court's role, in line with the separation of powers, was to interpret the meaning of existing Irish law as it relates to birth registration and not to create new law to regulate surrogacy arrangements. The Supreme Court held that there was

---

2   *MR v An tArd Chláraitheoir* [2014] 3 IR 533.
3   *MR v An tArd Chláraitheoir* [2013] 1 ILRM 449 at para 100.
4   *MR v An tArd Chláraitheoir* [2013] 1 ILRM 449 at para 104.
5   *MR v An tArd Chláraitheoir* [2013] 1 ILRM 449 at para 104.
6   *MR v An tArd Chláraitheoir* [2014] 3 IR 533 at para 113 per Denham CJ.

no provision in the existing law to allow for a genetic mother, as distinct from a gestational mother, to be registered as the legal mother. The existing law defined the mother in terms of giving birth to a child and so the court concluded that the birth mother was to be regarded as the legal mother.[7] As MacMenamin J noted

> "It is self-evident that, in day to day reality, the role of a mother goes far further than this. But for the purposes of this discussion, it is the connection with birth which is material in discerning the context, intent and purpose of the provisions in question. No other contrary interpretation appears in any Act of the Oireachtas."[8]

The applicability of the *mater semper certa est* presumption was discussed at length in each of the seven judgments handed down in this case. Denham J, for example, was of the view that *mater semper certa est* was never part of Irish common law. However, she noted that the applicability or otherwise of the presumption was not determinative in the case; "the words were a simple recognition of a fact which existed prior to the modern development of assisted human reproduction."[9] Similarly, Clarke J (who was in dissent), noted that "there is only sparse and limited authority for the proposition that the maxim mater semper ever formed part of the common law of Ireland."[10] MacMenamin J reached an equivalent conclusion, noting that "while the mater semper principle might not, as argued by counsel for the State, be an 'irrebuttable presumption', it was, nonetheless a premise, or implied meaning, on which reference to 'mother' was always predicated."[11] Thus, the judgement confirmed that *mater semper certa est* does not apply as a common law presumption in Ireland. Nonetheless, it was held that existing legislation defines the term "mother" as the woman that gives birth to a child, regardless of her genetic connection to the child.

2. Paternity

Where a man is married to a woman who gives birth to a child, the maxim *pater est quem nuptiae demonstrant*[12] will operate to presume that he is the father of his wife's child. This presumption is given

---

[7] For example, see *MR v An tArd Chláraitheoir* [2014] 3 IR 533 at para 169 per Murray J and para 550 per MacMenamin J.
[8] *MR v An tArd Chláraitheoir* [2014] 3 IR 533 at para 550.
[9] *MR v An tArd Chláraitheoir* [2014] 3 IR 533 at para 110.
[10] *MR v An tArd Chláraitheoir* [2014] 3 IR 533 at para 462.
[11] *MR v An tArd Chláraitheoir* [2014] 3 IR 533 at para 539.
[12] This maxim translates as "the father is he whom the marriage points out."

legislative footing in Ireland under s 46 of the Status of Children Act 1987. This provision sets out that where a woman gives birth to a child during her marriage to a man or within 10 months after the marriage has ended, by death or otherwise, the husband is presumed to be the child's legal father. The presumption can be rebutted where the woman has been living apart from her husband for more than 10 months.[13] The presumption can also be rebutted where it is shown, on the balance of probabilities, that the man is not the father. DNA evidence can be used in this regard to rebut the presumption on the basis of genetics (or, rather, the absence of a genetic connection to the child).[14] In addition, where a man is listed as the father on the child's birth certificate, this gives rise to a presumption that he is the father of the child.[15] This presumption may be rebutted where it is shown, on the balance of probabilities, that he is not the father of the child.

On 22 May 2015, Ireland voted in favour of the Thirty-Fourth Amendment of the Constitution. The Marriage Act 2015 was subsequently enacted to give effect to this constitutional amendment and to enable same-sex couples to enter into civil marriages under Irish law. It should be noted, however, that while the husband of a woman who gives birth to a child is presumed to be the legal father, the female spouse of a woman who gives birth to a child is not automatically presumed to be the second legal mother—there is no presumption of parentage in the case of a married same-sex couple. However, as discussed later, the Children and Family Relationships Act 2015 makes provision for two women to be recognised as joint legal parents in cases of donor-assisted human reproduction.

The Right to Procreate

In Ireland, the courts have recognised that there is a right to found a family, but this right is not absolute and can be restricted where it is necessary and proportionate to do so. The right to found a family was first recognised in *Murray v Ireland*.[16] In this case, a husband and wife who were both serving terms of life imprisonment, argued that they were entitled to conjugal rights in order to conceive a

---

[13] Status of Children Act 1987, s 46(1) amended by Children and Family Relationships Act 2015, s 88.

[14] Status of Children Act 1987, s 38 amended by Children and Family Relationships Act 2015, s 82.

[15] Status of Children Act 1987, s 46(3), amended by Children and Family Relationships Act 2015, s 88.

[16] *Murray v Ireland* [1991] ILRM 465.

child. The Supreme Court found that there is a right to procreate within marriage flowing from the unenumerated personal rights guaranteed by Art 40.3 of the Irish Constitution. McCarthy J noted that this right is "essential to the human condition and personal dignity. It is independent of and antecedent to all positive law; it is of the essence of humanity."[17] However, like many other constitutional rights, it was held that the right to procreate is not absolute and can be suspended where a person is imprisoned and thereby deprived of personal liberty in accordance with law. Thus, the right to procreate may be qualified by proportionate and legitimate restrictions.

In *Murray*, the right to procreate was expressed as a right that arose as a consequence of marriage. This would seem to suggest that the right to procreate only applies to married couples. It is notable, however, that the Supreme Court found that the right flowed from Art 40.3 of the Irish Constitution, which protects personal rights, and not from Art 41, which protects the marital family. Thus, it could be argued that the right to procreate extends equally to unmarried couples and single persons; however, this argument has not been specifically addressed by the Irish courts.[18]

The European Court of Human Rights (ECtHR) considered limitations imposed on a prisoner's right to procreate using assisted reproductive technologies in the case of *Dickson v United Kingdom*.[19] In this case, the applicants were a married couple serving sentences of imprisonment in different prisons. They applied to Mr Dickson's prison to be allowed access to artificial insemination so that Mrs Dickson (who had since been released from prison) could conceive a child. This request was refused by the Secretary of State on the basis of a general policy that was applied to such requests. The applicants brought their case to the ECtHR claiming that the refusal violated their rights under Art 8 (right to respect for private and family life) and Art 12 (right to marry and to found a family) of the European Convention on Human Rights (ECHR). The ECtHR began by noting that a person retains his or her ECHR rights on imprisonment. It may sometimes be necessary to impose restrictions on those rights, for example for reasons of security or for the prevention of crime and disorder, but any restriction on those rights must be justified in each individual case. The ECtHR

---

[17] *Murray v Ireland* [1991] ILRM 465 at 476.

[18] Andrea Mulligan, "From Murray v Ireland to Roche v Roche: Re-Evaluating the Right to Procreate in the Context of Assisted Reproduction" (2012) 35 *Dublin University Law Journal* 261.

[19] *Dickson v United Kingdom* App no 44362/04 (ECtHR, 4 December 2007).

noted that the ECHR had not yet been interpreted as requiring States to provide conjugal visits for prisoners, and thus States have a margin of appreciation in that area.[20] At the same time, the court noted that the provision of artificial insemination facilities would not involve any security issues nor would it impose any significant administrative or financial demands on the State.[21] Overall, the ECtHR found that the policy in question, which prevented the applicants from accessing artificial insemination, placed "an inordinately high 'exceptionality' burden" on them: they had to establish that the deprivation of artificial insemination facilities might prevent conception altogether and that the circumstances of their case were otherwise "exceptional" within the meaning of the policy.[22] This created a high threshold that "did not allow a balancing of the competing individual and public interests and a proportionality test by the Secretary of State or by the domestic courts in their case, as required by the Convention."[23] As such, the principle of proportionality had not been adhered to and the ECtHR held that there was a violation of Art 8 ECHR. This judgment does not mandate that States must automatically provide prisoners with access to artificial insemination facilities in order to be ECHR compliant but it establishes that, when considering any such requests, the State must weigh up the competing individual and public interests and assess the proportionality of any restriction in any individual case.

One of the earliest cases to come before the Irish courts concerning assisted reproductive technologies was *Roche v Roche*,[24] which concerned the use of frozen embryos. In this case, a married couple underwent IVF treatment using their own gametes which resulted in the creation of six embryos. Three embryos were implanted and the wife became pregnant and gave birth to a daughter. The remaining embryos were frozen. The couple later separated and the wife sought to have the remaining frozen embryos implanted in her uterus but the husband objected to this as he did not want to become the father of another child with the wife now that they were separated. The wife instituted proceedings seeking to use the remaining frozen embryos.

---

[20] *Dickson v United Kingdom* App no 44362/04 (ECtHR, 4 December 2007) at para 81.
[21] *Dickson v United Kingdom* App no 44362/04 (ECtHR, 4 December 2007) at para 74.
[22] *Dickson v United Kingdom* App no 44362/04 (ECtHR, 4 December 2007) at para 82.
[23] *Dickson v United Kingdom* App no 44362/04 (ECtHR, 4 December 2007) at para 82.
[24] *Roche v Roche* [2010] 2 IR 321.

The central question for the Supreme Court in *Roche v Roche* was whether the constitutional protection afforded to the life of the unborn in Art 40.3.3° of the Constitution (since repealed) extended to fertilised embryos stored in a clinic such that the embryos had to be implanted in the plaintiff wife's womb in order to vindicate their right to life. Article 40.3.3° of the Irish Constitution provided that

> "The State acknowledges the right to life of the unborn and, with due regard to the equal right to life of the mother, guarantees in its laws to respect, and, as far as practicable, by its laws to defend and vindicate that right."

The Supreme Court unanimously dismissed the appeal and found that a frozen embryo was not "unborn" for the purposes of Art 40.3.3° of the Irish Constitution and did not, therefore, attract protection under that article. In addition, the court held that the husband's consent to the first round of IVF treatment and to the freezing of embryos was not an agreement to the implantation, years later, of any surplus embryos.

In this case, Murray CJ noted that there is no consensus as to precisely when life begins, in particular whether it begins at conception or implantation.[25] The Chief Justice did not think that this was a matter for the courts to determine but felt that the point in time when human life should be legally protected was a policy choice for the Oireachtas to determine.[26] Indeed, this was a sentiment echoed throughout the five judgments handed down in this case: each judge called on the Oireachtas to introduce legislation to regulate the use and storage of fertilised embryos and the provision of IVF treatment.

In her judgment, Denham J noted that the "mischief" to which Art 40.3.3° was addressed was that of "the termination of pregnancy, the procuring of a miscarriage, an abortion."[27] Denham J noted that the life of the "unborn" in Art 40.3.3° was to be considered alongside the life of the mother and that the article

> "applies to a relationship where one life may be balanced against another. This relationship only exists, this balance only applies, where there is a physical connection between the mother and the unborn. This occurs only subsequent to implantation of the embryo. Thus the balancing of the right

---

[25] *Roche v Roche* [2010] 2 IR 321 at para 42.
[26] *Roche v Roche* [2010] 2 IR 321 at paras 49–54.
[27] *Roche v Roche* [2010] 2 IR 321 at para 134.

to life described in Article 40.3.3 may only take place after implantation. Therefore an unborn under Article 40.3.3 is established after an embryo is implanted."[28]

Similarly, Hardiman J held that the mother referred to in Art 40.3.3°

"is the mother of the 'unborn' and that their physical relationship is such that the right to life of the unborn is capable of impinging on the right to life of the mother. This, it appears to me, requires a physical relationship. The only relevant physical relationship is that of pregnancy."[29]

This case was concerned with the legal status of embryos and did not focus on the right to procreate. Denham J did, however, make some comments in this regard. For example, the judge noted that the right to procreate was accompanied by an equal and opposite right *not* to procreate. In the instant case, the exercise of the husband's right not to procreate was found to be a proportionate interference with the wife's right to procreate. In addition, Denham J noted that, if the frozen embryos were found to be protected by Art 40.3.3°, the implication would be that the State would have to intervene to facilitate their implantation in all cases, irrespective of the wishes of the parents. This, however, would not be consistent with the rights of the marital family under Art 41.[30] That said, the judge also noted that, if a similar case was to come before the courts in future, all circumstances would have to be taken into account and that "[i]f a party had no children, and had no other opportunity of having a child, that would be a relevant factor for consideration."[31] This seemingly leaves open the possibility that in another case, where a woman does not already have children, implantation might be ordered by the court notwithstanding that the other spouse has a right not to procreate. This point was not, however, addressed by the remainder of the court and so the significance (if any) of the statement remains to be seen.

A similar set of facts to those considered in *Roche* came before the ECtHR three years earlier in the case of *Evans v UK*.[32] In this case, the applicant had suffered from pre-cancerous tumours on her ovaries which meant that her ovaries had to be removed. Prior to this operation, she had undergone a procedure to extract her eggs

---

[28] *Roche v Roche* [2010] 2 IR 321 at para 139.
[29] *Roche v Roche* [2010] 2 IR 321 at para 172.
[30] *Roche v Roche* [2010] 2 IR 321 at para 146.
[31] *Roche v Roche* [2010] 2 IR 321 at para 114.
[32] *Evans v the United Kingdom* App no 6339/05 (ECtHR, 10 April 2007).

and underwent IVF treatment with her partner at the time to create and freeze a number of embryos for future use. The couple later separated and the partner requested that the embryos be destroyed. The applicant applied to have her former partner's initial consent to the use and storage of the embryos restored. She was unsuccessful before the domestic courts and subsequently brought her case to the ECtHR claiming that the legal provision requiring the consent of both parties to the implantation of the embryos violated her rights under Art 8 ECHR.[33]

The ECtHR noted that the case involved a conflict between the Article 8 rights of two private individuals and that each person's interest was entirely irreconcilable with the other's: if the applicant was permitted to use the embryos, her former partner would become a father against his wishes and if the former partner's withdrawal of consent was upheld, the applicant would be denied the opportunity of becoming a genetic parent. The ECtHR noted that there was no European consensus on the use of IVF treatment and further that such treatment gives rise to "sensitive moral and ethical issues against a background of fast-moving medical and scientific developments."[34] This meant that the State had a wide margin of appreciation or discretion to regulate the area. This margin extended to the State's decision on whether or not to enact legislation governing the use of IVF treatment in the first place and, having intervened, to the detailed rules it lays down in that regulation. In assessing the proportionality of the UK legislation and requirements for consent, the ECtHR noted that

> "Respect for human dignity and free will, as well as a desire to ensure a fair balance between the parties to IVF treatment, underlay the legislature's decision to enact provisions permitting of no exception to ensure that every person donating gametes for the purpose of IVF treatment would know in advance that no use could be made of his or her genetic material without his or her continuing consent."[35]

---

[33] In her original application to the ECtHR, the applicant also complained that the provisions of English law requiring the embryos to be destroyed once her partner withdrew his consent to their continued storage violated the embryos' right to life, contrary to Art 2 of the Convention. The ECtHR noted that, following the decision in *Vo v France* App no 53924/00 (ECtHR, 8 July 2004), because there is no European consensus on the scientific and legal definition of the beginning of life, the issue of when the right to life begins comes within the margin of appreciation of each Member State. As such, there was no violation of Art 2 ECHR.

[34] *Evans v the United Kingdom* App no 6339/05 (ECtHR, 10 April 2007) at para 81.

[35] *Evans v the United Kingdom* App no 6339/05 (ECtHR, 10 April 2007) at para 89.

The legislation in question sought to promote legal certainty and to avoid inconsistency and so was found to pursue legitimate aims consistent with Art 8 ECHR. Overall, the ECtHR held that the legal provisions struck a fair balance between the competing interests and so there was no violation of Art 8 ECHR.

Parentage in Donor-Assisted Human Reproduction

Before 2015, there was no specific legislation in place in Ireland governing the allocation of parentage in situations where donor-assisted human reproduction (DAHR) was used. This meant that where a couple conceived a child by way of a donor procedure (using donated sperm/ovum/embryo), the rules of parentage set out above would apply: woman who gave birth was regarded as the legal mother, if she was married, her husband was presumed to be the legal father, and if she was unmarried, the man listed on the child's birth certificate was presumed to be the legal father. This approach often failed to accommodate the second intended parent (male or female) who was not genetically or gestationally connected to the child. In particular, where same-sex couples engaged in this process, the partner of the birth mother had no opportunity to be recognised as a legal parent or to acquire legal parental responsibilities towards the child.

The Children and Family Relationships Act 2015 (the "2015 Act") now provides detailed rules to determine the parentage of children born via DAHR. These rules allow children who are conceived via DAHR to automatically acquire a legal relationship with both of their intended parents from the moment of birth.

For the purpose of the 2015 Act, a DAHR procedure is defined as one where

> "(a) one of the gametes from which the embryo has been or will be formed has been provided by a donor,
> (b) each gamete from which the embryo has been or will be formed has been provided by a donor, or
> (c) the embryo has been provided by a donor."[36]

The term "gamete" refers to the male (sperm) or female (ovum) reproductive cell. The term embryo refers to the organism created in the 28-week period after fertilisation of the ovum by the sperm.

---

[36] Children and Family Relationships Act 2015, s 4.

1. The Legal Mother

The 2015 Act sets out that the parents of a child who is born following a DAHR procedure shall be the mother (the woman who gives birth) and the spouse, civil partner or cohabitant, as the case may be, of the mother. If the mother is single, she alone shall be the parent of the child. The "mother" for the purposes of DAHR is defined as the woman who gives birth to the child.[37]

The intended mother in the DAHR procedure must be over 21 years of age and she must be informed of the following before the procedure can take place:

- That her name, date of birth, address and contact details will be transmitted to the Minister for Health;
- That where she consents to the DAHR procedure, she will be the parent of the child;
- That the donor of a gamete or embryo used in the DAHR procedure shall not be the parent of the child;
- That information regarding the birth of the child, the parent(s) and donor(s) will be recorded in the National Donor-Conceived Person Register;
- That when the child reaches the age of 18 years, he or she may access information in relation to the donor and may seek to contact him or her;
- That the mother may request information from the register before the child reaches the age of 18 years in respect of non-identifying information about the donor and the number of persons who have been born as a result of a gamete donated by the relevant donor, and the sex and year of birth of each of them;
- That the mother must inform the DAHR facility whether the DAHR procedure resulted in a pregnancy and birth and, if so, must provide the facility with specific information concerning the birth;
- That the mother may revoke her consent to the procedure at any time until the DAHR procedure is performed.[38]

Having been provided with this information, the intended mother must consent and make a declaration to her recognition as the legal mother of the child and agree that the donor of genetic material will

---

[37] Children and Family Relationships Act 2015, s 4.
[38] Children and Family Relationships Act 2015, s 13.

not be recognised as a legal parent.[39] In addition, where applicable, the intended mother must consent to the recognition of her spouse, civil partner or cohabitant, as the case may be, as the second legal parent of the child.[40]

2. The Second Legal Parent

The 2015 Act provides that where a couple engage in DAHR, the spouse, civil partner or cohabitant, as the case may be, of the mother will be regarded as the child's second legal parent. The second legal parent must be provided with the same information set out above in the case of the intended mother before the procedure can be performed,[41] and must also consent and make a declaration to the effect that he or she agrees to his or her recognition as the child's second legal parent and also that he or she understands that the donor of genetic material will not be regarded as a parent.[42]

3. Gamete Donors

Where a DAHR procedure is performed under the 2015 Act, the donor of genetic material will not be regarded as a parent of the child nor will he or she have any parental rights and duties in respect of the child.[43] The gamete donor must be over the age of 18 years and must have been provided with the following information in respect of the DAHR process:

- That where he or she consents to the use of his or her gamete in a DAHR procedure, he or she is entitled to request information from the National Donor-Conceived Person Register on the number of persons who have been born as a result of the use in a DAHR procedure of a gamete donated by the donor, and the sex and year of birth of each of them;
- That his or her ability to access information from the Register is dependent on the child, who has attained the age of 18 years, requesting the Minister to record on the Register a statement of his or her name, date of birth and contact details and confirming that he or she consents

---

[39] Children and Family Relationships Act 2015, s 9(3)(c).
[40] Children and Family Relationships Act 2015, s 9(3)(d) amended by Marriage Act 2015, s 23.
[41] Children and Family Relationships Act 2015, s 13.
[42] Children and Family Relationships Act 2015, s 11, amended by Marriage Act 2015, s 23.
[43] Children and Family Relationships Act 2015, s 5.

to the release of that information to the relevant donor should the donor request it under s 36;

- That his or her name, his or her date and place of birth, his or her nationality, the date on which, and the place at which, he or she provided the gamete, and his or her contact details provided under s 24 will be provided to the Minister for Health and will be recorded on the National Donor-Conceived Person Register;
- That he or she shall not be the parent of the child born as a result of the DAHR procedure;
- That when the child reaches the age of 18 years, he or she may access information in relation to the donor and seek to contact him or her;
- That upon being notified of the request by a child for such information, the donor may make representations to the Minister for Health setting out why his or her safety, the safety of the child, or both, requires that the information not be released;
- That it is desirable that he or she keep updated, in accordance with s 38(1), the information in relation to him or her that is recorded on the Register;
- That he or she may revoke consent to the procedure at any time until the DAHR procedure is performed.[44]

The donor of genetic material must also consent and make a declaration to the use of his or her gamete in a DAHR procedure and must declare that he or she understands that he or she will not be a parent of any child born through the use of such material following a DAHR procedure.[45]

These rules of parentage only apply in situations where the DAHR procedure is performed in a clinical setting. The 2015 Act does not expressly set out that the DAHR procedure *must* be performed in a DAHR facility but this requirement can be implied from various provisions. For example, the term "DAHR facility" is defined as "a place at which a DAHR procedure is performed."[46] In addition, in order for the above-mentioned parentage provisions to operate, the requisite consents must be duly obtained and retained by "the operator of the DAHR facility."[47] As such, in order for the parentage provisions mentioned above to apply, the conception must have taken place in a DAHR facility. This means that children conceived

---

44 Children and Family Relationships Act 2015, s 7.
45 Children and Family Relationships Act 2015, s 6.
46 Children and Family Relationships Act 2015, s 4.
47 Children and Family Relationships Act 2015, s 28.

through DAHR in non-clinical settings, for example where the procedure is performed at home, are not covered by the parentage provisions set out in the 2015 Act and the traditional rules of parentage will apply.[48]

4. Retrospective Parentage

The 2015 Act also allows for the retrospective allocation of parentage of children who were born following the use of a DAHR procedure at any time prior to the coming into force of the legislation. Where certain criteria are met, an application may be made to either the District Court[49] or the Circuit Court[50] for a declaration of parentage which sets out that the intended parents are the legal parents of a child. The criteria for the making of such a declaration are as follows:

- the child must have been born as a result of a DAHR procedure that was performed (either within or outside of the State) before the date on which the relevant section came into operation;
- at the time when the DAHR procedure was performed, a person, other than the intended mother, was an intended parent of the child;
- the gamete donor must have been unknown to the intended parents and must not have been an intended parent at the time of the procedure, and the donor must remain unknown to the intended parents at the time of the application; and
- the intended mother must be recorded as the legal mother in the Register for Births and no person, or no person other than the second intended parent, can have been recorded in that register as the child's father or second legal parent.[51]

Where these criteria are satisfied, the intended parents may jointly apply to the District Court for a declaration of parentage that sets out that the second intended parent is a legal parent.[52] Alternatively, the child or the intended parents may individually apply to the Circuit Court for such a declaration.[53] Where the declaration is

---

48 See Lydia Bracken, "In the Best Interests of the Child? The Regulation of DAHR in Ireland" (2016) 23 *European Journal of Health Law* 391.
49 Children and Family Relationships Act 2015, s 21.
50 Children and Family Relationships Act 2015, s 22.
51 Children and Family Relationships Act 2015, s 20
52 Children and Family Relationships Act 2015, s 21.
53 Children and Family Relationships Act 2015, s 22.

granted by either court, the second intended parent shall be deemed to be a legal parent from the date of the order and the order will set out that the gamete donor is not a parent of the child and that he or she has no parental rights or duties.[54]

These provisions allow for a person not previously recognised as a second legal parent to be recognised as such in circumstances where the child was born before the 2015 Act was commenced. In order for the retrospective declaration of parentage to be granted, the gamete donor must have been unknown to the intended parents at the date of the procedure and he or she must remain unknown at the time of the application.[55] Therefore, where a known donor has been used, the declaration cannot be granted.

The Child's Right to Identity

The child's right to identity is an important aspect of the legal regulation of assisted reproduction. Children conceived using donor gametes often express a strong desire for information about their origins and it is generally accepted that the earlier that donor-conceived children learn about the nature of their conception, the more favourable the outcomes in terms of identity formation and fostering positive family relationships.[56]

The Children and Family Relationships Act 2015 contains a range of provisions that are designed to protect the child's right to identity. Perhaps most significant is the prohibition on the use of anonymous donor gametes and embryos set out in s 24. This section provides that a donated gamete or embryo cannot be acquired by a DAHR facility for use in a DAHR procedure unless identifying information about the donor is also acquired.[57] Therefore, DAHR can only take place where the identity of the donor is known and recorded.

The 2015 Act does, however, provide for a limited exception to the above. It allows a DAHR facility to use anonymous gametes for a period of three years after the commencement of the relevant sections of the 2015 Act, in circumstances where an intended parent already has a child conceived using gametes from the same donor and where they wish to have a genetic sibling for that child. In

---

[54] Children and Family Relationships Act 2015, s 23.
[55] Children and Family Relationships Act 2015, s 20(1)(d)–(e).
[56] Diane Beeson, Patricia Jennings and Wendy Kramer, "Offspring searching for their sperm donors: how family type shapes the process" (2011) 26 *Human Reproduction* 2415.
[57] Children and Family Relationships Act 2015, s 24.

this situation, the gamete must have been acquired before the commencement of the section and the donor of the gamete must have consented to the use of the gamete in a DAHR procedure.[58] Similarly, the prohibition on the use of anonymous embryos does not apply where the embryo was formed before the commencement of the section, once the donor, or each donor of the embryo, has consented to the use of the embryo in a DAHR procedure.[59] Outside of these limited circumstances, anonymous donation is prohibited, thereby ensuring that a record will be kept of information relevant to the child's genetic background.

Section 33 of the 2015 Act sets out that the Minister for Health shall cause to be established and maintained a National Donor-Conceived Person Register (the "Register"). The purpose of this Register is to record information relating to donor-conceived children which shall include personal details, donor information and recipient parent information.[60] Furthermore, an obligation is imposed on the operator of the DAHR facility to keep a record of donor information and recipient parent information. This information must subsequently be transmitted to the Minister for Health for inclusion in the Register.[61]

The child is given the right to request information from the Register. Once the child has reached the age of 18 years, he or she may request both identifying and non-identifying information about the donor, as well as certain limited details about other persons who may have been conceived using material from the same donor.[62] The parents of a child who has not reached the age of 18 years may request non-identifying information from the Register.[63] Where the child seeks identifying information, the donor will be notified of this request and may request that the Minister does not issue such information in circumstances where "the safety of the relevant donor or the donor-conceived child, or both, requires that the information not be released."[64] Where the Minister is satisfied that sufficient reasons exist to withhold the information concerned, he or she shall refuse to issue same.[65] As such, the child's ability to access information pertaining to his or her identity may be impeded in certain limited circumstances.

---

58 Children and Family Relationships Act 2015, s 26(5).
59 Children and Family Relationships Act 2015, s 26(6).
60 Children and Family Relationships Act 2015, s 33(3).
61 Children and Family Relationships Act 2015, ss 28(3)–28(5).
62 Children and Family Relationships Act 2015, ss 34–35.
63 Children and Family Relationships Act 2015, s 34.
64 Children and Family Relationships Act 2015, s 35(2)(b).
65 Children and Family Relationships Act 2015, s 35(3)(a).

A notable feature of the 2015 Act is that it provides for interaction between the National Donor-Conceived Person Register and the Register for Births. Section 39(1) of the 2015 Act provides that where the Minister for Health records information relating to the birth of a donor-conceived person in the Register, he or she is obliged to notify an tArd Chláraitheoir (the Registrar General) of this record. Upon receiving this notification, an tArd Chláraitheoir is then obliged to "note in the entry in the register of births in respect of the child that the child is a donor-conceived child and that additional information is available from the Register in relation to the child."[66] Subsequently, where a person over the age of 18 years applies for a copy of his or her birth certificate, and a note exists in relation to him or her, an tArd-Chláraitheoir shall, when issuing a copy of the birth certificate requested, inform the person that further information relating to him or her is available from the Register.[67]

The notification process is an innovative measure that will facilitate donor-conceived persons to acquire knowledge of their genetic origins. After all, although the donor-conceived person may apply for information from the Register, they will only know to access the Register if they have first been told that they were donor-conceived. As Bainham has noted, "the right to information ... is largely illusory in the case of donor-conceived children unless they know that they are donor-conceived."[68] Of course, if a person has not previously been told that they are donor-conceived, it may cause distress to discover this upon application for a birth certificate. It is to be hoped, however, that the notification process will foster openness among intended parents and encourage them to tell their children of their donor conception as they will know that this information cannot be supressed forever. Research suggests that, for some people, discovering the fact of donor conception later in life and/or in unplanned ways can result in long-term psychological distress and can damage family relationships.[69] It is to be hoped therefore that the new provisions will encourage intended parents to be more open and proactive in telling their children of their donor conception earlier in life.

---

[66] Children and Family Relationships Act 2015, s 39(2).
[67] Children and Family Relationships Act 2015, s 39(4).
[68] Andrew Bainham, "Arguments about Parentage" (2008) 67(2) *Cambridge Law Journal* 322 at 335.
[69] Eric Blyth, Marilyn Crawshaw, Iolanda Rodino, and Petra Thorn, "Donor-conceived people do benefit from being told about their conception" *Bionews* 30 May 2017 <http://www.bionews.org.uk/page_845387.asp>

Parentage in Surrogacy

Surrogacy is a process where a woman agrees to carry a child on behalf of another person or couple. Currently in Ireland, surrogacy is permitted but there is no specific legislation in place to regulate its use. As a result, the traditional rules of parentage continue to apply in surrogacy such that the woman who gives birth to the child will always be regarded as the child's legal mother.[70] If she is married, her husband (but not her wife) is presumed to be the child's legal father,[71] and if she is not married, the man listed on the birth certificate will be presumed to be the legal father.[72] Both presumptions can be rebutted where it is shown, on the balance of probabilities, that the man is not the father of the child.

The application of the traditional parentage laws in cases of surrogacy does not adequately accommodate these arrangements as it means that at least one of the intended parents in the surrogacy arrangement (the non-gestational intended mother or non-genetic intended father) might not have any legal connection to the child at birth. This was seen in the case of *MR and An tArd Chláraitheoir*, discussed above, where the intended mother could not be recognised as the legal mother of twins born to the surrogate, despite being genetically related to the children. The absence of specific rules to determine parentage in surrogacy also affects male couples who engage in surrogacy as the intended father who is not genetically related to the child has no opportunity to be legally recognised as a parent upon the birth of the child.

In the absence of specific legislation to address surrogacy, intended parents who are not genetically or gestationally related to the child have to rely on guardianship or adoption laws to establish a legal relationship with the child. Guardianship, discussed in detail in Chapter 4, can be extended to a person who is not legally related to the child. However, the appointment of this person as an *additional* guardian is only possible where the adult is married to, or is a civil partner or cohabitant of, the legal parent and has shared responsibility for the child's day-to-day care for a period of at least two years.[73] Thus, a two-year waiting period applies. This means that the intended parent seeking guardianship cannot

---

[70] *MR v An tArd Chláraitheoir* [2014] 3 IR 533.
[71] Status of Children Act 1987, s 46(1).
[72] Status of Children Act 1987, s 46(3), amended by Children and Family Relationships Act 2015, s 88.
[73] Guardianship of Infants Act 1964, s 6C, inserted by Children and Family Relationships Act 2015, s 49.

acquire rights and responsibilities in respect of the child for some time after the birth.

An alternative option would be for the intended parent to apply to adopt the child. As is discussed in Chapter 5, the Adoption (Amendment) Act 2017 puts a new scheme in place to facilitate step-parent adoptions and so an intended parent could avail of these new provisions to acquire a legal relationship with the child.[74] It should be noted, however, that step-parent adoption is only possible where the spouse, civil partner or cohabitant of the birth parent has lived with the birth parent for a continuous period of not less than two years.[75] Moreover, an adoption order is not designed to address surrogacy situations.

In the *MR* case, each of the seven judges expressed concern in relation to the current lack of legal regulation in the area of surrogacy and they called for legislation to be introduced to regulate the complex family relationships arising. O'Donnell J, for example, expressed the view that it was

> "surely most clearly and profoundly wrong from the point of children born through an unregulated process into a world where their status may be determined by happenstance, and where simple events such as registration for schools, attendance at a doctor, consent to medical treatment, acquisition of a passport and even joining sports teams may involve complications, embarrassment and the necessity for prior consultation with lawyers resulting in necessarily inconclusive advice."[76]

Denham CJ noted that there is currently "a lacuna in the law as to certain rights, especially those of the children" born via surrogacy and she called for legislation to be introduced to address this lacuna.[77] Similarly, MacMenamin J found that "[t]he human situation in this case, and others, renders it incumbent on the legislature to attempt to address these questions."[78]

Surrogacy legislation has been discussed in Ireland for many years.[79] When the Children and Family Relationships Bill 2014

---

[74] Adoption Act 2010, s 58A, inserted by Adoption (Amendment) Act 2017, s 26.
[75] Adoption Act 2010, s 37(b) as amended by Adoption (Amendment) Act 2017, s 18.
[76] *MR v An tArd Chláraitheoir* [2014] 3 IR 533 at para 211 per O'Donnell J.
[77] *MR v An tArd Chláraitheoir* [2014] 3 IR 533 at para 116 per Denham CJ.
[78] *MR v An tArd Chláraitheoir* [2014] 3 IR 533 at para 582 per MacMenamin J.
[79] See: Commission on Assisted Human Reproduction, *Report of the Commission on Assisted Human Reproduction* (Dublin, 2005).

was initially published, it contained proposals for the regulation of surrogacy. The Bill set out that, in a surrogacy arrangement, the woman who gives birth to the child would be regarded as the legal mother at birth.[80] The intended parents could then apply for a declaration of parentage after the birth to terminate the surrogate's parental status and to transfer parental status to themselves.[81] The surrogate's consent would be required before this declaration could be made, and the application for the declaration could be sought not less than 30 days after and not more than six months after the child's birth.[82] In essence, the Bill made provision for what might be termed a "delayed model" of parentage whereby parentage would be transferred after birth. The Bill also proposed that the declaration of parentage could only be granted in circumstances where at least one of the intended parents had a genetic connection to the child and where evidence was provided to the court that the surrogate was not genetically related to the child.[83] Therefore, the Bill only allowed for "full" surrogacy to be used, that is where either the intended mother provided her egg to enable the conception of the child or a donor egg was used.

The surrogacy proposals were subsequently removed from the 2014 Bill, as it was felt that further policy work and consultations were required in relation to surrogacy. As such, the regulation of surrogacy was deferred to the Assisted Human Reproduction Bill 2017 (the "2017 Bill"), which was approved for drafting on 3 October 2017. The General Scheme of the Assisted Human Reproduction Bill 2017 proposes a new framework for the regulation of surrogacy in Ireland. The model of parentage proposed is broadly similar to that which was put forward in the 2014 Bill—in that parentage would be transferred after the birth of the child—but the 2017 Bill also requires that all surrogacy agreements would be pre-authorised by a new Assisted Human Reproduction Regulatory Authority. The main elements of the proposed regulation of surrogacy set out in the 2017 Bill are detailed below.

The 2017 Bill provides that surrogacy would only be permitted where a number of conditions are met. Among the conditions are that:

---

[80] General Scheme of the Children and Family Relationships Bill 2014, Head 12(1).
[81] General Scheme of the Children and Family Relationships Bill 2014, Head 13.
[82] General Scheme of the Children and Family Relationships Bill 2014, Heads 13(9)(b) and 13(5).
[83] General Scheme of the Children and Family Relationships Bill 2014, Head 13(8).

- the surrogacy must be domestic, gestational, and non-commercial[84];
- the surrogacy agreement must be approved in advance of treatment by the Assisted Human Reproduction Regulatory Authority[85];
- the surrogate must be habitually resident in Ireland; must have previously given birth to a child; must be least 25 years of age but under 45 years of age; and must have been assessed and approved as suitable to act as a surrogate by a registered medical practitioner and also by a counsellor[86];
- the intended parent(s) must be at least 21 years of age and at least one of them must be under 47 years of age; at least one intended parent must be habitually resident in Ireland; at least one intended parent must have contributed a gamete to the child's conception; and the intended parents must be either unable to gestate a pregnancy, unable to conceive a child for medical reasons, include a woman who is unlikely to survive a pregnancy or childbirth, or include a woman who is likely to have her health significantly affected by a pregnancy or by childbirth[87];
- the personal details of each intended parent, the surrogate, donor (where applicable) and any child born under the surrogacy agreement must be recorded in the National Surrogacy Register.[88]

Thus, the model of surrogacy that is proposed is a restrictive one that would only apply to certain surrogacy arrangements. The proposed regulation would not apply in situations where international surrogacy is used nor would it apply in cases of "traditional" surrogacy, that is where the surrogate provides her egg to enable the conception of the child. One of the intended parents would have to be genetically related to the child and only "reasonable expenses" could be paid to the surrogate.[89] The Bill also requires that the surrogate and intended parent(s) would undergo counselling and receive independent legal advice at each

---

[84] General Scheme of the Children and Family Relationships Bill 2014, Head 36.
[85] General Scheme of the Children and Family Relationships Bill 2014, Head 37.
[86] General Scheme of the Children and Family Relationships Bill 2014, Head 38.
[87] General Scheme of the Children and Family Relationships Bill 2014, Head 39.
[88] General Scheme of the Children and Family Relationships Bill 2014, Head 36.
[89] "Reasonable expenses" are defined in Head 41 of the General Scheme to include medical expenses, travel expenses, loss of earnings, and legal advice among other things.

stage of the surrogacy agreement.[90] The stages referred to are (i) before the agreement; (ii) after the birth of the child but before the child is living with the intended parents; and (iii) at the time of the application for the transfer of parentage of the child.[91]

The model of parentage proposed under the 2017 Bill is broadly similar to that which had been put forward in the 2014 Bill. It is a "delayed" model of parentage whereby the surrogate would be recognised as the legal mother on the birth of the child, and if she is married to a man, her husband would be presumed to be the legal father. The intended parents might not automatically have any legal connection to the child at birth. Following the birth of the child, the surrogate would be required to provide her consent to the child living with the intended parent(s).[92] Thereafter, the intended parent(s) (or the surrogate) could apply to the court for a parental order to transfer parentage from the surrogate to the intended parent(s). This application could not be made earlier than six weeks and not more than six months after the child's birth.[93] The application would have to be accompanied by evidence demonstrating that the surrogate is not the genetic mother of the child and evidence showing that at least one of the intended parents is a genetic parent.[94] The consent of the surrogate (and her husband if applicable) would be required before the parental order could be granted. This requirement could be waived in certain circumstances, such as where the surrogate is deceased or cannot be located.[95]

A notable difference between the 2017 Bill and the earlier proposals to regulate surrogacy is the proposed requirement for pre-authorisation of the surrogacy agreement from the Regulatory Authority. Under the 2017 Bill, an AHR treatment provider would be required to apply to the Regulatory Authority and receive written authorisation for a surrogacy agreement before any treatment could be provided under that agreement.[96] The Regulatory Authority would only provide authorisation where all of the conditions set out in Head 36 of the Bill are met and where the agreement has been signed by the surrogate, and each intended parent. Once the authorisation is issued, it would only be valid for the period

---

90 General Scheme of the Children and Family Relationships Bill 2014, Head 43.
91 Explanatory note accompanying Head 43, General Scheme of the Assisted Human Reproduction Bill 2017.
92 General Scheme of the Assisted Human Reproduction Bill 2017, Head 46.
93 General Scheme of the Assisted Human Reproduction Bill 2017, Head 47.
94 General Scheme of the Assisted Human Reproduction Bill 2017, Head 47(4).
95 General Scheme of the Assisted Human Reproduction Bill 2017, Head 48.
96 General Scheme of the Assisted Human Reproduction Bill 2017, Head 37.

specified in the authorisation, up to a maximum period of two years. The pre-authorisation of the surrogacy agreement would not impact on the allocation of parentage in any way.

The 2017 Bill also makes provision for a "surrogacy certificate" to be issued to the intended parents following the grant of a parental order.[97] The surrogacy certificate would be similar to an adoption certificate, which is issued by an tArd-Chláraitheoir following the grant of an adoption order, in that it would replace the child's birth certificate for identification purposes. It would list the intended parents (who have obtained the parental order) as the child's legal parents. The certificate would be identical to a standard birth certificate, with nothing to indicate that the child to whom the certificate relates was born under a surrogacy agreement.[98] An tArd-Chláraitheoir is also directed to establish and maintain an index to the register of births linking each parental order with the relevant entry in the register of births. This index would not be open to public inspection.[99]

Another notable feature of the 2017 Bill is the proposed creation of a National Surrogacy Register. This Register would record all information relating to surrogate-born children including information on the surrogate, each intended parent and, where applicable, the donor.[100] The Register would also contain information concerning parental orders and applications for same. The new Register would operate alongside the National Donor Conceived Person Register but would be completely separate from it.[101] Thus, where donated gametes are used to create the embryo as part of a surrogacy agreement, it is proposed that details of that donor would be recorded in the National Surrogacy Register and not in the National Donor Conceived Person Register. If the same donor separately acted as a donor in the context of a DAHR procedure under the Children and Family Relationships Act 2015, his or her details would separately be recorded in the National Donor Conceived Person Register.[102]

---

[97] General Scheme of the Assisted Human Reproduction Bill 2017, Head 52.

[98] Explanatory note accompanying Head 52 General Scheme of the Assisted Human Reproduction Bill 2017.

[99] General Scheme of the Assisted Human Reproduction Bill 2017, Head 52(3).

[100] General Scheme of the Assisted Human Reproduction Bill 2017, Head 50.

[101] As was discussed earlier in this Chapter, the purpose of the National Donor Conceived Person Register is to record information relating to donor-conceived children born through a DAHR procedure for the purpose of the Children and Family Relationships Act 2015.

[102] Explanatory note accompanying Head 50, General Scheme of the Assisted Human Reproduction Bill 2017.

The 2017 Bill proposes that a surrogate-born child who has reached the age of 18 years, or the parent of a surrogate-born child who is under the age of 18 years, would be able to apply to the Regulatory Authority for certain information contained in the National Surrogacy Register.[103] Separate procedures are proposed in respect of applications concerning non-identifying information about a donor,[104] identifying information about a donor,[105] information relating to the surrogate or an intended parent,[106] and information concerning donor-siblings.[107] These provisions are similar to those that apply under the 2015 Act in respect of children born following a DAHR procedure.

1. "Delayed" Model of Parentage

The model of parentage proposed under the 2017 Bill can be described as a "delayed" or "post-birth" model of parentage as it proposes that parentage would be transferred from the surrogate (and her husband, if applicable) to the intended parents after birth via the parental order. A broadly similar model of parentage operates in England and Wales under the Human Fertilisation and Embryology Act 2008. In England and Wales, the law provides that the surrogate is automatically regarded as the legal mother upon the birth of a child. The intended parents may then apply for a parental order to transfer legal parentage to them. This order cannot be made for the first six weeks after the child's birth but it must be made within six months of the birth and the surrogate's consent is required for the order to be granted.[108]

It is notable, however, that the English regulation of surrogacy has attracted increased criticism over the years. It is seen to disproportionately favour the surrogate at the expense of other stakeholders in the process and to create uncertainty as to the child's future upbringing. The delayed transfer of parentage means that intended parents remain unsure of whether the surrogate will consent to the parental order up until the point that the order is made, while the surrogate may be concerned that the intended parents will change their mind about the process and never seek the order leaving her, quite literally, holding the baby. These apprehensions have led both intended parents and surrogates to

---

[103] General Scheme of the Assisted Human Reproduction Bill 2017, Head 53.
[104] General Scheme of the Assisted Human Reproduction Bill 2017, Head 53.
[105] General Scheme of the Assisted Human Reproduction Bill 2017, Head 55.
[106] General Scheme of the Assisted Human Reproduction Bill 2017, Head 54.
[107] General Scheme of the Assisted Human Reproduction Bill 2017, Head 56.
[108] Human Fertilisation and Embryology Act 2008, s 54(7) and s 54(11).

favour reform of the English surrogacy laws.[109] It should also be noted that England's surrogacy laws are currently under review by the Law Commission of England and Wales and the Scottish Law Commission.[110]

The 2017 Bill puts forward a slightly different model of parentage to that which is contained in the English Human Fertilisation and Embryology Act 2008. The 2017 Bill proposes that a surrogacy agreement would be signed by the surrogate and the intended parents before the surrogacy is undertaken and the surrogacy agreement would have to be authorised by the Regulatory Authority before any treatment could be provided. For the purpose of the Bill, a surrogacy agreement is defined as "an agreement under which a woman agrees to attempt to become pregnant and, if successful, to act as a surrogate and to transfer the parentage of any child born as a result of the pregnancy to an intended parent or intended parents."[111] As such, it might be the case that this pre-authorisation would help to alleviate some of the difficulties noted in respect of the English system above. The pre-authorisation would not, however, affect the allocation of parentage in any way, nor would the surrogacy agreement contractually bind the surrogate to her original undertaking to consent to the transfer of parentage after birth. In fact, Head 41 of the Bill expressly states that a surrogacy agreement would not be an enforceable contract, except in relation to the payment of the surrogate's reasonable expenses, and then only if the agreement was made before the transfer of the embryo. As such, the surrogate could still change her mind and refuse to consent to the parental order. It should be noted, however, that in England and Wales, the surrogate has a veto over the making of the parental order and the order cannot be made without her consent. By contrast, Head 48 of the 2017 Bill would allow a court to waive the requirement for consent to be provided by the surrogate or her husband where he or she:

(a) is deceased;
(b) lacks the capacity to provide consent;
(c) cannot be located after reasonable efforts have been made to find him or her; or
(d) for any other reason the court considers to be relevant.

---

[109] Surrogacy UK, *Surrogacy in the UK: Myth busting and reform: Report of the Surrogacy UK Working Group on Surrogacy Law Reform* (Surrogacy UK, 2015).
[110] See: Law Commission "Surrogacy laws set for reform as Law Commissions get Government backing" https://www.lawcom.gov.uk/surrogacy-laws-set-for-reform-as-law-commissions-get-government-backing/
[111] General Scheme of the Assisted Human Reproduction Bill 2017, Head 35.

The last clause would allow the court to grant the parental order in a case in which the surrogate does not consent, and where there are exceptional reasons to do so. Furthermore, the Irish surrogate would have some additional protections ahead of her English counterpart in that she could herself apply for the parental order should the intended parents neglect to do so.[112] However, the proposed model of parentage does not afford the surrogate any opportunity to avoid becoming a legal mother in the first place.

2. Other Models of Surrogacy

Some jurisdictions have dealt with the question of the allocation of parentage in surrogacy arrangements through the use of pre-conception court orders. This approach would appear to have greater potential to respect the interests of all the stakeholders in the surrogacy process than the delayed model. This pre-conception approach allows for the child's legal parental status to be determined prior to conception and it gives the intended parents all of the necessary legal tools that they need to protect that child from birth. It also provides certainty, as the parties know who the child's legal parents will be at the outset and it avoids post-birth litigation to establish who the legal parents are.

Pre-conception court orders are adopted in jurisdictions such as California and South Africa. In South Africa, surrogacy agreements must be validated by the High Court before the surrogacy is undertaken.[113] Where the pre-conception order is granted, the intended parents will be recognised as the legal parents upon the birth of the child[114] and the surrogate does not acquire any legal parental status. It should be noted, however, that the South African law distinguishes between "full" and "partial" surrogacy. In the latter case, where the surrogate is also the genetic mother of the child, she retains the right to terminate the surrogate motherhood agreement by filing written notice with the court within 60 days of the birth of the child.[115]

The pre-conception model of parentage in surrogacy has numerous advantages over the delayed model given that it allows the intended parents to acquire full joint parental responsibilities and rights from the moment of the child's birth, which offers security and protection to the child.

---

[112] General Scheme of the Assisted Human Reproduction Bill 2017, Head 47(2).
[113] Children's Act 2005, s 292.
[114] Children's Act 2005, ss 295 and 297.
[115] Children's Act 2005, s 298.

Overview

The recognition of parentage in Ireland has changed dramatically since the introduction of the Children and Family Relationships Act 2015. Once the relevant provisions are fully commenced, this Act will recognise a wide variety of family relationships that were previously overlooked by the legislature. The General Scheme of the Assisted Human Reproduction Bill 2017 proposes to introduce further changes to Irish law to reflect the ever-changing makeup of modern Irish families. In addition to the proposals to regulate surrogacy discussed in this chapter, the 2017 Bill seeks to regulate:

- gamete and embryo donation for use in assisted human reproduction treatment and research;
- posthumous assisted reproduction involving the gametes or embryos of a deceased person under certain conditions;
- pre-implantation genetic diagnosis and sex selection;
- embryo and stem cell research.

If enacted, this Bill will provide long overdue regulation and clarity in these areas and will enable a greater range of parent-child relationships to be created and legally recognised.

CHAPTER 4

PARENTAL RESPONSIBILITIES: GUARDIANSHIP, CUSTODY AND ACCESS

Introduction

Adults caring for children take on particular legal responsibilities and they are given certain legal rights that allow them to properly exercise the caring role. In Ireland, these responsibilities and rights are separated into three distinct concepts or statuses: guardianship, custody and access. These concepts are primarily governed by the Guardianship of Infants Act 1964 (the "1964 Act"), as amended.[1] Guardianship refers to the responsibilities, rights and duties associated with raising a child. It is concerned with the most significant aspects of the child's life, such as where the child is to be educated, the child's religious upbringing (if any) and healthcare decision-making. Custody refers to the right and duty of an adult to exercise day-to-day care and control of a child and is a separate concept to that of guardianship. Access is the means of ensuring that the child can visit and maintain contact with carers with whom he or she is not residing. The three concepts are separate and distinct such that a person with guardianship will not always have custody of the child (and vice versa) but he or she may have access to the child.

Traditionally, guardianship and custody in Ireland flowed from, and were almost exclusively available to, the legal parents of a child. Before 2015, a person who was not a legal parent could only a become a guardian in limited circumstances under ss 7 or 8 of the 1964 Act. Under s 7 of the 1964 Act, a guardian can appoint any person to act as a testamentary guardian in the event of his or her death, while section 8 allows for a court to appoint a person as a guardian where the child has no existing guardian. The Children and Family Relationships Act 2015 (the "2015 Act") has now extended the categories of persons who may apply for guardianship and custody, thereby recognising the changing nature of Irish family relationships. In addition, although a greater range of individuals could always apply for access to a child,[2] the 2015

---

[1] Provisions of the Guardianship of Infants Act 1964 have been amended, substituted, inserted and deleted by a number of statutes including: the Marriage Act 2015; the Children and Family Relationships Act 2015; the Child and Family Agency Act 2013; the Adoption Act 2010; the Health Act 2004; the Courts and Court Officers Act 2002; Protection of Children (Hague Convention) Act 2000; the Children Act 1997; the Family Law (Divorce) Act 1996; the Family Law Act 1995; the Child Care Act 1991; the Courts Act 1991; the Judicial Separation and Family Law Reform Act 1989; the Status of Children Act 1987; the Courts (No 2) Act 1986; the Age of Majority Act 1985; the Courts Act 1981; the Health Act 1970; the Succession Act 1965; and by numerous statutory instruments.

[2] Guardianship of Infants Act 1964, s 11B provided that persons "in loco parentis" could apply for access.

Act has now streamlined this process. This is important because access is a right of the child, and not of the adult. The reforms recognise the importance for children of maintaining an array of different family relationships.

The 2015 Act has, to a large extent, modernised the Irish law governing guardianship, custody and access. In addition to recognising a wider range of adult-child relationships, the 2015 Act expressly provides that in any proceedings concerning the guardianship, custody, upbringing, or access to a child, the court "shall regard the best interests of the child as the paramount consideration."[3] This legislative provision gives effect to Art 42A.4.1° of the Irish Constitution, which requires that provision shall be made by law that in proceedings concerning the adoption, guardianship or custody of, or access to, any child, "the best interests of the child shall be the paramount consideration."[4]

This chapter will begin by outlining the requirements of the best interests principle in the context of guardianship, custody and access, before turning to consider the operation of these concepts in more detail.

The Best Interests of the Child

Traditionally in Ireland, the courts were obliged to consider the "welfare of the child" in proceedings concerning guardianship, custody and access. Section 3 of the 1964 Act (since amended) originally provided that

> "[w]here in any proceedings before any court the custody, guardianship or upbringing of an infant, or the administration of any property belonging to or held on trust for an infant, or the application of the income thereof, is in question, the court, in deciding that question, shall regard the welfare of the infant as the first and paramount consideration."

Section 2 of the 1964 Act defined "welfare" as comprising "the religious and moral, intellectual, physical and social welfare of the infant." In considering the welfare of the child, the courts would examine these factors but they would not do so in isolation. Instead, the courts would examine all relevant circumstances of the case

---

[3] Guardianship of Infants Act 1964, s 3, amended by Children and Family Relationships Act 2015, s 45.

[4] Bunreacht na hÉireann, Art 42A.4.1°.

in order to ascertain the "totality of the picture presented."[5] The welfare of the child was the "first and paramount" consideration, but it was not the only consideration.

The reference to the "religious welfare" of the child in s 2 of the 1964 Act required that the religious upbringing of the child should be maintained following any application for guardianship, custody or access. As such, the courts were unwilling to award custody to a parent of a different religion to the child unless that parent was committed to maintaining the child's religious upbringing. For example, in *Cullen v Cullen*,[6] a mother whose religious faith had lapsed was awarded custody, but she had to give an undertaking that the child would continue to receive religious instruction while in her care. "Moral welfare" was another component of religious upbringing and many of the cases involving this factor concerned parents in adulterous relationships. For example, in *JJW v BMW*,[7] custody was awarded to a father in a situation where the mother had committed adultery. However, in later cases, the courts moved away from deciding custody on the basis of the "moral" behaviour of the parents, such that living with a non-marital partner, in itself, became largely irrelevant in matters of custody.[8]

The other factors to be taken into account under s 2 of the 1964 Act were: intellectual welfare, which concerned the child's education and intellectual needs; physical welfare, which was concerned with the health and physical wellbeing of the child; and social welfare, which referred to promoting the capacity of the child to become a better member of the society in which he or she lived. Emotional welfare was not referred to in s 2 of the 1964 Act but it was added to the list of welfare considerations by the courts over the years. In *DFO'S v CA*, for example, McGuinness J suggested that the parents should attend professional counselling in order to secure the child's emotional welfare.[9]

Section 3 of the 1964 Act was subsequently amended by s 45 of the 2015 Act to provide that in any proceedings concerning the guardianship, custody, upbringing, or access to a child, the best interests of the child shall be "the paramount consideration."[10] In determining the best interests of the child in such proceedings, the

---

5   *MBO'S v POO'S* (1976) ILTR 57 at 61.
6   *Cullen v Cullen* (SC, 8 May 1970).
7   *JJW v BMW* (1976) 109 ILTR.
8   See, for example *EK v MK* (SC, 31 July 1974).
9   *DFO'S v CA* (HC, 20 April 1999, McGuinness J).
10 Guardianship of Infants Act 1964, s 3, amended by Children and Family Relationships Act 2015, s 45.

courts are directed to consider a list of factors set out in Pt V of the 1964 Act.[11] This new Pt V essentially creates what might be termed a "best interests checklist" for the courts. It obliges the court, when determining the best interests of the child, to have regard to all of the factors or circumstances that it regards as relevant to the child concerned and his or her family, and it sets out a non-exhaustive list of factors which may be taken into account in this assessment. These factors include:

"(a) the benefit to the child of having a meaningful relationship with each of his or her parents and with the other relatives and persons who are involved in the child's upbringing and, except where such contact is not in the child's best interests, of having sufficient contact with them to maintain such relationships;

(b) the views of the child concerned that are ascertainable (whether in accordance with section 32 or otherwise);

(c) the physical, psychological and emotional needs of the child concerned, taking into consideration the child's age and stage of development and the likely effect on him or her of any change of circumstances;

(d) the history of the child's upbringing and care, including the nature of the relationship between the child and each of his or her parents and the other relatives and persons referred to in paragraph (a), and the desirability of preserving and strengthening such relationships;

(e) the child's religious, spiritual, cultural and linguistic upbringing and needs;

(f) the child's social, intellectual and educational upbringing and needs;

(g) the child's age and any special characteristics;

(h) any harm which the child has suffered or is at risk of suffering, including harm as a result of household violence, and the protection of the child's safety and psychological well-being[12];

---

[11] Guardianship of Infants Act 1964, Pt V, inserted by Children and Family Relationships Act 2015, s 63.

[12] For the purposes of s 31(2)(h), the court shall have regard to household violence that has occurred or is likely to occur in the household of the child, or a household in which the child has been or is likely to be present, including the impact or likely impact of such violence on: the safety of the child and other members of the household concerned; the child's personal well-being, including the child's psychological and emotional well-being; the victim of such violence; the capacity of the perpetrator of the violence to properly care for the child and the risk, or likely risk, that the perpetrator poses to the child. Guardianship of Infants Act 1964, Pt V, s 31(3), inserted by Children and Family Relationships Act 2015, s 63.

   (i)   where applicable, proposals made for the child's custody, care, development and upbringing and for access to and contact with the child, having regard to the desirability of the parents or guardians of the child agreeing to such proposals and co-operating with each other in relation to them;

   (j)   the willingness and ability of each of the child's parents to facilitate and encourage a close and continuing relationship between the child and the other parent, and to maintain and foster relationships between the child and his or her relatives;

   (k)   the capacity of each person in respect of whom an application is made under this Act—
     (i) to care for and meet the needs of the child,
     (ii) to communicate and co-operate on issues relating to the child, and
     (iii)to exercise the relevant powers, responsibilities and entitlements to which the application relates."[13]

The new best interests checklist will help to guide the Irish courts in determining the best interests of the child in cases concerning guardianship, custody and access and it will ensure that all matters of relevance to the child's best interests will be taken into account. The concept of the "best interests of the child" is often criticised as a vague standard which leaves a large amount of discretion to the decision-maker to determine what is "best" for a particular child or group of children. This is because society lacks a clear consensus as to what is best for children and therefore value judgments are necessary in the decision-making process. The new best interests checklist will help to guide decisions relating to the best interests of the child, but it is notable that no guidance is given as to how much weight is to be given to each factor on the checklist. As such, it might be questioned whether the new checklist will significantly reduce the indeterminacy of the best interests principle in practice as there is nothing to prevent Judge A from giving more weight to one of the factors, while Judge B focuses on a different factor.

The above should not be taken to suggest that the best interests checklist is unsuitable. It would not be appropriate for the legislature to set down a strict definition of what is meant by the "best interests of the child" because the best interests principle must be flexible and adaptable so that it can adjust to suit the needs and interests of individual children. The courts must engage in

---

[13] Guardianship of Infants Act 1964, Pt V, s 31(2), inserted by Children and Family Relationships Act 2015, s 63.

an individualised assessment of what is best for a particular child or group of children—this would not be possible if judges were obliged to apply the same strict definition in every case. In this way, the indeterminacy of the best interests principle—and the fact that the checklist leaves room for indeterminacy—is favourable as it allows for flexibility and adaptability in the decision-making process. As such, the best interests checklist is to be welcomed as it clarifies factors to be considered when determining the child's best interests *and* because it does not strictly prescribe the approach to be taken by the decision-maker.

The Right of the Child to be Heard

Among the factors to be taken into account in assessing the best interests of the child under the best interests checklist are "the views of the child concerned that are ascertainable."[14] In addition, s 25 of the 1964 Act provides that in any case where s 3 (the best interests of the child) applies, "the court shall, as it thinks appropriate and practicable having regard to the age and understanding of the child, take into account the child's wishes in the matter."[15] These provisions reflect the requirements set out in Art 42A.4.2° of the Constitution that:

> "Provision shall be made by law for securing, as far as practicable, that in all proceedings [concerning the adoption, guardianship or custody of, or access to, any child] in respect of any child who is capable of forming his or her own views, the views of the child shall be ascertained and given due weight having regard to the age and maturity of the child."[16]

The child's right to be heard is of vital importance. Allowing children to express their views makes them active participants in the decision-making process and gives them a voice in the most important matters affecting their upbringing. The child's right to be heard allows the child to participate in decision-making in a manner that reflects their age and maturity. The child's right to be heard is also expressly referred to in Art 12(1) of the United Nations Convention on the Rights of the Child (UNCRC), which provides that

> "States Parties shall assure to the child who is capable of

---

[14] Guardianship of Infants Act 1964, Pt V, s 31(2)(b), inserted by Children and Family Relationships Act 2015, s 63.

[15] Guardianship of Infants Act 1964, s 25, inserted by Children Act 1997, s 11.

[16] Bunreacht na hÉireann, Art 42A.4.2°.

forming his or her own views the right to express those views freely in all matters affecting the child, the views of the child being given due weight in accordance with the age and maturity of the child."[17]

In order to give effect to this right, Art 12(2) UNCRC provides that the child must be given

"the opportunity to be heard in any judicial and administrative proceedings affecting the child, either directly, or through a representative or an appropriate body, in a manner consistent with the procedural rules of national law."[18]

Thus, States parties are required to put in place mechanisms to facilitate the child's right to be heard directly or indirectly in legal proceedings. The child's right to be heard is discussed in detail in Chapter 7.

The child's right to be heard does not, however, mean that the child's views will be determinative of the matter, and indeed most children would not want to have the final say in legal matters concerning them. Furthermore, attaching too much weight to the views of the child may run contrary to the European Convention on Human Rights. In *C v Finland*,[19] for example, a Finnish court awarded custody of two children to their father after the death of their mother. Upon appeal, the Finnish Supreme Court overturned those decisions, granting custody to the mother's female partner, on the basis of the views clearly expressed by the children. The European Court of Human Rights found that the Finnish Supreme Court had violated the father's right to respect for his private and family life under Art 8 ECHR by giving absolute weight to the views of the children without properly considering the father's position and interests.

In Ireland, the case of *FN and EB v CO (Guardianship)*[20] established that children (of a certain age and understanding) have a constitutional right to express their views in cases concerning guardianship, custody or upbringing of the child under Art 40.3 of the Constitution. This case concerned an application by maternal grandparents to be appointed guardians of their grandchildren pursuant to s 8 of the 1964 Act following the death of the children's

---

[17] United Nations Convention on the Rights of the Child, Art 12(1).
[18] United Nations Convention on the Rights of the Child, Art 12(2).
[19] *C v Finland* App no 18249/02 (ECtHR, 9 May 2006).
[20] *FN and EB v CO (Guardianship)* [2004] 4 IR 311.

mother. Having interviewed the children, Finlay Geoghegan J was satisfied that "each of the girls is of an age and maturity at which it is appropriate to take into account their wishes."[21] The girls both stated that they wanted their grandparents to continue to be involved in the making of any important decisions as to their welfare. In considering the weight to be afforded to their views, Finlay Geoghegan J noted that s 25 of the 1964 Act only requires a court to "take into account" the wishes of the child. The judge noted that this provision did "not mean that a court must or should make the relevant decision in accordance with the wishes of the child."[22] That said, the judge noted that an individual in respect of whom a decision of importance is being taken has a personal right within the meaning of Art 40.3 of the Constitution to have such decision taken in accordance with the principles of constitutional justice. This was found to include

> "the right of a child, whose age and understanding is such that a court considers it appropriate to take into account his/her wishes, to have such wishes taken into account by a court in taking a decision to which s. 3 of the Act of 1964 applies."[23]

Ultimately, the applicant grandparents were appointed guardians of the children to act jointly with their father.

In the context of guardianship, custody and access proceedings in Ireland, there are various ways for the child's views to be ascertained but difficulties remain. In particular, as will be seen below, issues of cost and an absence of official judicial guidelines pose considerable barriers to the realisation of the child's right to be heard in private family law proceedings.

Representing the Child's Views

(a) Guardian ad litem

Section 28 of the 1964 Act, inserted by s 11 of the Children Act 1997, provides for the appointment of a guardian ad litem in proceedings concerning guardianship, custody and access.[24] A guardian ad litem is a person who helps the child to have his or her voice heard and views considered in certain types of legal proceedings. The guardian ad litem also provides the court with an independent assessment of the child's interests. A major difficulty with s 28 of

---

21 *FN and EB v CO (Guardianship)* [2004] 4 IR 311 at 321.
22 *FN and EB v CO (Guardianship)* [2004] 4 IR 311 at 321.
23 *FN and EB v CO (Guardianship)* [2004] 4 IR 311 at 322.
24 Guardianship of Infants Act 1964, s 28, inserted by Children Act 1997, s 11.

the 1964 Act is that the provision was never commenced, meaning that it is not in operation. Therefore, a guardian ad litem may be appointed in child care proceedings,[25] but not in private family law cases concerning guardianship, custody and access.

(b) Expert Reports

There is provision in Irish law for the child's views to be indirectly presented to the court through expert reports. Under s 47 of the Family Law Act 1995, the courts have the power (although the use of the section has been limited to date)[26] to order a "section 47 report" whereby an expert is appointed to assess "any question affecting the welfare of a party to the proceedings or any other person to whom they relate."[27] These reports can be ordered by the Circuit Court or High Court, but not by the District Court. Section 26 of the 1964 Act, inserted by s 11 of the Children Act 1997, extended s 47 to District Court proceedings, but that section was never commenced. This is unfortunate given that many family law cases are heard in the District Court.

Section 32 of the 1964 Act, inserted by s 63 of the 2015 Act, provides for a new type of expert report in cases concerning guardianship, custody or access. This section provides that the court may, of its own motion or on application to it, "give such directions as it thinks proper for the purpose of procuring from an expert a report in writing on any question affecting the welfare of the child" or "appoint an expert to determine and convey the child's views."[28] In deciding whether to make such an order, the court will have regard to the following factors.

(a) the age and maturity of the child;
(b) the nature of the issues in dispute in the proceedings;
(c) any previous expert report concerning the welfare of the child;
(d) the best interests of the child;
(e) whether the making of the order will assist the child in expressing his or her views;

---

[25] Child Care Act 1991, s 26.
[26] Geoffrey Shannon, *Children and Family Relationships Law in Ireland: Practice and Procedure* (Clarus Press, Dublin, 2016), p 33.
[27] Family Law Act 1995, s 47(1).
[28] Guardianship of Infants Act 1964, s 32(1), inserted by Children and Family Relationships Act 2015, s 63.

(f)   the views expressed by any party to the proceedings or person to whom those views relate.[29]

The expert reports referred to in s 32 of the 1964 Act, inserted by s 63 of the 2015 Act, differ from the s 47 reports, in that the former may address "any question affecting the welfare of the child" and can be ordered in all courts, including the District Court.

In addition to the above, s 32(1)(b) of the 1964 Act, inserted by s 63 of the 2015 Act, empowers the court to "appoint an expert to determine and convey the child's views." The role of this expert is to:

"(a)   ascertain the maturity of the child,
(b)   where requested by the court, ascertain whether or not the child is capable of forming his or her views on the matters that are the subject of the proceedings, and report to the court accordingly,
(c)   where paragraph (b) does not apply, or where paragraph (b) applies and the expert ascertains that the child is capable of forming his or her own views on the matters that are the subject of the proceedings—
    (i)   ascertain the views of the child either generally or on any specific questions on which the court may seek the child's views, and
    (ii)   furnish to the court a report, which shall put before the court any views expressed by the child in relation to the matters to which the proceedings relate."[30]

In respect of either category of expert, the 2015 Act allows the Minister for Justice and Equality, in consultation with the Minister for Children and Youth Affairs, to specify, among other things, the qualifications and experience of such an expert and the fees and allowable expenses that they may charge.[31]

Where an expert report is ordered, that report will be considered by the court but it will not be determinative of the matter—it is the role of the court to determine the child's best interests. As Denham J stated in *JMcD v PL and BM*

[29]   Guardianship of Infants Act 1964, s 32(3), inserted by Children and Family Relationships Act 2015, s 63.
[30]   Guardianship of Infants Act 1964, s 32(6), inserted by Children and Family Relationships Act 2015, s 63.
[31]   Guardianship of Infants Act 1964, s 32(10), inserted by Children and Family Relationships Act 2015, s 63.

"The court is the decision maker. The court is required to consider all the circumstances and evidence. The s. 47 report is part of the evidence to be considered by the court. It is for the court to determine in accordance with law, what is in the best interests of the child."[32]

Notably, where an expert is appointed to facilitate the expression of the child's views under s 32 of the 1964 Act or s 47 of the Family Law Act 1995, the fees and expenses of the expert appointed must be paid by the parties to the proceedings.[33] This is significant because s 47 reports typically cost between €2500 and €3000, which creates difficulties for those who cannot pay that amount.[34] Where the parties cannot afford to pay for the report, the court will not be able to appoint an expert to compile it and this would clearly impede the court in its assessment of the child's views. In its Concluding Observations on Ireland's combined third and fourth periodic reports, the Committee on the Rights of the Child recommended that provisions should be put in place to cover the cost of an expert to hear the child's views in family law proceedings.[35] At the time of writing, no proposals have been put forward to address this issue.

(c) Hearing the Child Directly

In private law proceedings, the voice of the child may also be heard by speaking directly with the judge in chambers. This can be particularly useful in cases where the parties cannot afford to pay for an expert report and so the judge must find another way to ascertain the child's views (and hence satisfy all factors on the best interests checklist).

In *O'D v O'D*,[36] Abbott J in the High Court set out a number of guidelines that he found useful to apply when speaking with children:

"1. The judge shall be clear about the legislative or forensic framework in which he is embarking on the role of talking to the children as different codes may require or only permit different approaches.

---

[32] *JMcD v PL* [2010] 2 IR 199 at 268.
[33] Guardianship of Infants Act 1964, s 32(9), inserted by Children and Family Relationships Act 2015, s 63; Family Law Act 1995, s 47(4).
[34] Geoffrey Shannon, *Children and Family Relationships Law in Ireland: Practice and Procedure* (Clarus Press, Dublin, 2016), p 33.
[35] Committee on the Rights of the Child, *Concluding observations on the combined third and fourth periodic reports of Ireland* (1 March 2016), para 31.
[36] *O'D v O'D* [2008] IEHC 468.

2. The judge should never seek to act as an expert and should reach such conclusions from the process as may be justified by common sense only, and the judge's own experience.

3. The principles of a fair trial and natural justice should be observed by agreeing terms of reference with the parties prior to relying on the record of the meeting with children.

4. The judge should explain to the children the fact that the judge is charged with resolving issues between the parents of the child and should reassure the child that in speaking to the judge the child is not taking on the onus of judging the case itself and should assure the child that while the wishes of children may be taken into consideration by the court, their wishes will not be solely (or necessarily at all) determinative of the ultimate decision of the court.

5. The judge should explain the development of the convention and legislative background relating to the courts in more recent times actively seeking out the voice of the child in such simple terms as the child may understand.

6. The court should, at an early stage ascertain whether the age and maturity of the child is such as to necessitate hearing the voice of the child. In most cases the parents in dispute in the litigation are likely to assist and agree on this aspect. In the absence of such agreement then it is advisable for the court to seek expert advice from the s. 47 procedure, unless of course such qualification is patently obvious.

7. The court should avoid a situation where the children speak in confidence to the court unless of course the parents agree. In this case the children sought such confidence and I agreed to give it them subject to the stenographer and registrar recording same. Such a course, while very desirable from the child's point of view is generally not consistent with the proper forensic progression of a case unless the parents in the litigation are informed and do not object, as was the situation in this case."[37]

The comments above do not represent official guidelines, but simply reflect one judge's experience of speaking with children. There are no official guidelines available to judges to guide the process of

---

[37] *O'D v O'D* [2008] IEHC 468, para 10.

speaking with children. As such, there is a lack of consistency among the judiciary about whether and how the child's views are to be ascertained. Some judges remain wary of interviewing children. As McGuinness J stated in the case of *M(TM) v D(M)*,

> "I have interviewed children on a number of occasions in regard to family matters, although it is not a practice that I would go in for very often. I am well aware of the danger that children may be coached in what they are to say to the Court."[38]

It is also possible that the child's views may be given as direct evidence during the court proceedings. However, this approach is rarely an appropriate way of hearing the voice of the child in private family law proceedings as it may involve him or her expressing a preference for one parent over another in open court which may be stressful, or indeed distressing, to the child.

The child's right to be heard is considered in further detail in Chapter 7 of this book.

Defining Guardianship, Custody and Access

The terms "guardianship", "custody" and "access" are sometimes criticised as being outdated and unclear. These terms have connotations of ownership and control and do not seem to fit with the modern trend of recognising that parents and other adults not only have rights in respect of their children but are also duty bound to protect and provide for them. Furthermore, the concepts of guardianship, custody and access are not defined by statute, which often leads to confusion about what the respective roles entail.[39]

The suitability of the terms guardianship, custody and access were reviewed by the Law Reform Commission (LRC) in a Report on Legal Aspects of Family Relationships in 2010. In this Report, the LRC recommended that the existing Irish term of "guardianship" should be replaced with that of "parental responsibility" so as to better convey that parents and guardians have both rights and responsibilities towards their children. The Commission also recommended that the term "day-to-day care" should be used in place of "custody" and the term "contact" should replace "access".[40]

---

[38] *M(TM) v D(M)* [1999] IEHC 88, para 26.
[39] Law Reform Commission, *Consultation Paper on Legal Aspects of Family Relationships* (LRC CP 55–2009), Ch 1.
[40] Law Reform Commission, *Report on Legal Aspects of Family Relationships* (LRC

The LRC felt that the proposed terms would be "a more accurate reflection of what is entailed in each of the concepts and would, therefore, ensure greater clarity in the law."[41] The LRC noted that currently "there is confusion among members of the public as to the distinction between guardianship and custody, with many interpreting an order for joint custody as a joint parenting order."[42] The LRC argued that use of the term "parental responsibility" would make it clear that persons with such responsibility have a central decision-making role in the child's life, even where they do not care for the child on a day-to-day basis. Where an order for day-to-day care of the child is made, the LRC felt that it would be clear that the adult is responsible for caring for the child on a daily basis, while use of the term contact would place "greater emphasis on contact as a right of the child as well as a right of the parent."[43]

Many international instruments refer to the "responsibilities" of adults. For example, Art 5 of the UNCRC provides that "States Parties shall respect the responsibilities, rights and duties of parents" while Art 18(1) provides that "States Parties shall use their best efforts to ensure recognition of the principle that both parents have common responsibilities for the upbringing and development of the child."[44] In addition, Art 9 of the UNCRC emphasises that children have a right to maintain direct "contact" with their parents. As such, it would be in keeping with Ireland's international commitments if similar terms were adopted in this jurisdiction.

Both England and Wales and Scotland have replaced the older terminology of guardianship, custody and access with the terms "parental responsibility", "residence" and "contact."[45] The new terminology was adopted due to a lack of understanding among the public about the meaning of the older concepts. As the Scottish

---

101–2010), Ch 1.

[41] Law Reform Commission, *Consultation Paper on Legal Aspects of Family Relationships* (LRC CP 55–2009), para 1.38.

[42] Law Reform Commission, *Consultation Paper on Legal Aspects of Family Relationships* (LRC CP 55–2009), para 1.40.

[43] Law Reform Commission, *Consultation Paper on Legal Aspects of Family Relationships* (LRC CP 55–2009), para 1.40.

[44] See also Hague Convention on Protection of Children and Co-operation in Respect of Intercountry Adoption 1993; Hague Convention on Jurisdiction, Applicable Law, Recognition, Enforcement and Co-operation in Respect of Parental Responsibility and Measures for the Protection of Children 1996; Council Regulation (EC) No 2201/2003 concerning jurisdiction and the recognition and enforcement of judgments in matrimonial matters and in matters of parental responsibility ("Brussels II bis").

[45] See Children Act 1989; Children (Scotland) Act 1995; Family Law (Scotland) Act 1995.

Law Commission noted prior to the introduction of the new terms, some parents who had been awarded custody in that jurisdiction mistakenly believed that this gave them all parental responsibilities and rights when this was not the case.[46] The updated terminology more accurately describes the function and consequences of the different concepts and has played an important role in increasing understanding of the concepts among members of the public.

In Ireland, the 2015 Act provided an opportunity to update the terminology in this area but the legislature chose to retain the existing terms of guardianship, custody and access. The drafters of the legislation felt that it was necessary to retain this terminology because this is the language used in Art 42A of the Irish Constitution.[47] Arguably, this in itself should not have prevented the legislation from adopting different terms, particularly given that the older terminology lacks a children's rights focus. Updating the existing terms would serve an important role in emphasising the child-centred nature of the concepts and in highlighting that they give rise to responsibilities, as well as rights, to ensure that the child's rights and interests are protected.

Guardianship

Guardianship is concerned with the most significant aspects of the child's life, such as education, religion, and healthcare decision-making. Guardianship is not simply a right for the adult—it entails both rights and responsibilities. Until quite recently in Ireland, guardianship was primarily confined to the legal parents of a child, although the unmarried father always held a weaker position than other legal parents. A person who was not a legal parent could only be appointed as a guardian through testamentary guardianship or by court order where the child had no existing guardian.[48] The 2015 Act has introduced a number of legal reforms which have altered the framework for guardianship in Ireland. The position of the unmarried father is acknowledged (although it is open to debate whether it has been improved) and the 2015 Act has extended the categories of person who may be appointed as guardians. These reforms are designed to accommodate a wider range of family relationships in Ireland and acknowledge that, in some cases, a child may have more than two adults caring for him or her. Before

---

[46] Scottish Law Commission, *Report on Family Law* (Scot Law Com No 135, 1992), p 9.

[47] See Explanatory note accompanying Head 31 of the General Scheme of the Children and Family Relationships Act 2014.

[48] Guardianship of Infants Act 1964, ss 7 and 8.

turning to consider these reforms, this chapter will explain the role of the guardian and will outline the allocation of guardianship.

1. The Role of the Guardian

There is no statutory definition of guardianship in Ireland, but the 1964 Act explains the role of the guardian as follows:

> "as guardian of the person, [the guardian] shall, as against every person not being, jointly with him, a guardian of the person, be entitled to the custody of the infant and shall be entitled to take proceedings for the restoration of his custody of the infant against any person who wrongfully takes away or detains the infant and for the recovery, for the benefit of the infant, of damages for any injury to or trespass against the person of the infant."[49]

This description is imbued with connotations of ownership and control. The description fails to acknowledge that parents and other adults not only have rights in respect of their children but are also duty-bound to protect and provide for them. It also seems to ignore that children are themselves rights-holders and that actions and decisions made in respect of children should be made in their best interests.

The definition of the guardian's role as set out in the 1964 Act was not amended by the 2015 Act, but the new legislation does now provide a list of the "rights and responsibilities of a guardian", which are:

"(a) to decide on the child's place of residence;
(b) to make decisions regarding the child's religious, spiritual, cultural and linguistic upbringing;
(c) to decide with whom the child is to live;
(d) to consent to medical, dental and other health related treatment for the child, in respect of which a guardian's consent is required;
(e) under an enactment specified in subsection (12)[50];

---

[49] Guardianship of Infants Act 1964, s 10(2)(a).
[50] The enactments specified are: Firearms Act 1925, s 2A(2); Protection of Young Persons (Employment) Act 1996, s 5; International Criminal Court Act 2006, ss 50 and 50A; Criminal Justice (Mutual Assistance) Act 2008, ss 79, 79A and 79B; Passports Act 2008, s 14; and the Criminal Justice (Forensic Evidence and DNA Database System) Act 2014.

(f)   to place the child for adoption, and consent to the adoption of the child, under the Adoption Act 2010."[51]

This list is provided in the context of the appointment of additional guardians and so it would appear not to be an exhaustive list of the responsibilities and rights of a guardian but merely indicative of the powers that may be exercised. Although certainly an improvement on the definition in the 1964 Act, it is arguable that this list continues to emphasise the adult's rights, rather than focusing on his or her responsibilities towards the child. It is perhaps encouraging then that it seems not to be an exhaustive list, as this means that additional responsibilities could still be imposed on the guardian.

2. Allocation of Guardianship

Where the parents of a child are married to each other, both parents are automatically made joint guardians of the child.[52] Even if the parents subsequently separate or divorce, they remain joint legal guardians. Where the child is born outside of marriage, the mother is deemed to be the sole automatic guardian,[53] but the unmarried father does not acquire any automatic guardianship rights upon the birth of the child. There are, however, a number of ways for the unmarried father to acquire guardianship rights in relation to his child. As will be discussed below, he can obtain guardianship rights in relation to his child, either by subsequently marrying the mother, though co-habitation with the mother,[54] by agreement with her,[55] or by court order.[56]

(a) The Unmarried Father

The number of unmarried fathers in Ireland is increasing as more children are born outside of the traditional married family each year. Statistics for 2016 show that 36.5 percent of all births registered in that year were outside of marriage or civil partnership, an

---

[51]   Guardianship of Infants Act 1964, s 6C(11), inserted by Children and Family Relationships Act 2015, s 49.

[52]   Guardianship of Infants Act 1964, s 6(1), amended by Children and Family Relationships Act 2015, s 16.

[53]   Guardianship of Infants Act 1964, s 6(4), amended by Children and Family Relationships Act 2015, s 47.

[54]   Guardianship of Infants Act 1964, s 2(4A), inserted by Children and Family Relationships Act 2015, s 43.

[55]   Guardianship of Infants Act 1964, s 2(4), inserted by Children Act 1997, s 4.

[56]   Guardianship of Infants Act 1964, s 6A(1), inserted by Status of Children Act 1987, s 12, and substituted by Children and Family Relationships Act 2015, s 48.

increase of 0.1 percent from 2015.[57] As such, there are a growing number of fathers who do not have any automatic responsibilities and rights (other than the duty to contribute financially) towards their children.

The unmarried father is clearly in a weaker position than other parents. This weaker position stems from the fact that the relationship between the unmarried father and the child is not constitutionally protected. As Henchy J noted in *State (Nicolaou) v An Bord Uchtála*:

> "It has not been shown to the satisfaction of this Court that the father of an illegitimate child has any natural right, as distinct from legal rights, to either the custody or society of that child and the Court has not been satisfied that any such right has ever been recognised as part of the natural law."[58]

By contrast, in the same case, the Supreme Court held that the rights of an unmarried mother in relation to her child are personal rights protected by Art 40.3 of the Constitution.[59] Further, as discussed in Chapter 2, the rights of married parents are robustly protected by Arts 41 and 42 of the Constitution. These Articles safeguard the marital family—a family which does not include the unmarried father.

i. Guardianship through Cohabitation

Notwithstanding the lower constitutional standing of the unmarried father, the 2015 Act has attempted to improve his legal position. The 2015 provides for the unmarried father to be automatically appointed as a guardian in circumstances where he has cohabited with the mother

> "for not less than 12 consecutive months … which shall include a period, occurring at any time after the birth of the child, of not less than three consecutive months during which both the mother and father have lived with the child."[60]

This provision is notable as it allows for the unmarried father to automatically acquire guardianship for the first time. However, the

---

[57] Central Statistics Office, *Vital Statistics Yearly Summary 2016* (CSO, 2017).
[58] *State (Nicolaou) v An Bord Uchtála* [1966] IR 567 at 643.
[59] *State (Nicolaou) v An Bord Uchtála* [1966] IR 567 at 644. See also *G v An Bord Uchtála* [1980] IR 32.
[60] Guardianship of Infants Act 1964, s 2(4A) inserted by Children and Family Relationships Act 2015, s 43.

three month waiting period means that the unmarried father does not acquire guardianship upon the birth of the child and therefore will not automatically have all of the legal rights and responsibilities necessary to care for his child at birth. In these circumstances, the advantage of the provision may be questioned, in particular given that the unmarried father can acquire guardianship by agreement with the mother in a much shorter period.[61]

Therefore, although the 2015 Act acknowledges the position of the unmarried father, it arguably does not provide the best solution for the child, as the allocation of guardianship does not occur upon the birth of the child. Furthermore, the cohabitation requirement does little to benefit children whose parents do not live together. Their interests are ignored, suggesting that, in the eyes of the law, only children whose parents cohabitate have a right and a need to be cared for by their fathers, albeit subject to a three month waiting period.

ii. Guardianship by Agreement

In order for the unmarried father to acquire guardianship by agreement with the mother, the parents must make a statutory declaration that:

— They have not married each other,
— They declare that they are the father and mother of the child concerned,
— The mother agrees to the appointment of the father as a guardian of the child,
— They have entered into arrangements regarding the custody of and (if necessary) access to the child.[62]

This statutory declaration can be made at any time while the child is still a child. There is, however, no central register for these statutory declarations. Instead, the parent is given a copy which they must store themselves. This obviously creates difficulties if the parent's copy of the declaration is lost or destroyed. The failure of the State to create a central register was addressed in *ER O'B (a minor) v Minister for Justice, Equality and Law Reform*.[63] In this case, the

---

[61] For example, there is provision for a registrar to take and receive a statutory declaration within 14 days of the registration or re-registration of the birth of the child pursuant to Civil Registration Act 2004, s 27A, inserted by Children and Family Relationships Act, s 97. However, it should be noted that, at the time of writing, this provision has yet to be commenced.

[62] Guardianship of Infants Act 1964, s 2(4), inserted by Children Act 1997, s 4.

[63] *ER O'B (a minor) v Minister for Justice, Equality and Law Reform* [2009] IEHC 423.

applicant, whose father had been appointed as a guardian by way of statutory agreement with the mother, sought declarations from the High Court that the failure on the part of the State to establish and maintain a register of guardianship agreements constituted a breach of her constitutional rights under Arts 41.1, 40.3 and 40.1 of the Constitution and was a violation of her rights under Arts 8 and 14 of the European Convention on Human Rights. In the High Court, Peart J noted that the Constitution gives parents primary responsibility for their child's upbringing and so they are expected to take reasonable precautions in the interests of their children, which would include looking after a guardianship agreement. According to the judge

> "[a]ll that needs to be done is to create a numbers [*sic*] of copies, have them certified if desired and place them in safekeeping. Once steps are taken to safeguard the agreement all potential risks of its loss and destruction are eliminated."[64]

As such, the judge held that a central register was not necessary *per se* to avoid the risks associated with loss or destruction of the statutory agreement. Furthermore, the court noted that even if a guardianship agreement is lost or destroyed, secondary evidence of its existence can be given to establish who the guardians are. Ultimately, the Court found no breach of the applicant's rights and the reliefs were refused. The Court noted that the introduction of a central register may be desirable but this was a matter for the Oireachtas and not for the Court to determine having found no violation of constitutional or ECHR rights.

In 2014, the Joint Oireachtas Committee on Justice, Defence and Equality recommended that a central register for statutory declarations should be established,[65] but no such register is yet in place.

iii. Guardianship by Court Order

Where the unmarried mother and father do not cohabitate and where the mother does not agree to the father's appointment as a guardian, the only option available to the father is to apply to the court for guardianship. In *JK v VW*,[66] the Supreme Court

---

64 *ER O'B (a minor) v Minister for Justice, Equality and Law Reform* [2009] IEHC 423 at para 7.2.

65 Joint Oireachtas Committee on Justice, Defence and Equality, *Report on hearings in relation to the Scheme of the Children and Family Relationships Bill* (May 2014).

66 *JK v VW* [1990] 2 IR 437.

emphasised that the non-marital father has the right to apply for guardianship, but he does not have a right to be appointed as a guardian. According to Finlay CJ:

> "the correct construction of s. 6A is that it gives to the natural father a right to apply to the court to be appointed as guardian, as distinct from even a defeasible right to be a guardian. The discretion vested in the court on the making of such an application must be exercised regarding the welfare of the infant as the first and paramount consideration."[67]

Thus, the unmarried father may apply for guardianship but the success of his application will depend on an assessment of the best interests of the child. The best interests of the child must be the paramount consideration in any decision as to the guardianship, custody of or access to a child. If it is deemed to be in the child's best interests for the non-marital father to be appointed as a guardian, he will be.

At present, the majority of court applications for guardianship by unmarried fathers are successful. Figures for 2015 demonstrate that of the 2,367 guardianship applications by unmarried applicants in that year, 1,808 were successful.[68] In considering whether the father should be appointed as a guardian, the court will consider all of the circumstances of the case and must ensure that the best interests of the child are the paramount consideration. In *JK v VW*, the Supreme Court noted that:

> "The extent and character of the rights which accrue arising from the relationship of a father to a child to whose mother he is not married must vary very greatly indeed, depending on the circumstances of each individual case.
>
> The range of variation would, I am satisfied, extend from the situation of the father of a child conceived as a result of a casual intercourse, where the rights might well be so minimal as practically to be non-existent, to the situation of a child born as the result of a stable and established relationship and nurtured at the commencement of his life by his father and mother in a situation bearing nearly all of the characteristics

---

[67] *JK v VW* [1990] 2 IR 437 at 447. See also *WO'R v EH and An Bord Uchtála* [1996] 2 IR 248.
[68] Courts Service, *Annual Report 2015* (2015), p 44.

of a constitutionally protected family, when the rights would be very extensive indeed."[69]

This approach was endorsed in *WO'R v EH*.[70]

In *JK v VW*,[71] the unmarried father had planned the conception of a child with his partner and lived with the mother until their separation before birth. Upon the birth of the child, the mother had placed her for adoption without the father's knowledge. When the father discovered that the child had been placed for adoption, he applied for guardianship, with a view to halting the adoption. The case reached the Supreme Court by way of a case stated from the High Court, in which Barron J sought clarification as to the proper test to be applied in deciding whether to award guardianship of a child to the father under s 6A of the 1964 Act. The Supreme Court noted that the blood link and the possibility for the child "to have the benefit of the guardianship by and the society of its father" were among the factors to be taken into account when considering the welfare of the child.[72] In addition, the court noted that in a case such as the present one where the application for guardianship was linked to an application for custody

> "regard should not be had to the objective of satisfying the wishes and desires of the father to be involved in the guardianship of and to enjoy the society of his child unless the court has first concluded that the quality of welfare which would probably be achieved for the infant by its present custody, which is with the prospective adoptive parents, as compared with the quality of welfare which would probably be achieved by custody with the father, is not to an important extent better."[73]

The Supreme Court, having clarified the principles that should be applied in cases where an unmarried father applies for guardianship, remitted the case to the High Court for determination. Ultimately, the father's application for guardianship was denied by the High Court on the basis that "the welfare of the infant requires her to remain in her present custody [with the adoptive parents]" and the adoption was allowed to proceed.

---

[69] *JK v VW* [1990] 2 IR 437 at 447.
[70] *WO'R v EH and An Bord Uchtála* [1996] 2 IR 248.
[71] *JK v VW* [1990] 2 IR 437.
[72] *JK v VW* [1990] 2 IR 437 at 447.
[73] *JK v VW* [1990] 2 IR 437 at 447.

The father in this case subsequently brought an application to the European Court of Human Rights (heard as *Keegan v Ireland*)[74] claiming that his right to respect for his family life under Art 8 of the ECHR had been breached due to the fact that the Irish law allowed the child to be placed for adoption without his knowledge and consent. The European Court of Human Rights noted that the father had an opportunity to apply for guardianship and custody and that the High Court had fairly considered his interests in this application. However, the fact that the child was placed for adoption without his knowledge amounted to a violation of Art 8 ECHR as this caused the child to develop bonds with the adoptive parents and ultimately it was not in her best interests to disrupt those bonds by awarding custody to the father. This case led to a change in Irish law such that a father without guardianship must now be consulted in relation to the adoption of his child, although his consent to the adoption order is not required.[75]

The Irish courts have also found that, in the absence of legislation to the contrary,[76] the right to apply for guardianship extends to a man who donates sperm to an individual or couple. In *JMcD v PL and BM*,[77] a man, McD, donated sperm to a lesbian couple so that they could conceive a child. Prior to this, the parties had entered into an agreement that the respondents would be the child's parents, that McD would not have any responsibility for the child's upbringing, and that his role would be similar to that of a "favourite uncle". Over time, relations between the parties deteriorated and the respondents sought to travel to Australia with the child for a period of one year. McD applied to be appointed as a guardian of the child in an attempt to block the trip to Australia.

In the High Court, Hedigan J noted that, at the time, there was no Irish law that recognised the relationships between same-sex couples and their children. As such, he turned to the European Convention on Human Rights (ECHR) for guidance. The judge noted that, at the time of the hearing, the Strasbourg Court had yet to rule on whether a lesbian couple, living together in a committed relationship, would enjoy the status of a *de facto* family for the purpose of Art 8 ECHR. The most relevant decision which

---

[74] *Keegan v Ireland*, App no 16969/90 (ECtHR, 26 May 1994).
[75] Adoption Act 2010, s 30, substituted by Adoption (Amendment) Act 2017, s 13.
[76] Where a child is born after the provisions of the Children and Family Relationships Act 2015 that relate to donor-assisted human reproduction (DAHR) are commenced, a sperm donor will not be regarded as a legal parent and will not be eligible to apply for guardianship.
[77] *JMcD v PL* [2010] 2 IR 199.

existed at the time was *X, Y and Z v UK*[78] where the European Court of Human Rights (ECtHR) had found "family life" to exist between a female-to-male transsexual, his female partner and the child born to his female partner by donor insemination. Hedigan J felt that this ruling demonstrated a "substantial movement" towards the recognition of a same-sex couple as a *de facto* family for the purposes of Art 8 ECHR. He therefore concluded that the relationship between a same-sex couple, living together in a long-term committed relationship, amounted to *de facto* family life under Art 8 ECHR. In addition, the judge held that

> "where a child is born into such a family unit and is cared for and nurtured therein, then the child itself is a part of such a *de facto* family unit. Applying this to the case here it seems clear that between [the respondents and the child] there exist such personal ties as give rise to family rights under Article 8 of the European Convention on Human Rights."[79]

Hedigan J's recognition of the family as a *de facto* family under Art 8 ECHR ultimately had a strong influence on his conclusion that neither guardianship nor access should be granted to the applicant in this case. The judge noted that the integrity of the *de facto* family "would be seriously and even possibly fatally broken by such orders in this case."[80] This consideration, along with consideration of the welfare of the child, led the judge to refuse the orders sought.

Upon appeal, the Supreme Court was unanimous in dismissing the applicant's claim as to guardianship but the judges emphasised that the *de facto* family does not exist as a legal institution under Irish law. In his judgment, Murray CJ focused primarily on the status of the ECHR under Irish law. He noted that s 2 of the European Convention on Human Rights Act 2003 requires that existing statutory provisions must be interpreted in line with the ECHR. The judge observed that the trial judge did not identify any such rule of law which required interpretation for the purposes of s 2. On the contrary, it was the apparent absence of any statutory provision or rule of law that gave rise to the trial judge's interpretation and application of Art 8. Therefore, according to Murray CJ, the High Court had directly applied the ECHR to the instant case, which was outside of its jurisdiction.[81]

---

[78] *X, Y and Z v UK* App no 21830/93 (ECtHR, 22 April 1997).
[79] *JMcD v PL* [2010] 2 IR 199 at 235–236.
[80] *JMcD v PL* [2010] 2 IR 199 at 241.
[81] *JMcD v PL* [2010] 2 IR 199 at 255.

Denham J highlighted the fact that the ECtHR had itself yet to rule on whether a same-sex couple with a child would come within the ambit of Art 8 ECHR.[82] As such, she concurred that the trial judge had erred in his analysis of the Art 8 jurisprudence. She further noted, however, that even if that were not so, "the Irish law would conflict with such a scenario and would govern the situation."[83] The judge clarified that the *de facto* family was not a legal institution in Ireland and noted that the phrase *"de facto* family" was simply "a shorthand method of describing circumstances where a couple have lived together in a settled relationship for some time with a child."[84]

Although the *de facto* family was not regarded as a legal institution in Irish law, this did not mean that the Supreme Court did not consider the child's relationships within that family. As Murray CJ stated

> "That is not to say that the de facto position of [the birth mother's partner] could or should be totally ignored in considering the issues in this case since so much turns on the ultimate interests of the child. [Her] relationship with [the birth mother] and their relationship with the child are among the factors to be taken into account in that context.[85]

Ultimately, the best interests of the child determined that guardianship should not be granted to the applicant and the appeal was dismissed. Following a further hearing, the High Court (Hedigan J) granted access by the applicant to the child, subject to certain conditions.

As was discussed in Chapter 3, the legal position of a sperm donor is now addressed by the Children and Family Relationships Act 2015. Where a child is born following donor-assisted human reproduction (DAHR) as regulated under the 2015 Act, the sperm donor will not be regarded as a legal father[86] and therefore will not be able to apply for guardianship under s 6A of the 1964 Act. The relevant provisions of the 2015 Act relating to DAHR have, however, yet to be commenced. As such, the courts may continue to encounter similar applications for guardianship from sperm

---

[82] The ECtHR has since confirmed that a same-sex couple with a child enjoy family life for the purpose of Article 8. See, for example, *Gas and Dubois v France* App no 25951/07 (ECtHR, 15 March 2012).
[83] *JMcD v PL* [2010] 2 IR 199 at 274.
[84] *JMcD v PL* [2010] 2 IR 199 at 270.
[85] *JMcD v PL* [2010] 2 IR 199 at pp 255–256.
[86] Children and Family Relationships Act 2015, s 5.

donors of children born before the relevant parts of the 2015 Act are commenced.

iv. Birth Certificates

One might assume that where the father's name is listed on the child's birth certificate, he would acquire automatic rights and responsibilities in respect of the child, but this is not the case in Ireland (with the exception of maintenance responsibilities). Without acquiring guardianship, the unmarried father does not have any right to make decisions in respect of the child's upbringing; he cannot consent to medical treatment for the child, nor is his consent required should the child be placed for adoption — although he does have the right to be consulted should that occur.

In its 1982 Report on Illegitimacy, the Law Reform Commission (LRC) recommended that both parents should be regarded as automatic guardians of their children, whether married or not.[87] The LRC felt that this would be a significant improvement where the non-marital father is actively involved in the child's upbringing. Where he is not so involved, the LRC felt that automatic guardianship would make very little difference. The only potential difficulty noted by the LRC was the situation where the mother does not want the father to have any involvement in the child's upbringing. In these circumstances, the LRC recommended that the mother should be able to obtain a court order to displace the unmarried father's guardianship rights. This order would be granted where it was in the best interests of the child to do so, such as where the father took no active interest in the child or where he indicated that he had no desire to exercise any parental function.[88]

Interestingly, the 1982 Report also considered the possibility of conferring automatic guardianship rights on the unmarried father where he cohabited with the mother or where he was registered as the legal father on the child's birth certificate. These proposals were rejected as they were seen to perpetuate "the idea of differentiation between different kinds of parents."[89] In addition, the LRC felt that it would be difficult to define what exactly constitutes cohabitation.

Notwithstanding the LRC's 1982 position noted above, the 2015 Act extends guardianship to the unmarried father based on

---

[87] Law Reform Commission, *Report on Illegitimacy* (LRC 4–1982), p 144.
[88] Law Reform Commission, *Report on Illegitimacy* (LRC 4–1982), p 150.
[89] Law Reform Commission, *Report on Illegitimacy* (LRC 4–1982), p 152.

cohabitation. In addition, it should be noted that the LRC has since changed its position with regard to the consequences of registering the father on the birth certificate. In its 2010 *Report on Legal Aspects of Family Relationships*, the LRC recommended that that automatic parental responsibility should be linked to compulsory joint registration of the birth of a child.[90] In this Report, the LRC noted that compulsory joint birth registration "would ensure a clear publicly recorded means to verify the proposed automatic role for the father" and would mean that most unmarried fathers would automatically acquire guardianship.[91] The proposed compulsory joint registration would require two names to be present on the birth certificate of every child (with some exceptions).[92]

In other countries, the unmarried father can automatically acquire parental responsibility where he is listed as the father on the child's birth certificate. In England and Wales for example, since 1 December 2003, a non-marital father will automatically acquire parental responsibility where he is registered on the child's birth certificate, although his parental responsibility may be removed by court order in certain circumstances.[93]

In Ireland, the Civil Registration (Amendment) Act 2014 provides for the compulsory registration of the father's name on the birth certificate. This is not required in some exceptional circumstances, such as where the mother does not know the identity of the father of the child or where she believes that it would not be in the best interests of the child to provide details of his identity.[94] At the time of writing, this provision has not been commenced. Furthermore, even if the provision is commenced, it will not, in itself, bestow guardianship on the unmarried father. In the absence of further reforms, it will remain the case that registration of the father on the birth certificate does not give rise to automatic guardianship. Given that more and more children are born outside of marriage each year, and therefore an increasing number of unmarried fathers do not have automatic guardianship in respect of their children, it is arguable that the possibility of allowing for automatic guardianship

---

[90] Law Reform Commission, *Report on Legal Aspects of Family Relationships* (LRC 101–2010), para 2.08.

[91] Law Reform Commission, *Report on Legal Aspects of Family Relationships* (LRC 101–2010), para 2.08.

[92] Law Reform Commission, *Report on Legal Aspects of Family Relationships* (LRC 101–2010), para 2.09.

[93] Children Act 1989, s 4, amended by Adoption and Children Act 2002, s 111.

[94] Civil Registration Act 2004, s 22, amended by Civil Registration (Amendment) Act 2014, s 6.

to be linked to birth registration, subject to exceptions, should be revisited by the Irish legislature.

3. Guardianship following Donor-Assisted Human Reproduction

The 2015 Act is the first Irish legislation regulating the area of donor-assisted human reproduction ("DAHR"). As is discussed in Chapter 3, the 2015 Act sets out detailed rules to determine parentage in cases of DAHR. It sets out that the parents of a child who is born following a DAHR procedure shall be the mother (the woman who gives birth) and the spouse, civil partner or cohabitant, as the case may be, of the mother. If the mother is single, she alone shall be the parent of the child.[95] In addition to setting out who the parents of the child shall be, the 2015 Act amends the 1964 Act to address the allocation of guardianship in cases of DAHR. These provisions broadly mirror those that were outlined above:

- The spouse or civil partner of the woman who gives birth following a DAHR procedure, and who has consented to being recognised as the child's second parent under section 5 of the 2015 Act, will be recognised as a guardian upon the birth of the child[96];
- The cohabitant of the woman who gives birth following a DAHR procedure, who has consented to being recognised as the child's second legal parent under s 5 of the 2015 Act, and who has cohabited with the mother for 12 consecutive months (including a period of 3 months after the birth of the child), will be recognised as a guardian[97];
- Alternatively, the cohabitant of the woman who gives birth following a DAHR procedure, who is recognised as a second legal parent, may acquire guardianship by way of statutory declaration[98] or court order,[99] in the same manner as the unmarried father described above.

---

[95] Children and Family Relationships Act 2015, s 5.
[96] Guardianship of Infants Act 1964, s 6B(1) and s 6B(2)(a), inserted by Children and Family Relationships Act 2015, s 49 and amended by Marriage Act 2015, s 16(b).
[97] Guardianship of Infants Act 1964, s 6B(2)(b), inserted by Children and Family Relationships Act 2015, s 49.
[98] Guardianship of Infants Act 1964, s 6B(4), amended by Marriage Act 2015, s 16(b).
[99] Guardianship of Infants Act 1964, s 6A(1), substituted by Children and Family Relationships Act 2015, s 48.

4. Non-Parent Guardians

Before 2015, a person who was not a parent of a child could only be made a guardian in limited circumstances under ss 7 or 8 of the 1964 Act. Under s 7 of the 1964 Act, a guardian can appoint any person to act as a testamentary guardian in the event of his or her death, while s 8 allows for a court to appoint a person as a guardian where the child has no existing guardian.

The 2015 Act has introduced reforms that allow for a person who is not a legal parent to be appointed as an additional guardian during the lifetime of the legal parents in certain circumstances. The prospective guardian must be over the age of 18 years and the application will only be granted where:

"(a) on the date of the application, he or she—
  (i) is married to or is in a civil partnership with, or has been for over 3 years a cohabitant of, a parent of the child, and
  (ii) has shared with that parent responsibility for the child's day-to-day care for a period of more than 2 years,

or

(b) on the date of the application—
  (i) he or she has provided for the child's day-to-day care for a continuous period of more than 12 months, and
  (ii) the child has no parent or guardian who is willing or able to exercise the rights and responsibilities of guardianship in respect of the child."[100]

The first provision allows a person acting in the capacity of a step-parent to be appointed as an additional guardian, while the second provision may be used where a child is in long-term foster care or is cared for by a relative on a full-time basis. In applying for the appointment of an additional guardian, the consent of each guardian of the child will be required as will that of the proposed guardian.[101] The court may, however, dispense with the consent of one of the existing guardians where "it is satisfied that the consent is unreasonably withheld and that it is in the best interests of the child" to do so.[102] Notably, there is no limit set out in the legislation

---

[100] Guardianship of Infants Act 1964, s 6C(2), inserted by Children and Family Relationships Act 2015, s 49.
[101] Guardianship of Infants Act 1964, s 6C(6), inserted by Children and Family Relationships Act 2015, s 49.
[102] Guardianship of Infants Act 1964, s 6C(7), inserted by Children and Family Relationships Act 2015, s 49.

as to how many additional guardians may be appointed, reflecting the fact that a number of adults may be involved in the child's upbringing. The 2015 Act specifically sets out that the appointment by the court of a guardian "shall not, unless the court otherwise orders, affect the prior appointment ... of any other person as guardian of the child."[103] Therefore, where a non-parent guardian is appointed, he or she will act alongside the parent guardians and the appointment will not affect the parents' rights.

As was noted earlier in this chapter, the 2015 Act amends the 1964 Act to provide a definition of the rights and responsibilities of a guardian. It provides that a guardian has the right and responsibility:

"(a) to decide on the child's place of residence;
 (b) to make decisions regarding the child's religious, spiritual, cultural and linguistic upbringing;
 (c) to decide with whom the child is to live;
 (d) to consent to medical, dental and other health related treatment for the child, in respect of which a guardian's consent is required;
 (e) under an enactment specified in subsection 12[104];
 (f) to place the child for adoption, and consent to the adoption of the child, under the Adoption Act 2010."[105]

Where the court appoints a person as an additional guardian of a child, and one or both of the parents of that child are still living, the additional guardian will not automatically acquire all of the rights and responsibilities set out above. Rather, this guardian will only exercise such rights and responsibilities "where the court expressly so orders" and "to the extent specified in the order and in the case of the rights and responsibilities specified in any of paragraphs (a) to (e) of that subsection, subject to such limitations as are specified in the order."[106] Therefore, the extent of the court appointed guardian's rights and obligations will be at the discretion of the court. In deciding whether or not to limit the rights and

---

[103] Guardianship of Infants Act 1964, s 6C(5), inserted by Children and Family Relationships Act 2015, s 49.
[104] The enactments specified are: Firearms Act 1925, s 2A(2); Protection of Young Persons (Employment) Act 1996, s 5; International Criminal Court Act 2006, ss 50 and 50A; Criminal Justice (Mutual Assistance) Act 2008, ss 79, 79A and 79B; Passports Act 2008, s 14; and the Criminal Justice (Forensic Evidence and DNA Database System) Act 2014.
[105] Guardianship of Infants Act 1964, s 6C(11), inserted by Children and Family Relationships Act 2015, s 49.
[106] Guardianship of Infants Act 1964, s 6C(9), inserted by Children and Family Relationships Act 2015, s 49.

responsibilities of the additional guardian, the court will have regard to the relationship between him or her and the child and to the best interests of the child.[107]

5. Temporary Guardians and Testamentary Guardians

A temporary guardian may be appointed to temporarily exercise rights and responsibilities on behalf of another guardian in the event that he or she becomes incapable through serious illness or injury of exercising the rights and responsibilities of guardianship.[108] Only a "qualifying guardian", that is a guardian who is a legal parent and has custody of the child or who is not a legal parent but has custody of the child to the exclusion of any living parent,[109] may nominate a person to act as a temporary guardian. This nomination must be in writing and it must specify such limitations (if any) as the qualifying guardian wishes to impose on the rights and responsibilities of guardianship that the temporary guardian may exercise. The qualifying guardian or nominated person may subsequently apply to the court for an order confirming the appointment of the temporary guardian.[110]

Certain guardians[111] also have the power to appoint a testamentary guardian to act as a guardian in the event of his or her death.[112] The testamentary guardian will act jointly with any surviving guardians of the child. If a surviving guardian objects to the appointment of the testamentary guardian, or if the testamentary guardian has concerns about the legal powers of the surviving guardian, an application can be made to the court to resolve the situation. The court can make an order providing that:

"(a)   the appointment of the testamentary guardian is revoked

---

[107] Guardianship of Infants Act 1964, s 6C(10), inserted by Children and Family Relationships Act 2015, s 49.

[108] Guardianship of Infants Act 1964, s 6E, inserted by Children and Family Relationships Act 2015, s 49.

[109] Guardianship of Infants Act 1964, s 2, amended by Children and Family Relationships Act 2015 s. 43.

[110] Guardianship of Infants Act 1964, s 6E, inserted by Children and Family Relationships Act 2015, s 49.

[111] Testamentary guardians may be appointed by a guardian who is a parent of the child or by a guardian who is not the parent of the child but has custody of the child to the exclusion of any living parent of the child. Guardianship of Infants Act 1964, s 7, substituted by Children and Family Relationships Act 2015, s 50.

[112] Guardianship of Infants Act 1964, s 7, substituted by Children and Family Relationships Act 2015, s 50.

and the surviving guardian shall remain a guardian of
the child concerned,

(b)   the testamentary guardian shall act jointly with the
surviving guardian, or

(c)   the testamentary guardian shall act as guardian of the
child to the exclusion, insofar as the court thinks proper,
of the surviving guardian."[113]

Custody

Custody is generally understood as the right of a parent to exercise
care and control over the child on a day-to-day basis. In *RC v IS*,
Finlay Geoghegan J defined custody as "the right to physical care
and control" and emphasised that it is a concept distinct from
that of guardianship.[114] Although there is no statutory definition
of custody, it is clear that it does not amount to the authority to
make significant decisions affecting the child, as this is covered
by guardianship. A guardian will not always exercise custody of
a child, and a person with custody will not always be a guardian.
Where a guardian does not have custody, he or she remains entitled
to be involved in relevant decisions about the child's upbringing.[115]

Custody will typically vest in the parent with whom the child
resides, but the question of residence is separate to that of custody.
Thus, it is not uncommon for parents to be awarded joint custody
in circumstances where the child will live with one parent but
maintain regular contact with the other. The parents themselves will
usually decide these arrangements but, where there is a dispute,
the court will determine the matter on the basis of what is best for
the child or children concerned.

1. Who can exercise custody?

While a guardian does not always exercise custody, he or she is
entitled, as against all other non-guardians, to custody.[116] Thus,
married parents, as joint guardians, are entitled to shared custody
of their child. In *In re J (an infant)*, the High Court reiterated
that married parents enjoy rights under Arts 41 and 42 of the

---

[113] Guardianship of Infants Act 1964, s 7(5), substituted by Children and Family
Relationships Act 2015, s 50.
[114] *RC v IS* [2003] 4 IR 431 at 439.
[115] *RC v IS* [2003] 4 IR 431 at 439.
[116] Guardianship of Infants Act 1964, s 10(2)(a).

Constitution and that these include the right to custody of their child.[117] In that case, Henchy J noted that

> "it would be impossible, because of the age of the child (17 months), to give effect to the parents' right and duty of education [arising under Article 42 of the Constitution] if they are not given custody of the child."[118]

Similarly, in *G v An Bord Uchtála*, the Supreme Court (Henchy J) again recognised that the right and duty of married parents to provide for the religious and moral, intellectual, physical and social education of their children in Art 42 meant that the parents have "the primary right to custody."[119] Of course, the married parents' right to custody is not absolute. Pursuant to Art 42A.2.1° of the Constitution, the State can supply the place of the parents, in exceptional cases

> "where the parents, regardless of their marital status, fail in their duty towards their children to such extent that the safety or welfare of any of their children is likely to be prejudicially affected."[120]

The mother of a non-marital child, as the sole automatic guardian, is entitled to sole custody of the child at birth. In *State (Nicolaou) v An Bord Uchtála*, Walsh J held that the unmarried mother has a "natural right to the custody and care of her child" flowing from Art 40.3 of the Constitution.[121] The right of the unmarried mother to the custody of her child is, however, by no means absolute. An unmarried father does not have any constitutional right to custody but he has the right to apply for same, even if he has not been appointed as a guardian.[122]

Whereas previously only guardians (and the unmarried father who was not a guardian) could exercise custody of a child, the 2015 Act has now broadened the range of individuals eligible to apply for custody. Section 11E of the 1964 Act, inserted by s 57 of the 2015 Act, allows for the following persons to apply for custody:

- a relative of the child or

---

[117] *In re J (an infant)* [1966] IR 295.
[118] *In re J (an infant)* [1966] IR 295 at 307.
[119] *G v An Bord Uchtála* [1980] 1 IR 32 at 85.
[120] Bunreacht na hÉireann, Art 42A.2.1°.
[121] *State (Nicolaou) v An Bord Uchtála* [1966] IR 567 at 644.
[122] Guardianship of Infants Act 1964, s 11(4), inserted by Status of Children Act 1987, s 13 and amended by Children and Family Relationships Act 2015, s 53.

- a person with whom the child resides and who was or is married to, in a civil partnership with, or a cohabitant (for over three years) of the parent of the child and has shared with that parent responsibility for the child's day-to-day care for more than two years, or
- a person who has provided for the child's day-to-day care for a continuous period of more than 12 months in circumstances where the child has no parent or guardian who is willing or able to exercise the rights and responsibilities of guardianship in respect of the child.[123]

Where any of these individuals apply for custody, the court cannot make the order without the consent of each guardian of the child, unless it is deemed to be in the best interests of the child to dispense with that consent.[124] The court may also order that custody is exercised jointly between a person above and the child's parent. In this case, the court will specify the residential arrangements that are to apply in respect of the child (if these have not already been agreed) and, if the child is not to reside with one of the parents, specify the contact (if any) that is to take place between the child and that parent during that period.[125]

2. Custody Disputes

In any decision as to custody, the best interests of the child must be the paramount consideration as per s 3 of the 1964 Act, as amended by s 45 of the 2015 Act. Where a dispute arises as to custody between parents, for example upon the breakdown of a relationship, the courts generally favour joint custody arrangements whereby custody is shared between the adults.[126] However, as was recognised in *EP v CP*,[127] it may not be possible to award joint custody where there is a high level of conflict between the parties, although this is not an absolute rule. For example, in *DFO'S v CA*,[128] McGuinness J awarded joint custody to parents in the context of an acrimonious marital breakdown as it was felt that granting sole custody to one of the parties would simply add to the bitterness between them.

---

[123] Guardianship of Infants Act 1964, s 11E(1), inserted by Children and Family Relationships Act 2015, s 57.
[124] Guardianship of Infants Act 1964, s 11E(3)–(4), inserted by Children and Family Relationships Act 2015, s 57.
[125] Guardianship of Infants Act 1964, s 11E(5), inserted by Children and Family Relationships Act 2015, s 57.
[126] Joint custody may be awarded under s 11A of the Guardianship of Infants Act 1964, inserted by Children Act 1997, s 9 and substituted by Children and Family Relationships Act 2015, s 54.
[127] *EP v CP* (HC, 27 November 1998, McGuinness J).
[128] *DFO'S v CA* (20 April 1998, McGuinness J).

Where joint custody is awarded, this does not mean that each party is entitled spend an equivalent amount of time with the child. Indeed, this is rarely possible given that parties may not live within a close distance of one another or in close proximity to the child's school or recreational activities, so as to avoid disruptions to the child's everyday life. Therefore, in practice, although joint custody may be awarded, the child will reside with one parent and spend weekends and holidays with the other. However, the fact that joint custody is awarded means that both parents have equivalent responsibilities and rights towards the child. If it is not possible for custody to be shared, sole custody may be granted to one parent and access granted to the other.

If it is not possible to award joint custody, the best interests of the child will determine which party is to be awarded custody. As was noted above, previously, under s 3 of the 1964 Act, the court had to regard the welfare of the child as the first and paramount consideration in cases concerning the guardianship, custody of or access to a child. Section 2 of the 1964 Act defined "welfare" as comprising of "the religious and moral, intellectual, physical and social welfare of the infant." These factors had to be considered globally to make an order that best provided for the totality of the child's needs. Now, under the 2015 Act, the courts are required to consider the best interests of the child as the paramount consideration in cases of custody and are directed to refer to the best interests checklist in conducting this examination. Many of the older welfare factors feature (among other considerations) on this best interests checklist.

Whatever the outcome, a custody order is always open to variation to ensure that it remains in the best interests of the child.[129] The best interests of the child are not stagnant and will naturally evolve over time as the child develops and matures.

Access

Access is a right that allows the child to maintain contact with parents and other relatives. Access is a right of the child, and not of the adult.[130] In the event of relationship breakdown, it is important for the emotional wellbeing of children that they are able to maintain relationships with the adults who have raised and cared for them. As Denham J noted in *JMcD v PL and BM*:

---

[129] *B v B* [1975] IR 54 at 58.
[130] *MD v GD* (HC, 30 July 1992).

> "A child will know and have a relationship with the people with whom he or she lives—it will be an important aspect of his or her life, and therefore weigh heavily in determining his or her welfare [in the context of guardianship, custody and access]."[131]

The importance for the child in maintaining family relationships is also recognised in Art 9(3) of the UNCRC, which provides that:

> "States Parties shall respect the right of the child who is separated from one or both parents to maintain personal relations and direct contact with both parents on a regular basis, except if it is contrary to the child's best interests."[132]

The term "parents" is not defined in the UNCRC and so can be taken to including anyone acting *in loco parentis*. In Ireland, the best interests checklist set out in the 1964 Act, as amended by the 2015 Act, also acknowledges the importance of maintaining relationships, as it obliges the court to have regard to

> "the benefit to the child of having a meaningful relationship with each of his or her parents and with the other relatives and persons who are involved in the child's upbringing and, except where such contact is not in the child's best interests, of having sufficient contact with them to maintain such relationships."[133]

The Irish courts generally find in favour of granting access to those that request it, in particular where a parent who does not have custody of the child applies for access. Thus, for example, in *AMacB v AGMacB*,[134] access was granted to a father notwithstanding evidence presented to the court that the children feared him. Where direct access is not deemed to be suitable, the court may order supervised or indirect access or access with conditions attached. For example, in *O'D v O'D*,[135] supervised access was granted to the father in circumstances where there was a reasonable suspicion that he might have sexually abused his child. Notwithstanding the judicial trend in favour of granting access, the best interests of the child will always be the determining factor for the courts in considering any application. As with a custody order, an access

---

[131] *JMcD v PL* [2010] 2 IR 199 at 270.
[132] United Nations Convention on the Rights of the Child, Art 9(3).
[133] Guardianship of Infants Act 1964, s 31(2)(a), inserted by Children and Family Relationships Act 2015, s 63.
[134] *A Mac B v AG Mac B* (HC, 6 June 1984, Barron J).
[135] *O'D v O'D* [1994] 3 Fam LJ 81.

order is never final and may be varied over time according to the best interests of the child.

Parents and guardians may apply for access to a child where they do not have custody, but also a relative of the child or a person who resides (or used to reside) with the child may apply for access.[136] Previously, a two-step process was involved where a person who was not a legal parent sought an order for access: applicants first had to satisfy a leave stage and then the substantive application was heard. This requirement was intended to prevent frivolous applications from coming before the courts. The 2015 Act has now removed the leave requirement so that the application for access by a non-parent is a one-step application. This has resulted in a simplified procedure which makes it easier to apply for access and therefore better facilitates access between the non-parent and the child.

Enforcement of Custody and Access Orders

If one of the parties to a custody or access arrangement refuses to comply with the order of the court and seeks to frustrate that order, the other party may be able to apply for an enforcement order to remedy the situation. The 2015 Act allows a guardian or parent of a child who has been unreasonably denied custody or access to apply to the court for an enforcement order.[137] The court may grant the order where it is in the best interests of the child to do so. The order may require any or all of the following:

- that the applicant is granted additional access to the child to remedy any adverse effects that the denial of access has caused;
- that the respondent reimburse the applicant for any expenses incurred by the applicant in attempting to exercise the original custody or access order;
- that the respondent or the applicant, either individually or together: attend a parenting programme; avail of family counselling; or receive information on the possibility of availing of mediation as a way to resolving any future disputes between them.[138]

---

[136] Guardianship of Infants Act 1964, s 11B, inserted by Children Act 1997, s 9 and amended by Children and Family Relationships Act 2015, s 55.
[137] Guardianship of Infants Act 1964, s 18A, inserted by Children and Family Relationships Act 2015, s 60.
[138] Guardianship of Infants Act 1964, s 18A(4), inserted by Children and Family Relationships Act 2015, s 60.

If the court is of the opinion that the denial of custody or access was reasonable in the particular circumstances, it may refuse the application for the enforcement order.

Overview

The 2015 Act has introduced significant changes in the area of guardianship, custody and access. A greater range of persons can now be appointed as guardians, reflecting the changing reality of Irish families. However, despite the increase in births outside of marriage, the unmarried father remains in a weak position vis-à-vis guardianship. While the 2015 Act has improved his position to a certain extent, it is arguable that further reforms are required in this area.

ADOPTION

i

Introduction

Adoption is a process whereby a child is given the opportunity of an alternative family. The mechanism extinguishes the parental responsibilities and rights of the birth parents and transfers these to the adoptive family. There is no "right" to adopt a child, either under Irish law or international law. Certain individuals may be given a statutory right to *apply* for adoption, but the success of this application will depend on assessment of the person's eligibility and suitability to adopt. Adoption is a child-centred process and one in which the best interests of the child must be to the fore. This premise is recognised at an international level in Art 21 of the United Nations Convention on the Rights of the Child (UNCRC) which provides that States parties which recognise and/or permit a system of adoption "shall ensure that the best interests of the child shall be the paramount consideration."[1] Therefore, the child's best interests are to be the paramount focus in any decision concerning the adoption of a child.

In Ireland, adoption is legally regulated by the Adoption Act 2010, as amended by the Adoption (Amendment) Act 2017 (the "2017 Act"), the latter of which was signed into law on 19 July 2017. The Children and Family Relationships Act 2015 made a number of significant changes to Irish adoption law but the adoption provisions in that Act were never commenced. Instead, these provisions were transferred to the 2017 Act. This chapter will discuss these laws to provide a comprehensive overview of current Irish law and to highlight recent changes.

Adoption in the Best Interests of the Child

Article 21 of the UNCRC provides that "States Parties that recognize and/or permit the system of adoption shall ensure that the best interests of the child shall be the paramount consideration." As was seen in Chapter 2, Art 3 UNCRC provides that

> "In all actions concerning children, whether undertaken by public or private social welfare institutions, courts of law, administrative authorities or legislative bodies, the best interests of the child shall be a primary consideration."[2]

The Committee on the Rights of the Child has explained that where the best interests of the child are expressed as "a primary

---

[1]   United Nations Convention on the Rights of the Child, Art 21.
[2]   United Nations Convention on the Rights of the Child, Art 3(1).

consideration", this means that those interests "may not be considered on the same level as all other considerations" and must be accorded priority.[3] Where the best interests of the child are described as "the paramount consideration", they are to be afforded greater weight and must be "the determining factor when taking a decision."[4] Article 21 UNCRC therefore requires that greater protection is afforded to the child's best interests in cases of adoption.

In Ireland, Art 42A of the Constitution recognises the best interests principle, providing, among other things, that in cases of adoption, provision shall be made by law that "the best interests of the child shall be the paramount consideration."[5] This constitutional mandate is given effect by various legislative provisions. Previously, s 19 of the Adoption Act 2010 provided that in proceedings concerning adoption, the court had to "regard the welfare of the child as the first and paramount consideration." This provision was amended by s 9 of the 2017 Act, which now provides that, in adoption proceedings

> "the [Adoption] Authority or the court, as the case may be, shall regard the best interests of the child as the paramount consideration in the resolution of such matter, application or proceedings."[6]

This wording mirrors that in Art 42A and in Art 21 UNCRC and creates consistency in the language adopted.

Adoption in Ireland

In Ireland, statutory adoption was first introduced under the Adoption Act 1952. Before this, adoptions were privately organised and often agreed by way of a private adoption deed. These private arrangements did not have any formal legal status and were often shrouded in secrecy leading to doubts about their enforceability. In other cases, prior to the availability of formal adoption, the "adoptive parents" were simply registered as the birth parents of the child and a formal deed was never executed. The child would

---

[3] Committee on the Rights of the Child, *General comment No 14 (2013) on the right of the child to have his or her best interests taken as a primary consideration (art. 3, para. 1)* CRC/C/GC/14, paras 37 and 39.
[4] Committee on the Rights of the Child, *General comment No 14 (2013) on the right of the child to have his or her best interests taken as a primary consideration (art. 3, para. 1)* CRC/C/GC/14, para 38.
[5] Bunreacht na hÉireann, Art 42A.4.1°.
[6] Adoption Act 2010, s 19, amended by Adoption (Amendment) Act 2017, s 9.

be presented as if he or she was born to the new family without any mention of the actual circumstances of the child's birth.[7]

The Adoption Act 1952 introduced a formal adoption process into Irish law for the first time. It established statutory eligibility criteria for prospective adoptive parents[8] and it established An Bord Uchtála (the Adoption Board) as a body with power to grant or refuse to grant adoption orders.[9] The Adoption Act 1952 was followed by various other Adoption Acts which were finally consolidated by the Adoption Act 2010. This Act also dissolved An Bord Uchtála and replaced it with the Adoption Authority of Ireland (the "Adoption Authority").[10] The Adoption Authority has overall responsibility for granting adoption orders.[11]

The functions of the Adoption Authority include:

(a) performing the functions previously performed by An Bord Uchtála;
(b) performing in the State the role of a Central Authority under the Hague Convention on Protection of Children and Co-operation in respect of Intercountry Adoption 1993;
(c) providing general advice to the Minister for Children and Youth Affairs about adoption matters;
(d) undertaking or assisting in research projects and activities relating to adoption services;
(e) compiling statistical information and other records as to the proper planning, development and provision of those adoption services;
(f) maintaining the register of accredited bodies; and
(g) maintaining the register of intercountry adoptions.[12]

In order to exercise these functions, the Adoption Authority is given "all the powers as are necessary or expedient for the performance"

---

[7] Commission of Investigation into Mother and Baby Homes, *Second Interim Report* (September 2016), para 6.4. Indeed, this practice continued in some cases after the introduction of statutory adoption. For example, in 2018, it was revealed that 126 persons had their births incorrectly registered by St Patrick's Guild adoption society between 1946 and 1969. The registrations illegally listed the adoptive parents as the parents. It is speculated that many other illegal adoptions took place during this period.
[8] Adoption Act 1952, s 11.
[9] Adoption Act 1952, s 8.
[10] Adoption Act 2010, s 94.
[11] See: <https://www.aai.gov.ie/>.
[12] Adoption Act 2010, s 96(1).

of same.[13] Sections 97–102 of the Adoption Act 2010 regulate a number of other matters pertaining to the Adoption Authority, including its membership and meetings.

Types of Adoption

An adoption order may be domestic or intercountry in nature. Domestic adoption refers to the adoption of a child who is habitually resident in Ireland before his or her adoption and the adopters are also resident in the State. Intercountry adoption occurs where the adopters are resident in one country and seek to adopt a child who is resident in a different country. The different types of adoption are discussed individually below.

1. Domestic Adoption

Adoption was originally designed to give orphaned or abandoned children a new legal family. It is a permanent process that transfers all parental rights from the birth parents to the adoptive parents. Following the adoption order, the child is a permanent member of the new family and the adoptive parents have full parental responsibilities and rights as they would if the child was born to them.[14]

Increasingly, domestic adoption is used as a mechanism to regularise existing family relationships, for example where a step-parent who is married to one of the legal parents seeks to adopt the child. Figures in Ireland show that the majority of domestic adoption orders made in the years 2002–2016 were made in favour of a step-parent adopting jointly with a birth parent. In 2016, 65 of the 95 domestic adoption orders granted were step-parent adoptions.[15] The prevalence of this form of adoption could be explained by the fact that, before 2015, there was no mechanism other than adoption available to allow a step-parent to acquire a legal relationship with his or her partner's child. As discussed in Chapter 4, the Children and Family Relationships Act 2015 has introduced provisions that allow a person who is married to, in a civil partnership with, or a cohabitant (for over three years) of a parent of the child, and who has shared with that parent responsibility for the child's day-to-day care for a period of more

---

13 Adoption Act 2010, s 96(2).
14 Adoption Act 2010, s 58, amended by Adoption (Amendment) Act 2017, s 25.
15 Adoption Authority of Ireland, *Annual Report 2016* (Adoption Authority of Ireland, 2016), p 25.

than two years, to apply to become a guardian of the child.[16] Where the step-parent is made a guardian, he or she will exercise parental responsibilities and rights in respect of the child. Given that this alternative to adoption is now available in Irish law, it may lead to a reduction in the number of applications for step-parent adoption.

Before 2017, there was no specific legal provision for step-parent adoptions in Ireland. Step-parent or second-parent adoption, as generally understood, is a process that allows a birth parent's new spouse or partner to adopt the parent's biological or adoptive child in a manner that *does not affect* the parental rights and responsibilities of that parent. By contrast, in Ireland before 2017, where a step-parent adopted his or her partner's child, the effect of the adoption order was to terminate the legal parental rights and responsibilities of the birth parent and to transfer all parental rights to the step-parent. Consequently, in a situation where the step-parent wished to adopt the child, the birth parent (who already had full parental responsibilities and rights in respect of the child) was required to give up his or her existing parental rights and to jointly adopt the child alongside the step-parent. Clearly, this was an inadequate situation that created unnecessary steps and overly complicated the process.

The 2017 Act now specifically addresses step-parent adoption. Section 26 of the 2017 Act inserts a new s 58A into the Adoption Act 2010 to provide that where a child is adopted by a step-parent, the child is deemed to be the child of that step-parent and the step-parent's spouse, civil partner or cohabitant, as the case may be.[17] The step-parent is defined as the spouse, civil partner or cohabitant of a birth parent.[18] In order to be eligible to adopt, the child must have lived with the step-parent and the birth parent for a continuous period of not less than two years.[19] As a result of this amendment, it is no longer be necessary for a birth parent to adopt his or her own child in order to confer joint adoptive rights upon the step parent.

The eligibility and suitability of adopters is discussed in more detail later in the chapter.

---

[16] Guardianship of Infants Act 1964, s 6C(2), inserted by Children and Family Relationships Act 2015, s 49.

[17] Adoption Act 2010, s 58A, inserted by Adoption (Amendment) Act 2017, s 26.

[18] Adoption Act 2010, s 37(b), amended by Adoption (Amendment) Act 2017, s 18.

[19] Adoption Act 2010, s 37(b) as amended by Adoption (Amendment) Act 2017, s 18.

2. Intercountry Adoption

Intercountry adoptions are governed by the Hague Convention on Protection of Children and Co-operation in respect of Intercountry Adoption 1993 (the "Hague Convention"), which is given force of law in Ireland by s 9 of the Adoption Act 2010. The Hague Convention was developed to establish safeguards and to promote co-operation amongst contracting states in order to protect children and their families involved in intercountry adoptions. The Hague Convention strives to give practical effect to Art 21 UNCRC and to ensure that the best interests of the child are paramount in intercountry adoption.

The Hague Convention operates through a system of national Central Authorities that are required to co-operate with one another to ensure that the principles and objectives of the Hague Convention can be fulfilled. Individuals wishing to engage in intercountry adoption must apply to the Central Authority in the State of their habitual residence. In Ireland, the Adoption Authority of Ireland performs the role of the Central Authority.

Before an intercountry adoption can take place, the Central Authority of the "State of origin" (the country where the child was born) must establish that the child is adoptable, provide counselling to relevant parties and obtain the relevant consents to the adoption.[20] The Central Authority of the "receiving State" (the country where the adopters live) will assess the eligibility and suitability of the prospective adoptive parents to adopt[21] and must send a report providing details of the applicants to the Central Authority of the State of origin. This information will include details on the applicants' identity, eligibility and suitability to adopt, background, family and medical history, social environment, reasons for adoption, ability to undertake an intercountry adoption, and characteristics of the children for whom they would be qualified to care.[22] If the Central Authority of the State of origin is satisfied that the child is adoptable, it will transmit to the Central Authority of the receiving State its report on the child, proof that the necessary consents have been obtained and the reasons for its determination

---

[20] Hague Convention on Protection of Children and Co-operation in respect of Intercountry Adoption 1993, Art 4.

[21] Hague Convention on Protection of Children and Co-operation in respect of Intercountry Adoption 1993, Art 5.

[22] Hague Convention on Protection of Children and Co-operation in respect of Intercountry Adoption 1993, Art 15.

on the placement.[23] Thereafter the Central Authorities of the two States must work together to complete the adoption procedure in accordance with the Convention.[24]

There is also the possibility that an adoption might be conducted through a bilateral agreement with a country outside the Hague Convention, as long as this has "regard for the principles of the Hague Convention."[25]

In Ireland, intercountry adoptions are currently the most common form of adoption. In 2016, 214 intercountry adoptions were registered in the register of intercountry adoptions, while 95 domestic adoption orders were granted.[26] The prevalence of intercountry adoption is explained by the fact that fewer infants are placed for domestic adoption in Ireland than in previous years. In 2016, for example, just five of the 95 domestic adoption orders involved the adoption of infants placed for adoption in Ireland.[27]

However, it is important to recall that adoption must always be in the best interests of the child and that international law establishes that intercountry adoption must not be the first preference for a child who is deprived of his or her family environment. This acknowledges the fact that the child should not be removed from his or her national culture, language, traditions and heritage without proper consideration. Article 21(b) of the UNCRC provides that States parties must recognise "that inter-country adoption may be considered as an alternative means of child's care, if the child cannot be placed in a foster or an adoptive family or cannot in any suitable manner be cared for in the child's country of origin."[28] This approach is also recognised in Art 4(b) of the Hague Convention which provides that the State of origin must give "due consideration" to possibilities of placing the child within the State before considering intercountry adoption.[29] Therefore, there must always be an attempt to place the child in the country of origin before intercountry adoption is considered.

---

[23] Hague Convention on Protection of Children and Co-operation in respect of Intercountry Adoption 1993, Art 16.
[24] Hague Convention on Protection of Children and Co-operation in respect of Intercountry Adoption 1993, Arts 17–22.
[25] Adoption Act 2010, s 73.
[26] Adoption Authority of Ireland, *Annual Report 2016* (Adoption Authority of Ireland, 2016), p 29.
[27] Adoption Authority of Ireland, *Annual Report 2016* (Adoption Authority of Ireland, 2016), p 25.
[28] United Nations Convention on the Rights of the Child, Art 21(b).
[29] Hague Convention on Protection of Children and Co-operation in respect of Intercountry Adoption 1993, Art 4(b).

Who Can be Adopted?

In Ireland, the law allows for the adoption of children, defined as persons under the age of 18 years. This means that a person who has reached the age of 18 years cannot be adopted. Previously, different rules applied to the adoption of non-marital and marital children. Both types of adoption are now permitted due to changes introduced by Art 42A of the Irish Constitution and under the Adoption (Amendment) Act 2017. These changes are explained in the sections below.

1. Non-Marital Children

Previously, s 23 of the Adoption Act 2010 provided that, for an adoption order to be granted, the child had to reside in the State, be under seven years of age, and be an orphan or have been born to unmarried parents. There were some exceptions to these criteria. For example, having regard to the particular circumstances of a case, the Adoption Authority could make an adoption order in relation to a child who was over seven years of age,[30] and it retained the power to make an adoption order notwithstanding that the child had not been in the care of the applicants for the prescribed period.

The 2017 Act amended the criteria for a child to be eligible for adoption. Now, any child residing in the State who is under the age of 18 years may be adopted.[31] This provision allows for older children to be adopted without the adopters having to seek an exception to the general age limit as was previously the case. The provision also removes the requirement that the child must be an orphan or have been born to unmarried parents. The amendments are in keeping with Art 42A.3 of the Constitution which requires, *inter alia*, that provision shall be made by law for "the adoption of any child." Section 12 of the 2017 Act gives effect to this constitutional mandate as it removes many of the older restrictions on eligibility for adoption.

2. Marital Children

Until quite recently in Ireland, children born to married parents could not be adopted except in the most exceptional of circumstances. The barrier to such adoptions was created by Art 42 of the Irish Constitution which sets out that the parental rights and

---

[30] Adoption Act 2010, s 24.
[31] Adoption Act 2010, s 23, amended by Adoption (Amendment) Act 2017, s 12.

duties of married parents are "inalienable."[32] Further, under Art 42.5 of the Constitution (since removed), the State could only supply the place of parents where they failed in their duty towards the child. These Articles did not mean that marital children could never be adopted, but they set a high threshold for such adoptions. Under s 54 of the Adoption Act 2010, the High Court could authorise the Adoption Authority to make an adoption order where the married parents had failed in their duty towards the child for a continuous period of not less than 12 months; in circumstances where it was likely that the failure would continue until the child reached the age of 18 years; where the failure amounted to an abandonment on the part of the parents of all parental rights in relation to the child; and the failure was such that the State was required supply the place of the parents.[33] As such, before 2017, a child born to married parents could only be adopted in the most serious of cases.

The very high threshold previously set for the adoption of a marital child meant that, traditionally, the children who were subject to such applications tended to be older. Most were aged 17 years and fast approaching their 18th birthday. This trend emerged because it was it was easier to prove that the parents had failed in their duty towards the child for a substantial period, and easier to show that the parents would continue to fail in their duty until the child reached 18 years, where the application concerned an older child. Where a younger marital child was the subject of an involuntary application for adoption, there was always the possibility that the situation would change and so the child's best interests, as an evolving concept, usually dictated that the child should not be permanently deprived of a legal relationship with the birth parents as the family may yet come back together. Thus, adoptions concerning marital children tended to involve older children who were close to aging out of long-term foster care. Adoption in these circumstances allowed the child to be fully integrated into the new family and to maintain a secure and lifelong legal family relationship with that family.

Article 42A of the Irish Constitution has now removed the constitutional barrier to the adoption of marital children. Article 42A.2.2° places an obligation on the Oireachtas (the Irish parliament) to legislate for the adoption of any child where the

---

[32] Art 42.1 of Bunreacht na hÉireann provides that "[t]he State acknowledges that the primary and natural educator of the child is the Family and guarantees to respect the inalienable right and duty of parents to provide, according to their means, for the religious and moral, intellectual, physical and social education of their children."

[33] Adoption Act 2010, s 54(2)(b).

parents have failed in their duty towards the child for a specified period and where this is deemed to be in the best interests of the child. In addition, Art 42A.3 requires that legislation is put in place to allow for the voluntary placement for adoption, and the adoption of, any child. These constitutional provisions require that legislation is enacted to allow married parents to voluntarily place their children for adoption for the first time and permit the State to continue to supply the place of parents who have failed in their duty towards the child.

The 2017 Act gives effect to Arts 42A.2.2° and 42A.3 of the Constitution. Section 24 of the 2017 Act amends s 54 of the Adoption Act 2010 to set out that the High Court may authorise the Adoption Authority to make an adoption order and to dispense with the required consents for adoption in circumstances where:

"(a) for a continuous period of not less than 36 months immediately preceding the time of the making of the application, the parents of the child … have failed in their duty towards the child to such extent that the safety or welfare of the child is likely to be prejudicially affected,

(b) there is no reasonable prospect that the parents will be able to care for the child in a manner that will not prejudicially affect his or her safety or welfare,

(c) the failure constitutes an abandonment on the part of the parents of all parental rights, whether under the Constitution or otherwise, with respect to the child,

(d) by reason of the failure, the State, as guardian of the common good, should supply the place of the parents,

(e) the child —
(i) at the time of the making of the application, is in the custody of and has a home with the applicants, and
(ii) for a continuous period of not less than 18 months immediately preceding that time, has been in the custody of and has had a home with the applicants, and

(f) that the adoption of the child by the applicants is a proportionate means by which to supply the place of the parents."[34]

A notable difference between the above provision and the previous law is that the above does not require that the parental failure must be likely to continue until the child reaches the age of 18 years.

---

[34] Adoption Act 2010, s 54(2A), amended by Adoption (Amendment) Act 2017, s 24.

For this reason, it has been suggested that the threshold to be applied for involuntary adoptions arising under the 2017 Act will be lower and will make it easier for children to be adopted where their parents have failed in their duty towards them.[35] At the same time, it should be noted that the 2017 Act requires the parents to have failed in their duty towards the child for at least 36 months, whereas the Adoption Act 2010 specified that the failure had only to last for at least 12 months. As such, a longer period of failure is now required before the court will grant the adoption order. In addition, the 2017 Act increases the period of time that the child is to be in the custody of the applicants prior to the adoption from 12 to 18 months. The latter provision ensures that the child and the applicants have developed a strong relationship before the adoption order can be granted.

In addition, as was noted above, s 12 of the 2017 Act removes the older requirement that the child had to be an orphan or have been born to unmarried parents for an adoption order to be granted. This is a positive step forward for Irish law because many children in long-term foster care have married birth parents. These children can now be voluntarily placed for adoption by their parents, offering them a permanent "second chance" at stable family life with their foster carers.

Who Can Adopt? Eligibility and Suitability

As noted at the outset, no one has a "right" to adopt a child. Instead, certain individuals may apply to be assessed for adoption. In Ireland, the Adoption Act 2010 requires that prospective adoptive parent(s) hold a declaration of eligibility and suitability before they can adopt a child. Before 2017, only married couples or single persons were eligible to apply to adopt.[36] The Children and Family Relationships Act 2015 (the "2015 Act") made significant changes to the eligibility criteria for adoption. Section 114 of the 2015 Act amended s 33 of the Adoption Act 2010 to provide that married couples, single persons, civil partners and cohabiting couples were eligible to adopt. These provisions, however, were never commenced. The adoption provisions set out in 2015 Act have now been transferred to the 2017 Act. As a result, civil partners and cohabiting couples of the same or opposite sex are now eligible

---

[35] Geoffrey Shannon, "Paper on the Adoption Amendment Bill", (Seminar on the Implications for Children –Adoption Amendment Bill Foster Care to Adoption – A New Era, Dublin, 1 December 2016), pp 6–7.

[36] Adoption Act 2010, s 33.

to apply to jointly adopt a child for the first time in Ireland.[37] Married couples and single persons also remain eligible to apply for adoption.[38] Where any eligible couple jointly adopts a child, they are automatically recognised as joint guardians.

In addition to eligibility requirements, a person seeking to adopt a child must be deemed suitable to adopt. In this regard, a number of suitability criteria must be met. The Adoption Authority must be satisfied that each adopter:

> "(a) is a suitable person to have parental rights and duties in respect of the child, and
>
> (b) without prejudice to the generality of paragraph (a), is of good moral character, in good health and of an age so that he or she has a reasonable expectation of being capable throughout the child's childhood of—
>
>> (i) fulfilling his or her parental duties in respect of the child,
>>
>> (ii) promoting and supporting the child's development and well-being,
>>
>> (iii) safeguarding and supporting the child's welfare,
>>
>> (iv) providing the necessary health, social, educational and other interventions for the child, and
>>
>> (v) valuing and supporting the child's needs in relation to his or her
>>
>>> (I)   identity, and
>>>
>>> (II) ethnic, religious and cultural background,
>
> (c) has adequate financial means to support the child, and
>
> (d) has been provided with appropriate information, advice and counselling concerning adoption."[39]

The prospective adoptive parents must also be at least 21 years of age. There is no upper age limit set out in the legislation but, in practice, most adoption agencies apply their own upper age limits, with the maximum age for prospective adopters usually being set at 35 years of age.

In Ireland, the Child and Family Agency (Tusla) carries out the assessment of eligibility and suitability of prospective adopters. Based on this assessment, the Adoption Authority will decide whether to grant or refuse the declaration of eligibility and suitability. When issuing a declaration of eligibility and suitability,

---

[37] Adoption Act 2010, s 33, amended by Adoption (Amendment) Act 2017, s 16.
[38] Adoption Act 2010, s 33, amended by Adoption (Amendment) Act 2017, s 16.
[39] Adoption Act 2010, s 34.

the Adoption Authority may include in it a statement relating to the age or state of health of a child whom the Adoption Authority considers that the applicant or applicants are suited to parent.[40] The declaration lasts for a period of 24 months (with the possibility of a 12 month extension).[41] The applicant(s) must hold a valid declaration at the time that the adoption order is granted.

Procedures for a Valid Adoption Order

1. Domestic Adoption

In order for an adoption order to be granted, the consent of each guardian of the child is required.[42] A "relevant non-guardian" who does not exercise guardianship in relation to the child has the right to be consulted in relation to the adoption, but his or her consent to same is not required.[43] A "relevant non-guardian" includes a father of the child who is not a guardian; a parent of a child born through DAHR who is not a guardian; a person who is not a parent of the child but who has been appointed by the court as a guardian and the court order provides that his or her consent to the adoption of the child is not required; or a person appointed by the court to be a temporary guardian.[44] If the Adoption Authority believes that it would be inappropriate to consult with any relevant non-guardian, it can make the adoption order without consulting him or her with the approval of the High Court.[45]

There are two steps involved in the consent process: consent to the placement for adoption and consent to the final adoption order. In certain limited circumstances, the court can dispense with the required consent to the final adoption order.[46]

(a) Placement for Adoption

The child must be at least six weeks old before he or she is placed for adoption.[47] Where the child is placed for adoption, the parent or guardian placing the child must be fully informed of the

---

[40] Adoption Act 2010, s 40(3)
[41] Adoption Act 2010, s 41(1).
[42] Adoption Act 2010, s 26.
[43] Adoption Act 2010, s 30, substituted by Adoption (Amendment) Act 2017, s 13.
[44] Adoption Act 2010, s 3, amended by Adoption (Amendment) Act 2017, s 3.
[45] Adoption Act 2010, s 30(3), substituted by Adoption (Amendment) Act 2017, s 13.
[46] Adoption Act 2010, s 26.
[47] Adoption Act 2010, s 13.

consequences of this so that the agreement to the placement is free and informed consent. To ensure that the consent is free and informed, the person must be given a written statement explaining:

> "(i)   that a placement for adoption is the beginning of the adoption process,
>
> (ii)   the effect of a placement for adoption upon the rights of a mother or guardian,
>
> (iii) the effect of an adoption order upon the rights of a mother or guardian, and
>
> (iv) the requirements specified in sections 26 to 28 of the Adoption Act 2010 in respect of the consents necessary in relation to an adoption order (for example that consent may be withdrawn at any time before the making of an adoption order)."[48]

The parent or guardian must also be provided with information, advice and counselling and is required to sign a document indicating that he or she understands the consequences of the consent to the placement.

After a child has been placed for adoption, the accredited body (usually an adoption agency) is required to take all reasonable steps to consult with the "relevant non-guardian" of the child, informing him or her of the proposed adoption; explaining the legal implications of adoption; and ascertaining whether or not he or she objects to the proposed adoption.[49] If, after the accredited body consults with the relevant non-guardian, he or she objects to the placement, the accredited body must defer the placement of the child for adoption for such time as is necessary (at least 21 days) so that the relevant non-guardian can apply to the court for guardianship.[50] The child's birth parents must be notified of the deferral and the reasons for it.

If the relevant non-guardian chooses to apply for, and is awarded, guardianship his or her consent will be required before the adoption can proceed and so he or she would, at that stage, be in a position to block the making of the adoption order. In *JK v VW*,[51] for example, an unmarried father applied for guardianship in an attempt to prevent the adoption of his child. In this case, the mother had

---

48   Adoption Act 2010, s 14(a)

49   Adoption Act 2010, s 17, substituted by Adoption (Amendment) Act 2017, s 7.

50   Adoption Act 2010, s 17(3)(b), amended by Adoption (Amendment) Act 2017, s 7.

51   *JK v VW* [1990] 2 IR 437.

placed the child for adoption without the father's knowledge. When the father discovered that the child had been placed for adoption, he applied for guardianship but his application was refused by the High Court. The father subsequently brought a claim to the European Court of Human Rights (heard as *Keegan v Ireland*)[52] claiming that his right to respect for his family life under Art 8 of the European Convention on Human Rights (ECHR) had been breached due to the fact that the Irish law allowed the child to be placed for adoption without his consent. The European Court of Human Rights ruled that the Irish law allowing for the child to be placed for adoption without the father's knowledge amounted to a violation of Art 8 ECHR as it disrupted the relationship between the father and the child. This case ultimately led to a change in Irish law such that a father without guardianship must be consulted in relation to the adoption of his child as was seen above.

If the accredited body, having taken all reasonable steps, is unable to consult with the relevant non-guardian, the Adoption Authority may authorise the placement for adoption notwithstanding that the relevant non-guardian has not been consulted.[53] If the identity of the child's father is unknown to the accredited body and the mother (or other guardian) refuses to disclose his identity, the accredited body must advise the mother that, if the father's identity is not disclosed, the adoption may be delayed; the father of the child could contest the adoption at a later stage; and that the absence of information about the medical, genetic and social background of the child may be detrimental to the health, development or welfare of that child. If the mother still refuses to disclose the identity of the father, the Adoption Authority may apply for approval from the High Court to authorise the accredited body to place the child for adoption.[54]

The initial consent to the child's placement for adoption is regarded as interim in nature and it can be revoked by the birth parent(s) at any time prior to the making of the final adoption order.[55] In *G v An Bord Uchtála*, Henchy J explained that there is "nothing final" about the consent to the placement of a child for adoption. Rather, he noted that such consent

"acts to produce a temporary derogation or suspension of the mother's right to custody. It does not amount to a waiver or

---

[52] *Keegan v Ireland*, App no 16969/90 (ECtHR, 26 May 1994).
[53] Adoption Act 2010, s 18, substituted by Adoption (Amendment) Act 2017, s 8.
[54] Adoption Act 2010, s 18(5)–(6), amended by Adoption (Amendment) Act 2017, s 8.
[55] Adoption Act 2010, s 26(4).

abandonment so as to destroy the mother's rights; only the adoption order can have that effect."[56]

The provisional nature of the initial consent to adoption is demonstrated in the case of *N v Health Service Executive*,[57] known as the "Baby Ann" case. In this case, the unmarried parents of a child referred to as "Baby Ann" placed her for adoption. They later married and withdrew their initial consent to the adoption. The High Court held that the consent of the birth parents should be dispensed with on the basis that Baby Ann's best interests would be served through her adoption by the prospective adoptive parents. The Supreme Court, however, overruled this finding and ordered that Baby Ann be returned to her birth parents. The Supreme Court held that there is a constitutional presumption that it is in the best interests of the child to be raised by the married birth parents and that this presumption could only be rebutted where the parents were found to have failed for physical or moral reasons in their duty towards the child as per Art 42.5 of the Constitution.[58] The Court was satisfied that placing the child for adoption did not amount to such a failure of duty and ordered that the child be returned to the birth parents.

(b) Consent to the Adoption Order

The second consent required in the adoption process is consent to the making of the adoption order. Consent to the making of an adoption order is not valid unless given after the child concerned has attained the age of six weeks, and not earlier than three months before the application for adoption.[59]

In *G v An Bord Uchtála*,[60] an unmarried mother who had placed her child for adoption later sought to revoke this consent. The prospective adoptive parents sought an order to dispense with the mother's consent which was otherwise required before an adoption order could be made in their favour. The Supreme Court noted that the unmarried mother has a right to the custody and care of her child under Art 40.3 of the Constitution. The Court was satisfied that she had not abandoned this right in placing the child for adoption and so the child was returned to her.

---

[56] *G v An Bord Uchtála* [1980] IR 32 at 89.
[57] *N v Health Service Executive* [2006] 4 IR 374.
[58] Art 42.5 of Bunreacht na hÉireann has since been removed from the Constitution and replaced by Art 42A.2.1°.
[59] Adoption Act 2010, s 28.
[60] *G v An Bord Uchtála* [1980] IR 32.

This does not mean that an unmarried mother who has placed her child for adoption will always be successful in seeking to have the child returned to her custody. The ultimate test will be the best interests of the child. Where a parent or guardian has given their initial consent to placing the child for adoption, but refuses to consent to the final adoption order, the prospective adoptive parents may apply to the High Court for an order dispensing with that consent. If the Court is satisfied that it is in the best interests of the child to do so, it may make an order giving custody of the child to the applicants for a specified period, and authorising the Adoption Authority to dispense with the other person's consent.[61] In considering such an application, the best interests of the child must be the paramount consideration and the Court must have regard to a number of factors including:

"(i)   the relationship between the applicants and the child who is the subject of the application;

(ii)   the relationship between the child and his or her mother or guardian, as the case may be, and the efforts made by any of those persons to develop or maintain a relationship with the child;

(iii) the proposed arrangements of the applicants and the mother or guardian or other person whose consent to the making of the adoption order is necessary under section 26, as the case may be, for the future care of the child;

(iv) the rights, whether under the Constitution or otherwise, of the persons concerned (including the natural and imprescriptible rights of the child);

(v)   any other matter which the Court considers relevant to the application."[62]

In addition, this section requires that, in so far as is practicable, in a case where the child concerned is capable of forming his or her own views, those views must be give due weight, having regard to the age and maturity of the child.[63]

(c) The Adoption Certificate and Register of Adoptions

After the adoption order has been made, the child is legally regarded as the child of the adopter(s). This means that the

---

[61] Adoption Act 2010, s 31, substituted by Adoption (Amendment) Act 2017, s 14.

[62] Adoption Act 2010, s 31(4)(a), amended by Adoption (Amendment) Act 2017, s 14.

[63] Adoption Act 2010, s 31(4)(b), amended by Adoption (Amendment) Act 2017, s 14.

child's original birth certificate is no longer a valid document for identification purposes. A new birth certificate (referred to as the adoption certificate) will be issued by an tArd-Chláraitheoir (the Registrar General's Office) within four weeks. The adoption certificate has the status of a birth certificate for legal purposes. It gives the date of the adoption order and the names and addresses of the adoptive parents and is similar in all aspects to a birth certificate. In all instances where a birth certificate is required for official purposes, the adopted person should provide a copy of their adoption certificate.

Where a child has been adopted, an entry is made in the Adopted Children Register. This entry will contain all details relevant to the adoption such as the PPS number of the child; date of birth; details relating to the adopters; and date of the adoption order.[64] It is possible to inspect this Register by applying to the Registrar General and paying the prescribed fee but any "true copy" provided must omit any reference to a PPS number or any previous adoption.[65] The Registrar General is also required to keep an index tracing connections between each entry in the Adopted Children Register and the Register of Births. This index is not publicly available and no information from that index shall be given to any person except by order of a court or of the Adoption Authority.[66]

2. Intercountry Adoption

As discussed above, the requirements for an intercountry adoption are set by the Hague Convention on Protection of Children and Co-operation in respect of Intercountry Adoption 1993 and are given force of law in Ireland by the Adoption Act 2010. Once the intercountry adoption order has been made, particulars of the adoption must be entered in the register of intercountry adoptions.[67]

Section 92 of the Adoption Act 2010 provides that the High Court may direct the Adoption Authority to make, cancel or correct an entry in the register of intercountry adoptions. In *MO'C v Údarás Uchtála na hÉireann*,[68] Abbott J made an order under s 92 in relation to an adoption that did not comply with all of the requirements of the Hague Convention. In this case, the applicants had commenced the adoption process and received a declaration of eligibility and

---

[64] Adoption Act 2010, s 84 and Sch 3.
[65] Adoption Act 2010, s 85, amended by Adoption (Amendment) Act 2017, s 36.
[66] Adoption Act 2010, s 86.
[67] Adoption Act 2010, s 90.
[68] *MO'C v Údarás Uchtála na hÉireann* [2015] 2 IR 94.

suitability from the Adoption Authority to adopt a child from Mexico. After the child had been placed with the applicants, but before the final adoption order was made, the Adoption Act 2010 came into force thereby incorporating the Hague Convention into Irish law. The proposed adoption did not comply with the terms and conditions of the Hague Convention and so the adopters applied to the High Court to recognise the adoption and to make an entry in the register. In the High Court, Abbott J noted that

> "From the [Hague] Convention itself (which is a Convention of cooperation rather than of technical and inflexible jurisdiction rules) and from the explanatory memorandum it is clear that in relation to ensuring the broad objectives and fundamental principles of the Convention cooperation and flexibility may be required."[69]

Abbott J directed the registration of the adoption under s 92 on the basis that the adoption had complied in all respects with the requirements of a foreign adoption under the law as it stood before the commencement of the Adoption Act 2010 and the adoption broadly adhered to the requirements of the Hague Convention. Thus, there is an element of flexibility available in respect of the recognition of intercountry adoptions. However, where the requirements of the Hague Convention are clearly not met, for example where the adopters do not obtain a declaration of eligibility and suitability from the Central Authority in advance of the adoption, the court will not register the intercountry adoption.[70]

Origin and Tracing

Historically, adoption in Ireland has been characterised by confidentiality and secrecy. The effect of the adoption order was (and still is) to sever all legal ties with the birth family and, in order to protect the birth parents' right to privacy, the child had no contact with them after the adoption. It remains the case that adopted persons have no specific right of access to their birth records under Irish law, which impedes attempts at contact.

In the past, when a mother placed a child for adoption, she was usually assured confidentiality and, as a result of this, a culture of secrecy developed around adoption. As such, the principal difficulty that arises in the context of access to adoption records

---

[69] *MO'C v Údarás Uchtála na hÉireann* [2015] 2 IR 94 at 125.
[70] *JM v Adoption Authority of Ireland* [2017] IEHC 320.

and birth certificates is that such access gives rise to a potential conflict between two rights: the right to identity of the adopted person and the right to privacy of the birth parents. Neither right is expressly set down in the Constitution, but both rights have been recognised as coming within the scope of the "personal rights" guarantee contained in Art 40.3.1°.

The Supreme Court was called upon to consider whether adopted persons should have access to birth information in the case of *I'OT v B*.[71] In this case, two individuals who had been informally adopted sought access to their birth records but the requests were refused by the notice party, the Rotunda Girls Aid Society (the "Adoption Society") on the basis that the records were confidential. The Supreme Court found that "[t]he right to know the identity of one's natural mother is a basic right flowing from the natural and special relationship which exists between a mother and her child".[72] However, this right is not absolute and the Supreme Court noted that it may be restricted by reference to the constitutional rights of others, for example in order to safeguard the birth mother's right to privacy. This does not mean that the right to privacy is absolute but it was found to require that the two rights be balanced against one another. The Court has the task of balancing these rights and, where it is not possible to harmonise the rights, it must "determine which right is the superior having regard to all the circumstances of the case."[73] On the facts of this particular case, the Supreme Court held that the mother's right to privacy outweighed the rights of the adopted persons.

Since neither the right to privacy nor the right to identity are absolute, either right can be restricted. At present, Irish law prioritises the right to privacy of the mother such that, if she has expressed a desire for confidentiality, that will generally be respected and the right to identity of the adoptee will be subordinate. However, in *IO'T v B* the Supreme Court acknowledged that legislation could be enacted to shift this balance. As Keane J (who dissented on the recognition of a constitutional right to identity) noted:

> "Legislation, if it existed, would presumably afford a pivotal role in the process by which persons informally adopted could establish contact with their natural parents to An Bord Uchtála (which, rather than the courts, should be the agency of first resort) and would set out in detail the circumstances in which,

---

[71] *I'OT v B* [1998] 2 IR 321.
[72] *I'OT v B* [1998] 2 IR 321 at 348.
[73] *I'OT v B* [1998] 2 IR 321 at 349.

having regard to the requirements of the common good, the parent's rights to privacy should yield, in the particular case, to the child's wish to know his or her parentage."[74]

Thus, as O'Mahony has noted,

"[i]n principle, there seems no reason why the law could not constitutionally reverse [the current] situation so as to give absolute priority to the right to identity over the right to privacy, particularly given that the adoptee had no choice in the matter."[75]

The current situation is that the confidentiality guaranteed to the birth mother at the time of the adoption takes precedence over the adopted person's right to identity. This does not mean that an adopted person cannot access any information about their birth origins. In practice, adopted persons are able to request non-identifying information pertaining to their birth from their placing agency or from the Adoption Authority of Ireland. With this information, it may be possible to trace the birth family. There is, however, no legal right to obtain this information and identifying information will not be disclosed without the birth parent's permission.

In May 2005, the National Adoption Contact Preference Register was launched to facilitate contact between adopted persons and their birth family. Participation in the Register is voluntary and contact will only be possible where the birth parent(s) or family of the birth parent(s) and the adopted person choose to include their details on the Register. The parties must also be over the age of 18 years to participate. The parties can specify the level of contact that they would like to have and with whom (or indicate that they do not wish to have contact) and can indicate who they would like to share information with. The information contained on the Register is not accessible by the general public.

It could be argued that where the birth mother was assured confidentiality at the time that the child was placed for adoption, that agreement should not be retrospectively altered by later allowing the adopted person to access their birth information. Other countries have, however, successfully addressed this issue. In England and Wales for example, s 60 of the Adoption and Children

---

[74] *I'OT v B* [1998] 2 IR 321 at 379.
[75] Conor O'Mahony, *Submission to Joint Oireachtas Committee on Health and Children in relation to: The Adoption (Information and Tracing) Bill 2015* (2015), p 3.

Act 2002 gives adopted persons over the age of 18 years the right
to access any information about their birth. The Irish Government
has also signalled its intention to finally address this issue in the
Adoption (Information and Tracing) Bill 2016, discussed below.
This Bill proposes a number of changes to Irish law that would
allow adopted persons to access their birth information subject to
certain conditions.

Adoption (Information and Tracing) Bill 2016

The Adoption (Information and Tracing) Bill 2016 proposes to
provide for a scheme whereby adoption information, including
the information required to obtain a birth certificate, may be
provided to an adopted person in certain circumstances and
subject to conditions. Section 14 of the Bill provides that the Child
and Family Agency (Tusla) shall establish and maintain a register,
known as the Register of Adoption Contact Enquiries, to record the
names and contact details of persons who apply to be entered on
the register. It will also record the preferences of such persons to
share and receive information and whether they are seeking contact
with, or willing to be contacted by, a specified person. The Register
will be used to facilitate the gathering of information pertaining
to adopted persons. In addition, an entry previously made in the
National Adoption Contact Preference Register indicating that a
birth parent does not wish to have contact will be recorded on the
new Register of Adoption Contact Enquiries.

The Bill proposes that the following persons will be able to apply
to have an entry made on the register:

> "(a) a person who is, or who believes himself or herself to be,
>   a relevant person[76];
> (b) a person who is, or who believes himself or herself to be,
>   a birth parent of a relevant person;
> (c) a person who is a relevant guardian in relation to an
>   adopted person;
> (d) the adoptive parent of an adopted child;
> (e) a relative of a relevant person;
> (f) a relative of a birth parent of a relevant person."[77]

Where a person has made an entry in the Register, they may request

---

[76] A "relevant person" is defined in the Bill as an adopted person, a person who
is or was the subject of an incorrect registration, or a person who is or was the
subject of an informal care arrangement.

[77] Adoption (Information and Tracing) Bill 2016, s 14(3).

the Child and Family Agency (the "Agency") to facilitate contact between them and a person specified in that entry. Upon receiving such a request, the Agency will take all reasonable steps to locate the specified person. The Agency will determine whether or not the specific person is willing to have contact with the person requesting it (the "requester"). Where the specified person is willing to have contact, the Agency shall take action, as it considers appropriate to facilitate such contact. Where the specified person is unwilling to have contact, the Agency shall inform the requester of that fact.[78]

Section 23 of the Bill provides that a person who is over the age of 18 years and believes that he or she is an adopted person, a person who is or was the subject of an incorrect registration, or a person who is or was the subject of an informal care arrangement, may apply to the Child and Family Agency for information held by it relating to his or her birth relatives; birth parents; early life; medical information; medical information relating to a birth relative; provided items; birth certificate information; the forename and surname of his or her birth father; or for a copy of an adoption order made in respect of him or her.[79] Where the request for information relates to a birth relative, birth parent, early life or medical information, the Agency shall provide the applicant with a statement in accordance with s 40(1) of the Bill. This statement will set out the information applied for by the applicant that is contained in the relevant records held by the Agency and the Adoption Authority and will provide a statement as to the nature and likely accuracy of such records. The statement shall not contain any information that would identify a birth parent or a birth relative of the applicant.[80]

Where an application is made for the provision of birth certificate information or a copy of an adoption order, different conditions are set out in the Bill depending on whether the birth mother is alive and whether there is an entry on the Register. Where the Agency is satisfied that the applicant's birth mother is deceased, or where the adoption was effected before the relevant section comes into operation and there is no entry on the Register in respect of the applicant's birth mother, and the applicant has given an undertaking, in accordance with s 41, not to attempt to contact her, the Agency shall, where the application is for birth certificate information, provide a written statement in accordance with s 40(2). This statement will set out the information applied

---

[78] Adoption (Information and Tracing) Bill 2016, s 20.
[79] Adoption (Information and Tracing) Bill 2016, s 23(1).
[80] Adoption (Information and Tracing) Bill 2016, s 40(1).

for by the applicant that is contained in the relevant records held by the Agency and the Adoption Authority, and shall include a statement as to the nature and likely accuracy of the relevant records. Where the application is for a copy of an adoption order made in respect of the applicant, the Agency is obliged to provide the applicant with the document concerned.[81]

Where an application is made for the provision of birth certificate information or a copy of an adoption order and there is an entry in the register in respect of the applicant's birth mother, or the adoption was effected on or after the date on which the section comes into operation, the Agency will notify the birth mother that an application has been made and inform her that she is entitled to support and guidance. The birth mother will also be informed that she may provide a statement of compelling reasons as to why the information, or adoption order, should not be provided and that, if she does not avail of this entitlement, the information or adoption order shall be provided to the applicant. Where the birth mother is of the view that there are compelling reasons why the information should not be provided to the applicant, she may, within 12 weeks of the date of the notification, provide a written statement to the Agency of her reasons supporting that view. The Agency will determine whether there are compelling reasons not to provide the information or adoption order. Where the Agency determines that there are compelling reasons, it shall make an application to the Circuit Court seeking the approval of its determination to refuse to provide the requested information or adoption order to the applicant. If the Agency concludes that there are no compelling reasons as to why the requested information should not be disclosed, the information will be provided to the applicant.[82]

Where the applicant is an adopted person whose adoption was effected before the date on which the relevant section of the Bill comes into operation, and the entry in the register in respect of the birth mother records that she is not willing to be contacted by the applicant, the Agency shall only provide the applicant with his or her birth certificate information or adoption order where the applicant gives an undertaking to the Agency not to contact, or attempt to contact, the birth mother, birth father or relevant guardian concerned, or make arrangements with any other person for that person to contact, or attempt to contact, the birth

---

[81] Adoption (Information and Tracing) Bill 2016, s 25.
[82] Adoption (Information and Tracing) Bill 2016, s 26.

mother, birth father or relevant guardian concerned.[83] Equivalent procedures are set out where the adopted person applies for the forename and surname of his or her birth father.[84]

Many adopted persons have expressed dissatisfaction with the provisions proposed in the Adoption (Information and Tracing) Bill 2016, in particular the requirement that the adopted person must give an undertaking not to contact the birth parent in order to receive the information requested. It has been argued that this approach fails to fully vindicate the identity rights of the adopted person.[85] It should also be noted that the Bill is silent on whether a penalty, criminal or civil, would apply to an adopted person who breaches their undertaking.

Open Adoption

Ireland operates a "closed" system of adoption whereby there is no contact between the child, the adoptive parents and the birth parents after the adoption order has been made. This is a by-product of the traditional approach to adoption which was characterised by secrecy and confidentiality. Most adoptions nowadays concern older children who have been living with the prospective parents for some time, for example in step-families or in long-term foster care. In these situations, there has been a shift to a more "open" type of arrangement where the child can maintain some element of contact with the birth family. Irish adoption agencies now encourage open adoptions where the two families are given the opportunity to maintain some level of contact with one another.

Open adoption allows for contact and communication between the adoptive parents, the child, the birth parents, and in some cases the wider extended family. The level and frequency of contact will vary from case to case and can range from the exchange of letters, to telephone calls or visits with the child. There are a number of positives associated with open adoption. For example, it is suggested that open adoption can alleviate some of the difficulties experienced by adopted children such as identity confusion or feelings of abandonment by birthparents.[86] As Kilkelly notes, open adoption provides the adopted child

---

[83] Adoption (Information and Tracing) Bill 2016, ss 26(16) and 41.
[84] Adoption (Information and Tracing) Bill 2016, ss 27 and 28.
[85] Ronan McGreevy, "Zappone admits 'deep concern' over aspects of adoption bill" *The Irish Times* (Dublin, 3 May 2017).
[86] Marianne Berry, Debora Dylla, Richard Barth and Barbara Needell, "The Role

"with the best of both worlds; they benefit from belonging permanently to a supportive adoptive family while at the same time they can draw benefit from knowing and having contact with their birth family."[87]

At present in Ireland, there is no legal provision to facilitate open adoption. Instead, an open adoption agreement is a voluntary one between the adoptive family and birth family and the process is unregulated and unenforceable. The lack of regulation can leave the parties, particularly the birth family, in a weak position as there is nothing to bind the others to the agreement and so they can effectively be shut out of the child's life if the adoptive parents so wish. One way to facilitate open adoption would be to make it a condition of the adoption order. This, however, is not an ideal solution as the level of contact may need to be varied over time so as to reflect what is best for the child. As such, it may not be appropriate to strictly define the level of contact in a legal agreement. Open adoption can be time-consuming as the arrangements need to be continually reviewed. The adoptive and birth parents also require education, counselling and post-adoption support. These supports are essential to ensure that the child's best interests remain paramount in the process and so that the child can in fact benefit from the arrangement.

Although the 2017 Act does not introduce provisions to facilitate open adoption, s 42 provides that the Minister for Children shall initiate a review and consultation in respect of the potential introduction of open or semi-open adoption in Ireland within 10 months of the passing of the Act. A report on the findings of this review and public consultation must be presented to the Oireachtas within 18 months of the start of the review.[88] This provision imposes an obligation on the Minister to initiate consultations on the possible introduction of open adoption by May 2018 and to report on this matter by November 2019 at the latest.

Section 42 was introduced following an amendment to the Adoption (Amendment) Bill proposed in Seanad Éireann by Senator Alice Mary Higgins. The Minister for Children accepted the amendment and explained that the purpose of the review and consultations is to refine and clarify what is meant by the term "open adoption".[89]

---

of Open Adoption in the Adjustment of Adopted Children and Their Families" (1998) 20 *Children and Youth Services Review* 151.
[87] Ursula Kilkelly, *Children's Rights in Ireland* (Tottel Publishing, Dublin, 2008), p 390.
[88] Adoption (Amendment) Act 2017, s 42.
[89] Dáil Deb, 13 July 2017, vol 958 no 2.

The Minister indicated that the review would examine a number of other issues, including:

- retrospective application of open adoption provisions, having regard to the legal basis of existing adoptions and the constitutional and legal rights of those involved;
- possible implications for intercountry adoption;
- the identification of circumstances where it may not be in the best interests of the child to be subject to an open adoption.[90]

Overview

The 2017 Act has introduced a number of changes to Ireland's adoption laws and gives effect to many important requirements created by Art 42A of the Constitution. All children are now eligible for voluntary adoption, regardless of the marital status of the birth parents, and the threshold for involuntary adoptions has been lowered. The 2017 Act has also introduced important provisions regarding the eligibility criteria for prospective adopters and in relation to step-parent adoption.

It remains to be seen whether and how the law will respond to the issue of accessing birth information. Arguably, the Adoption (Information and Tracing) Bill 2016 does not go far enough to protect the identity rights of adopted persons and so it is hoped that the requirement for adopted persons to give an undertaking not to contact the birth parent(s) in exchange for birth information will be re-considered by the legislature. The outcome of the Minister for Children's consultations on open adoption is also awaited. As such, it might be that further changes to Irish adoption law will be introduced in years to come.

---

[90] Dáil Deb, 13 July 2017, vol 958 no 2.

CHAPTER 6

PROTECTING CHILDREN FROM HARM

Introduction

Over the years, there have been many high-profile cases and public enquiries concerning the abuse and neglect of children in Ireland.[1] These scandals underline the need for a robust legal and policy framework for child protection that is comprised of legislative and administrative measures designed to protect children from abuse and neglect. Ireland must also remain cognisant of its international obligations in this area, in particular those arising under the United Nations Convention on the Rights of the Child (UNCRC). Article 19(1) of the UNCRC provides that

> "States Parties shall take all appropriate legislative, administrative, social and educational measures to protect the child from all forms of physical or mental violence, injury or abuse, neglect or negligent treatment, maltreatment or exploitation, including sexual abuse, while in the care of parent(s), legal guardian(s) or any other person who has the care of the child."[2]

This provision places a clear obligation on States to protect children from all forms of harm. This protection may take the form of legislation or it may require the State to embark on social and/or educational programmes to ensure that children are protected. The obligation to protect extends to all children, whether they are in the care of their parents or other individuals. Therefore, although the family (in particular the marital family) is typically an autonomous, private unit, and parents are generally trusted to uphold the best interests of their children, Art 19(1) makes it clear that the State must intervene in family life where this is necessary to protect children.

Ireland also has clear obligations in the area of child protection under the European Convention of Human Rights. The case of *O'Keeffe v Ireland*, for example, established that the State is under a duty to protect children in all circumstances and that it cannot circumvent this duty by delegating responsibility to a private entity.[3] In *O'Keeffe*, the applicant had suffered sexual abuse by the

---

[1] These cases include situations where children have been abused or neglected by their parents as well as where they have suffered abuse and/or neglect while in State care. See, for example: *Report of the Commission to Inquire into Child Abuse* (Ryan Report, 2009); *Report of the Kilkenny Incest Investigation* (McGuinness, 1993); *Kelly – A Child is Dead* (Joint Committee on the Family, 1996); *Roscommon Child Care Case* (Gibbons, 2010) among many others.

[2] United Nations Convention on the Rights of the Child (UNCRC), Art 19(1).

[3] *O'Keeffe v Ireland*, App no 35810/09 (ECtHR, 28 January 2014).

principal of her primary school in the 1970's. The Irish Supreme Court had found that the State was not liable for the applicant's suffering because the school was under the patronage of the Catholic Church. The European Court of Human Rights (ECtHR), however, found that the mechanisms of detection and reporting of child protection concerns that were in place at the time were inadequate and ineffective. The ECtHR found that Art 3 ECHR (prohibition of torture or inhuman or degrading treatment or punishment) gives rise to a positive obligation on the State "to ensure [the protection of children] from ill treatment, especially in a primary education context, through the adoption, as necessary, of special measures and safeguards."[4] Thus, the Irish State had failed to fulfil its positive obligation to protect the applicant from abuse and a violation of Art 3 ECHR was found.

The Irish Constitution also places obligations on the State to protect children and to intervene in family life where it is necessary to do so. Article 42A.2.1° of the Irish Constitution provides that:

> "In exceptional cases, where the parents, regardless of their marital status, fail in their duty towards their children to such extent that the safety or welfare of any of their children is likely to be prejudicially affected, the State as guardian of the common good shall, by proportionate means as provided by law, endeavour to supply the place of the parents, but always with due regard for the natural and imprescriptible rights of the child."[5]

The language used in Art 42A.2.1° makes it clear that the State *shall* intervene in the circumstances mentioned. It is an obligation and not a choice. Primarily, the State is enabled to supply the place of parents through the making of care orders whereby the child is removed from the family home and placed in State care. These orders are governed by the Child Care Acts 1991 to 2015 and are discussed in detail in this chapter.

Sadly, there are some failings in Ireland's child protection system which mean that vulnerable children do not always receive adequate alternative care in a timely manner. The main problems within the current system are addressed in this chapter, along with suggestions for reform where relevant. The chapter also addresses other areas of child protection law that apply to children inside and outside of the family home. Article 19 of the UNCRC demands that

---

[4]   *O'Keeffe v Ireland*, App no 35810/09 (ECtHR, 28 January 2014), para 146.
[5]   Bunreacht na hÉireann, Art 42A.2.1°.

children are protected from *all* forms of abuse and so this chapter considers Ireland's complete prohibition of corporal punishment, as well as legislation providing for mandatory reporting of child abuse and Garda vetting, as these enactments ensure that children are protected in all settings.

Taking Children into Care

Where a child is not receiving adequate care and protection, they may be removed from the care of their family and taken into the care of the State under the Child Care Acts 1991 to 2015 (the "Child Care Acts"). Since 2014, the Child and Family Agency (Tusla) has responsibility for providing care and protection to children in circumstances where their parents are not able to do so. Section 3 of the Child Care Act 1991, as amended by the Child and Family Agency Act 2013, sets out the functions of Tusla in the context of child protection: it is required to take steps to identify children who are not receiving adequate care and protection and to co-ordinate information from all relevant sources relating to children. In doing so, the welfare of the child must be the first and paramount consideration, the wishes of the children must be given due consideration, as far as practicable, and Tusla must have regard to the principle that "it is generally in the best interests of a child to be brought up in his own family."[6] As of September 2017, there were 6,230 children in care in Ireland.[7]

A number of options are available under the Child Care Acts to ensure that children are protected. These include:

- Emergency care;
- Care orders;
- Supervision orders;
- Voluntary care;
- Special care orders.

1. Emergency Care

(a) Removal from the Home

Under s 12 of the Child Care Act 1991, a member of An Garda Síochána may enter any building or vehicle without a warrant in order to remove a child to safety where there are reasonable

---

[6] Child Care Act 1991, s 3, amended by Child and Family Agency Act 2013, s 97 and Sch 2.

[7] Tusla, *National Performance and Activity Dashboard* (September 2017).

grounds for believing that there is an immediate and serious risk to
the health or welfare of a child, and where it would not be sufficient
to wait for Tusla to apply for an emergency care order under s 13
of the Act. This provision allows Gardaí to immediately remove
children from situations of harm or potential harm. After the child
has been removed from the home by An Garda Síochána, he or she
must be placed in the care of Tusla "as soon as possible" so that
Tusla can make an application for an emergency care order at the
next sitting of the District Court.[8] Usually, the child is placed in
emergency foster care prior to the court hearing. A protocol is in
place between an Garda Síochána and Tusla that details how they
co-operate and interact in dealing with child welfare and protection
concerns.[9]

In 2017, Dr Geoffrey Shannon, Special Rapporteur on Child
Protection, published the findings of an audit of the use of s 12
of the Child Care Act 1991 by An Garda Síochána (the "Audit").
Overall, the Audit commended the work of An Garda Síochána,
and it noted that s 12 was only invoked after careful consideration
of individual circumstances and was by no means used in an
"over-zealous manner."[10] The Audit did, however, highlight
some significant failings in Ireland's child protection system. For
example, the Audit found that there was a lack of formal training for
members of An Garda Síochána in child protection, with a reliance
instead on "on-the-job" learning. The Audit also highlighted
the lack of information-sharing and co-operation between the
different agencies involved in child protection. Members of An
Garda Síochána reported difficulties, and sometimes resistance,
when seeking follow-on services for children removed under s
12. As noted above, when a child is removed under s 12, they
are to be delivered into the care of Tusla "as soon as possible."
However, it was noted that children often had to remain in the
Garda station for long periods of time while attempts were made
to contact the appropriate supports.[11] Since most removals take
place in the evenings or at weekends, the Garda station or a
hospital is often the only place of safety available when the child is
initially removed. There was, however, an acknowledgement that
these are not appropriate locations to remove highly vulnerable

---

[8] Child Care Act 1991, s 12(3)–(4), amended by Child and Family Agency Act 2013, s 97 and Sch 2.
[9] *Joint Working Protocol for An Garda Síochána/Tusla – Child and Family Agency Liaison.*
[10] Geoffrey Shannon, *Audit of the exercise by An Garda Síochána of the provisions of Section 12 of the Child Care Act 1991* (2017), p xiii.
[11] The audit found that the average time children spend at the initial place of safety (usually a Garda station or hospital) is between one to six hours.

children to. Despite this, members of An Garda Síochána are not given any formal guidance on "how children should be treated when in an environment such as a Garda station to avoid greater traumatisation."[12] The Audit noted that there are some specialist child protection units currently in existence in parts of the country that operate effectively. However, these units are only available "in a handful of Garda stations throughout the State", and do not operate on a 24-hour basis.[13]

In some cases, children were subject to repeated removals under s 12 indicating "systemic failings with regard to the child protection systems in Ireland."[14] There was also a perception among some members of An Garda Síochána that, in some cases, Tusla social workers delayed addressing a particular risk to a child, so that the matter would fall outside of their working hours and become a matter for An Garda Síochána (who operate on a 24-hour basis).[15]

In response to these findings, the Audit made a number of recommendations, including that:

- The whole child protection system is in need of a cultural change and each individual must take responsibility for his or her own role in promoting the welfare of children;
- There is a need for greater interagency co-operation between An Garda Síochána and Tusla;
- Members of An Garda Síochána should receive comprehensive training on child protection as part of their initial training programme;
- Specialist child protection units within An Garda Síochána should be established on a national basis and consideration should be given to having social workers assigned to the specialist child protection units;
- A social work service that is directly accessible to at risk children or families outside of office hours should be developed as a matter of priority to ensure a comprehensive and unified child protection system.

The Minister for Children and Youth Affairs published

---

[12] Geoffrey Shannon, *Audit of the exercise by An Garda Síochána of the provisions of Section 12 of the Child Care Act 1991* (2017), p 247.

[13] Geoffrey Shannon, *Audit of the exercise by An Garda Síochána of the provisions of Section 12 of the Child Care Act 1991* (2017), p xviii.

[14] Geoffrey Shannon, *Audit of the exercise by An Garda Síochána of the provisions of Section 12 of the Child Care Act 1991* (2017), p 247.

[15] Geoffrey Shannon, *Audit of the exercise by An Garda Síochána of the provisions of Section 12 of the Child Care Act 1991* (2017), p 174.

an Implementation Plan for Tusla arising from these recommendations.[16] This Plan identified a number of actions to address the recommendations including that:

- The Strategic Liaison Committee, the forum for high level liaison between An Garda Síochána and the Child and Family Agency (Tusla), has been asked to implement the recommendation regarding cultural change in the child protection system;
- A revised protocol, reflecting the Children First Act 2015, has been compiled to enhance inter-agency co-operation.
- Specialist child protection units are in the process of being established by An Garda Síochána;
- The Department of Children and Youth Affairs has requested that Tusla examine, as a matter of priority, the level of demand for out-of-hours services and identify the most appropriate and child-friendly manner in which supports can be provided in the application of s 12.[17]

The Implementation Plan does not specify actions to address all of the audit's recommendations. The remaining recommendations in the report are noted for implementation by An Garda Síochána.

(b) Emergency Care Order

Children who are removed by An Garda Síochána under s 12 of the Child Care Act 1991 (the "1991 Act") must subsequently be delivered into the care of Tusla. Tusla must then either return the child to the care of the parents or apply to the District Court for an emergency care order under s 13 of the 1991 Act. The Court will grant the application providing for the short-term emergency care of the child where the judge is of the opinion that:

"(a)   there is an immediate and serious risk to the health or welfare of a child which necessitates his being placed in the care of the Child and Family Agency, or

(b)   there is likely to be such a risk if the child is removed from the place where he is for the time being."[18]

---

[16]   Department of Children and Youth Affairs, *Implementation Plan for Tusla Actions arising from Dr. Shannon's audit of the application of section 12 by An Garda Síochána* (June 2017).

[17]   Department of Children and Youth Affairs, *Implementation Plan for Tusla Actions arising from Dr. Shannon's audit of the application of section 12 by An Garda Síochána* (June 2017).

[18]   Child Care Act 1991, s 13(1), amended by Child and Family Agency Act 2013, s 97 and Sch 2.

If the emergency care order is granted, it lasts for a maximum period of eight days or for a shorter period as specified by the Court. As the emergency care order is a temporary measure, the threshold for granting the order is lower than that required for other care orders under the 1991 Act, discussed later. The application can also be made ex parte,[19] though Tusla are required under s 14 to inform the parent(s) in the event that the order is granted unless the parent(s) cannot be located. Where necessary, the court may direct that the child's location is not to be disclosed to the parents; impose conditions on any access between the child and the parents; and may give directions in respect of the medical or psychiatric examination, treatment or assessment of the child.[20]

Applications for emergency care orders are not always granted. This is because it is not always necessary to take the child into care to avoid an immediate and serious risk to his or her health or welfare. In some cases, the risk can be alleviated by removing an abusive or dangerous adult from the home through a barring or safety order, rather than removing the child. This approach was endorsed in *State (D and D) v Groarke*, where the Supreme Court noted that, if there is a suspicion of ill-treatment or abuse by one parent only, "there is a very definite and positive obligation on a court ... carefully to consider whether the welfare of the child clearly requires its removal from the custody of the innocent parent."[21]

2. Care Orders

Where Tusla is of the view that a child requires care or protection, there is a duty on it to apply for a care order or supervision order in respect of that child.[22] A care order is one where the child is removed from the care of the parents and transferred to the care of the State. The first step is usually to apply for an interim care order providing for the short-term, transitional care of the child, and this is typically followed by a care order.

(a) Interim Care Order

Section 17 of the 1991 Act provides for interim care orders.

---

[19] *Ex parte* applications are made without notice to the other side and are only allowed in exceptional circumstances.

[20] Child Care Act 1991, s 13(7)(a), amended by Child and Family Agency Act 2013, s 97 and Sch 2.

[21] *The State (D and D) v Groarke* [1990] 1 IR 305 at p 318.

[22] Child Care Act 1991, s 16, amended by Child and Family Agency Act 2013, s 97 and Sch 2.

Generally, the interim care order will protect the child from the time that an emergency care order ends until the making of the care order. The interim care order generally lasts for 29 days but may exceed this period where the parents consent to the longer period.[23]

The interim care order will be made where:

> "(a) an application for a care order in respect of the child has been or is about to be made (whether or not an emergency care order is in force), and
>
> (b) there is reasonable cause to believe that any of the circumstances mentioned at paragraph (a), (b) or (c) of section 18(1) exists or has existed with respect to the child and that it is necessary for the protection of the child's health or welfare that he be placed or maintained in the care of Child and Family Agency pending the determination of the application for the care order."[24]

The circumstances listed in s 18(1) are:

> "(a) the child has been or is being assaulted, ill-treated, neglected or sexually abused, or
>
> (b) the child's health, development or welfare has been or is being avoidably impaired or neglected, or
>
> (c) the child's health, development or welfare is likely to be avoidably impaired or neglected."[25]

The duration of the interim care order can be extended in circumstances where the parents consent to the extension and where the court is satisfied that the grounds for the making of an interim care order continue to exist with respect to the child.[26]

(c) Care Order

The full care order will be granted where the District Court is satisfied that any of the criteria listed in s 18(1) above are met and that the child requires care or protection which he or she is unlikely to receive unless the court makes the care order. The care

---

[23] Child Care Act 1991, s 17(2), amended by Child Care (Amendment) Act 2013, s 1.

[24] Child Care Act 1991, s 17(1), amended by Child and Family Agency Act 2013, s 97 and Sch 2.

[25] Child Care Act 1991, s 18(1), amended by Child and Family Agency Act 2013, s 97 and Sch 2.

[26] Child Care Act 1991, s 17(2)(b), amended by Child and Family Agency Act 2013, s 97 and Sch 2 and Child Care (Amendment) Act 2013, s 1.

order commits the child to the care of Tusla for so long as he or she remains a child or for such shorter period as the court may determine. If the care order is not granted by the court, it may grant a supervision order, discussed below, in the alternative.[27]

Where a care order is made, Tusla assumes the role of parent in respect of the child and is obliged to do what is reasonable in all the circumstances for the purpose of safeguarding or promoting the child's health, development or welfare. Tusla will decide on the type of care to be provided for the child; give consent to any necessary medical or psychiatric examination, treatment or assessment with respect to the child; and will have authority to give consent to the issue of a passport to the child.[28]

Once a child is in care, there are four types of living arrangements specified in s 36 of the 1991 Act:

(a) placement with a foster parent, or
(b) placement in residential care, or
(c) placement with a suitable person with a view to the child's adoption, or
(d) placement with a relative or such other arrangements as Tusla thinks proper in the circumstances.[29]

Tusla will determine the most appropriate placement for the child in light of his or her best interests. Every child is unique and so all of that child's circumstances must be taken into account in making this decision. Approximately 92 percent of children in care are cared for in foster placements, either by relative foster parents or by approved foster families.[30]

As noted above, when a child is taken into care, Tusla assumes parental responsibility for that child. Where a child is placed in foster care or placed with a relative and has been in the care of the same foster parent or relative for five years or more, that carer may apply to the court to obtain parental responsibility in respect

---

[27] Child Care Act 1991, s 18(5), amended by Child and Family Agency Act 2013, s 97 and Sch 2.
[28] Child Care Act 1991, s 18(3), amended by Child and Family Agency Act 2013, s 97 and Sch 2.
[29] Child Care Act 1991, s 36(1), amended by Child and Family Agency Act 2013, s 97 and Sch 2.
[30] Department of Children and Youth Affairs, *Foster Care* <https://www.dcya.gov.ie/viewdoc.asp?fn=/documents/Children_In_Care/FosterCare.htm>

of the child.[31] If granted, the order will authorise the foster parent or relative to:

> (a) have, on behalf of Tusla, control over the child as if the foster parent or relative were the child's parent, and
>
> (b) do what is reasonable to safeguard and promote the child's health, development or welfare by giving consent to any necessary medical or psychiatric examination, treatment or assessment with respect to the child and to the issue of a passport to the child.[32]

Where this order is granted, the court can impose any conditions or restrictions as to the extent of the authority of the foster parent or relative.[33] This is an important provision as it gives the adult caring for the child the full range of legal powers necessary to exercise that role without having to continuously seek the consent of Tusla.

Tusla will only assume parental responsibility for a child where a *full* care order is made; an interim care order does not transfer parental responsibility to Tusla. This can be seen in the case of *CFA v M & J*,[34] where parents refused to give their consent to their children (who were subject to interim care orders) travelling for a holiday with their foster carers. In the absence of such consent, the foster carers applied to the District Court under s 47 of the Child Care Act 1991 for a direction permitting the children to travel outside of the jurisdiction for the purpose of the holiday. The judge granted the order dispensing with the parents' consent for the children to go on the holiday on the basis that there was nothing to suggest that the proposed holiday would not be in the interests of the children. However, in doing so, the judge noted that

> "Interim care orders do not have the effect of vesting parental responsibility in the CFA [Child and Family Agency] or its agents. The rights of parents must be respected by the CFA at all times in the context of whatever type of order (or none) which requires that their children be in the care of the CFA."[35]

---

[31] Child Care Act 1991, s 43A, inserted by Child Care (Amendment) Act 2007, s 4.

[32] Child Care Act 1991, s 43A(5), inserted by Child Care (Amendment) Act 2007, s 4.

[33] Child Care Act 1991, s 43A(6), inserted by Child Care (Amendment) Act 2007, s 4.

[34] *CFA v M&J* [2015] IEDC 03.

[35] *CFA v M&J* [2015] IEDC 03.

3. Supervision Order

A supervision order allows Tusla to periodically visit the child at home to ensure that his or her welfare is maintained and to advise the parent(s) regarding the care of the child. This order does not remove the child from the home; it is used in situations where there are concerns about a child's welfare but those concerns do not require that the child is removed and taken into care.

Supervision orders are provided for under s 19 of the 1991 Act. Under this section, the court may grant a supervision order where there are reasonable grounds for believing that:

> "(a) the child has been or is being assaulted, ill-treated, neglected or sexually abused, or
> (b) the child's health, development or welfare has been or is being avoidably impaired or neglected, or
> (c) the child's health, development or welfare is likely to be avoidably impaired or neglected,
> and it is desirable that the child be visited periodically by or on behalf of the Child and Family Agency."[36]

The supervision order ensures ongoing supervision and involvement by Tusla in the child's life but it does not require that he or she is removed from the home. As it is a less interventionist order, the threshold for the application is lower than that required for a care order. Section 19 requires that there must be "reasonable grounds for believing" that the child has suffered harm, whereas under s 18 (care order), the court must be "satisfied that" harm has occurred. The supervision order will last for up to 12 months and may be extended on the application of Tusla to the court, taking into account the best interests of the child.[37] The supervision order may also contain directions as to the care of the child, for example requiring the child to attend for medical or psychiatric examination, treatment or assessment.[38] However, there are limits on the nature of the directions that can be imposed. For example, in *JG v Judge Kevin Staunton*,[39] the District Court granted a supervision order containing a direction that the parents attend for parenting assessments and psychometric testing and receive counselling and

---

[36] Child Care Act 1991, s 19(1), amended by Child and Family Agency Act 2013, s 97 and Sch 2.
[37] Child Care Act 1991, ss 19(6)–19(7), amended by Child and Family Agency Act 2013, s 97 and Sch 2.
[38] Child Care Act 1991, s 19(4), amended by Child and Family Agency Act 2013, s 97 and Sch 2.
[39] *JG v Judge Kevin Staunton* [2014] 1 IR 390.

psychotherapy. The High Court found that there was no legislative basis for imposing such obligations on the parents and therefore the directions were invalid.

4. Voluntary Care

It is also open to the parents of a child to voluntarily place him or her in the care of the State without the need for a court order. Under s 4 of the 1991 Act, there is a duty on Tusla to take a child into care where that child requires care or protection that he or she is unlikely to receive unless taken into care. The consent of the parents is required and the parents are entitled to withdraw this consent and resume care of the child at any point. Where a child is placed in voluntary care, the parents continue to exercise parental responsibility and so Tusla must consider the parents' wishes as to how the care is provided. A child may also be taken into care under s 4 where he or she is lost, the parent who has custody is missing or it appears that the child has been deserted or abandoned. In these circumstances, Tusla must endeavour to reunite the child with the parent(s) so long as this is in the child's best interests.[40]

5. Special Care Orders

Special care is available where a child requires special care and attention due to his or her own behaviour. Essentially, it is a short-term, therapeutic intervention for vulnerable 11 to 17-year olds with complex psychological and sociological profiles. It is used where other forms of care would not adequately address the child's behaviour and risk of harm. Special care addresses the child's behaviour and risk of harm to him/herself; the child's care requirements including medical and psychiatric assessment, examination and treatment; and the child's educational supervision. Special care is provided in a special care unit.[41]

Special care orders are provided for under Pt IVA of the Child Care Act 1991, as inserted by the Child Care (Amendment) Act 2011. Tusla may apply for a special care order in circumstances where:

(a)   it is satisfied that there is reasonable cause to believe that the behaviour of the child poses a real and substantial risk of harm to his or her life, health, safety, development or welfare;

---

[40]   Child Care Act 1991, s 4(4).
[41]   Child Care Act 1991, s 23C, inserted by Child Care (Amendment) Act 2011, s 10.

(b) it is satisfied that there is reasonable cause to believe that other forms of care and mental health services would not adequately address that behaviour and risk of harm and the child's care requirements; and

(c) it is satisfied that special care is required to address that behaviour and risk of harm and the child's care requirements.[42]

Before Tusla can apply for the special care order, it must arrange for the convening of a family welfare conference, unless it is not in the best interests of the child do so.[43] The functions of a family welfare conference are to:

(a) consider whether a child in respect of whom the conference is being convened requires special care;

(b) if it is considered that the child requires special care, recommend that Tusla applies for a special care order;

(c) make any other recommendations as are appropriate in respect of the care and protection of the child, such as recommending that Tusla should apply for a care order, a supervision order, a special care order or other care under the Act of 1991 in respect of the child; and

(d) if it is considered that the child does not require special care, make such recommendations to Tusla in relation to the care or protection of the child as the conference considers necessary, including, where appropriate, care, other than special care, under the Act of 1991.[44]

The family welfare conference may be attended by the child concerned, the parents/guardians of the child, any guardian ad litem appointed for the child, officers of Tusla, other relatives as determined by the co-ordinator of the conference and any other persons that the co-ordinator, after consultation with the child and his or her parents or guardian, believes would make a positive contribution to the conference.[45] The family welfare conference allows the child to be included in the discussions on his or her welfare and allows the child and his or her family to have a voice in the decision-making process.[46]

---

[42] Child Care Act 1991, s 23F(2), inserted by Child Care (Amendment) Act 2011, s 10.
[43] Child Care Act 1991, s 23F(5), inserted by Child Care (Amendment) Act 2011, s 10.
[44] Children Act 2001, s 8, amended by Child Care (Amendment) Act 2011, s 29.
[45] Children Act 2001, s 9.
[46] The Children (Family Welfare Conference) Regulations 2004 (SI No 549 of 2004) further regulate the operation of a family welfare conference.

The special care order places the child in the care of Tusla to be detained in a special care unit for his or her appropriate care, education and treatment. In 2015, there were 18 special care beds in Ireland.[47] Where the child is placed in special care, he or she will be provided with individualised supports and therapeutic interventions. These supports may include counselling for substance abuse, psychological supports, social work and social care supports, speech and language therapy, and educational services. All interventions are designed to address the individual needs of the young person in special care and to promote his or her welfare.

Care Plan and Review of Care

Where a child is placed in care, a written document known as a care plan is drawn up containing all details of the child's placement such as where they are to live, access arrangements with family and where and how they will be educated. The care plan will initially be reviewed as part of a child in care review meeting after the child has been in care for two months and is subsequently reviewed every six months for the first two years. If the child is in care for more than two years, the care plan is reviewed once a year.[48] The child in care review meeting is conducted by Tusla.

Section 47 of the Child Care Act 1991 allows the District Court, of its own motion or on the application of any person, to give such directions and make such order on any question affecting the welfare of the child as it thinks proper, and it may vary or discharge any such direction or order.[49] This provision gives the District Court a supervisory function in respect of children in the care of Tusla. This role was confirmed by the High Court in *Eastern Health Board v Judge JP McDonnell*,[50] which held that s 47 gave the District Court full authority to give directions to the HSE (now Tusla) in all matters pertaining to the welfare of the child who is in care. In the case in question, the District Court was found to have authority to direct that a care plan be prepared and reviewed by a child psychiatrist.

---

[47] Tusla, *Annual Review on the Adequacy of Child Care and Family Support Services Available 2015* (Child and Family Agency 2015), p 61

[48] Child Care Act 1991, s 42; Child Care (Placement of Children in Residential Care) Regulations 1995 (SI No 259 of 1995); Child Care (Placement of Children in Foster Care) Regulations 1995 (SI No 260 of 1995); Child Care (Placement of Children with Relatives) Regulations 1995 (SI No 261 of 1995).

[49] Child Care Act 1991, s 47, amended by Child and Family Agency Act 2013, s 97 and Sch 2.

[50] *Eastern Health Board v McDonnell* [1999] 1 IR 174.

Aftercare

Aftercare refers to the support provided to a young person who has aged out of the care system that allows them to transition into adulthood. It is usually provided to adults between the ages of 18 years and 21 years, though the upper age limit may be extended to 23 years where the person is engaged in a course of education. Childhood ends at 18 and so children effectively "age out" of the care system at this point. While some young people in foster care may remain living with their foster family after the age of 18 years, others will not and will move to an aftercare residential placement or on to independent living. For many, the transition from care to independent living can be difficult. Research shows that people who exit care are more at risk of entering homelessness than persons not in care, they may have gaps in their education and are likely to become reliant on social welfare for their main source of income.[51] It is therefore vitally important that appropriate aftercare support is available to them.

The Child Care Act 1991, in its original form, made provision for a limited form of aftercare support but there was no obligation on the State to provide such support.[52] The Child Care (Amendment) Act 2015 now provides a comprehensive legislative basis for the provision of aftercare services. This Act amends the 1991 Act to provide that Tusla "shall" prepare an aftercare plan for an eligible child or an eligible adult setting out the assistance that may be provided by Tusla after he or she attains the age of 18 years.[53] An "eligible child" is a child aged 16 years or over who:

"(a) is in the care of the Child and Family Agency and has been in the care of the Agency for a period of not less than 12 months since attaining the age of 13 years, or

(b) was in the care of the Child and Family Agency for a period of not less than 12 months since attaining the age of 13 years but is no longer in the care of the Agency."[54]

An "eligible adult" is defined as:

"a person aged 18, 19 or 20 years who was in the care of the

51 EPIC, *'MY VOICE HAS TO BE HEARD': Research on outcomes for young people leaving care in North Dublin* (EPIC, 2012).
52 s 45 of the Child Care Act 1991 originally provided that a health board "may" provide support where a child left its care.
53 Child Care Act 1991, s 45, substituted by Child Care (Amendment) Act 2015, s 5.
54 Child Care Act 1991, s 2, inserted by Child Care (Amendment) Act 2015, s 2.

Child and Family Agency for a period of not less than 12 months in the 5 year period immediately prior to the person attaining the age of 18 years."[55]

Before the aftercare plan is prepared, the eligible child or adult will be assessed in terms of his or her needs (if any) in respect of:

"(a) education,
(b) financing and budgeting matters,
(c) training and employment,
(d) health and well-being,
(e) personal and social development,
(f) accommodation, and
(g) family support."[56]

Where an eligible child is in the care of Tusla, it must prepare an aftercare plan at least six months before he or she attains the age of 18 years, or within three months of that child having become an eligible child, whichever is the later.[57] An eligible adult may request that Tusla prepares an aftercare plan for them and it shall do so within three months of receiving such a request.[58]

In addition to the support provided in the aftercare plan, Tusla provides a Standardised National Aftercare Allowance currently set at €300 per week for young people who have been in care for 12 months on their 16th birthday or for 12 consecutive months prior to their 18th birthday. The Aftercare Allowance continues to be paid up to the age of 21 years (with the possibility of a further two years of support) provided that the young adult is engaging in education or training.[59]

Child Care Law Reporting Project

Traditionally, there was a lack of transparency in respect of child care proceedings in Ireland due to the strict operation of the *in camera* rule in child care cases. The dearth of information on such proceedings is now addressed by the Child Care Law Reporting

---

[55] Child Care Act 1991, s 2, as inserted by Child Care (Amendment) Act 2015, s 2.
[56] Child Care Act 1991, s 45A(3), inserted by Child Care (Amendment) Act 2015, s 6.
[57] Child Care Act 1991, s 45B(5), inserted by Child Care (Amendment) Act 2015, s 7.
[58] Child Care Act 1991, s 45C(1), inserted by Child Care (Amendment) Act 2015, s 8.
[59] See: Tusla, *Guidance Document for the Implementation of Aftercare Allowance.*

Project (CCLRP). This project was established in 2013 in accordance with s 3 of the Child Care (Amendment) Act 2007 (the "2007 Act"). Section 3 of the 2007 Act amended s 29 of the Child Care Act 1991 to allow for the publication of reports and decisions of child care proceedings.[60]

CCLRP produces reports on child care proceedings in the Irish courts in a manner that maintains the anonymity of the children and families involved. The aims of the project are, *inter alia*, to provide information to the public on child care proceedings in the courts and to make recommendations to address any shortcomings in the child care system identified by the research. Case reports are published on the project website (www.childlawproject.ie). The reports contain information on child care proceedings, the nature of cases that come before the courts and the reasons why care orders are granted or refused in particular cases. The project does not report on all child care proceedings that come before the Irish courts as there are simply too many cases to feasibly do so. Instead, the reporters attend and report on a representative sample of cases.

The Case Histories and Reports published by the Child Care Law Reporting Project often highlight shortcomings in Ireland's care system. In 2017, two Reports were issued. Among other matters, these Reports contained details of cases where there were significant delays for children in accessing supports, where they were subject to lengthy legal proceedings, and where there was a lack of co-ordination between service providers, which meant that child victims of sexual abuse were interviewed multiple times by different professionals.[61] In one case, notwithstanding the commencement of the Child Care (Amendment) Act 2015 in September 2017 (discussed above), no aftercare plan had been formulated for a young woman with mental health needs who would turn 18 within two months. In many of the cases reported, children were placed in special care units abroad as there was no suitable placement for them within the State.[62]

---

[60] Child Care Act 1991, s 29, amended by Child Care (Amendment) Act 2007, s 3.

[61] This practice would seem to run contrary to the advice of the Committee on the Rights of the Child which has stated that "a child should not be interviewed more often than necessary, in particular when harmful events are explored. The 'hearing' of a child is a difficult process that can have a traumatic impact on the child." Committee on the Rights of the Child, *General Comment No. 12 (2009) The right of the child to be heard (1 July 2009)* CRC/C/GC/12, para 24.

[62] Child Care Law Reporting Project, *Case Histories 2017 Volume 2* <https://www.childlawproject.ie/publications/>.

Problems similar to those identified in the 2017 Case Summaries have been noted in other research. As was discussed above, related issues were identified by Dr Geoffrey Shannon in his audit of s 12 of the Child Care Act 1991, and, as is discussed below, similar failings have been repeatedly identified by expert groups over the years. It is clear that greater efforts are required to fully protect children in need of care and to adequately address their needs.

Shortcomings in the Care System

Children in care are among the most vulnerable members of society. It is vital, therefore, that the care that is provided to them is monitored to ensure that it operates in their best interests. Pursuant to s 69 of the Child Care Act 1991, the Minister for Health may cause to be inspected any service maintained by Tusla and to examine the treatment of children therein. Foster care services[63] are monitored by the Health Information and Quality Authority (HIQA) against the National Standards for Foster Care 2003. HIQA's reports do not always paint a positive picture of the care system. For example, the 2017 inspection report on the foster care services operated by Tusla in the Mid-West Service Area revealed a number of inadequacies in the provision of foster care services in that region.[64] Many areas (including child protection), were found to be majorly non-compliant with the National Standards. Among the findings were that:

- Foster care assessments were often delayed;
- There was no record of Garda vetting for a number of foster carers and a substantial number of household members aged 16 years and over did not have Garda vetting;
- In many cases, there was no social worker allocated to the foster carers or the children;
- Child protection concerns and allegations of abuse and neglect were not managed in line with *Children First*.[65]

There were similar findings in other geographical regions.[66] Indeed,

---

[63] Foster care is defined in s 36(2) of the Child Care Act 1991 as the situation where a person other than a relative of a child takes care of the child on behalf of Tusla.

[64] The Mid-West Service Area comprises the counties of Clare, Limerick, North Tipperary and the city of Limerick. See: HIQA, *Statutory foster care service inspection report. Mid-West Region* (13 March–16 March 2017).

[65] HIQA, *Statutory foster care service inspection report. Mid-West Region* (13 March–16 March 2017).

[66] For example, similar problems were identified in Cavan, Monaghan and

in Dublin South Central, HIQA found that of the 26 standards assessed, only one standard had been met.[67] This represents significant non-compliance with the national standards.[68]

Unfortunately, this is not the first time that inadequacies have been found in Ireland's care system. In 2010, the Independent Child Death Review Group highlighted a number of failings in the child protection system and made several recommendations for reform.[69] This review examined the deaths of 196 children during the period of 1 January 2000 to 30 April 2010 who were in the care of the State (36 deaths), in receipt of aftercare (32 deaths) or known to the child protection services at the time of their death (128 deaths). The review found that there were inconsistencies in the procedures adopted throughout the care system. For example, of the 36 young people who had died in care, 15 had not had a care plan and appropriate procedures were not always followed (such as medical examination) when a child was initially taken into care. The review also found that aftercare was not always provided to young people who left care. Where aftercare was provided, there was poor record-keeping about the services provided. The review also identified failings in respect of children who were known to child protection services. For example, files were closed in a number of cases where parents had drug or alcohol problems and were not adequately followed up. Often, no social worker was assigned to such families. The review also found that children experienced delays in accessing services and there was found to be a lack of professional supervision or supports for social workers.

Ireland's child protection system is also kept under review by the Special Rapporteur on Child Protection, Dr Geoffrey Shannon, who submits an annual report to the Oireachtas examining developments and trends in child protection nationally and internationally. This annual report also makes recommendations for the reform of existing laws, where appropriate. As was outlined above, Dr Shannon published the findings of an audit of the use of s 12 of the Child Care Act 1991 by An Garda Síochána in 2017.

Dublin North City in 2017. Mark Hilliard, "'Significant non-compliance' in safeguarding children in care" *Irish Times* (Dublin, 5 April 2018).
[67] HIQA, *Statutory foster care service inspection report. Dublin Mid-Leinster–Dublin South Central* (29 November–1 December 2016).
[68] Many other cases demonstrating systemic failings in the foster care system can be found in media reports. See, for example, Paul Cullen, "Tragic story of Grace: the HSE does not do accountability" *Irish Times* (Dublin, 1 March 2017); Marie O'Halloran and Elaine Edwards, "Woman raped as foster child urges commission of investigation" *Irish Times* (Dublin, 25 April 2018).
[69] Geoffrey Shannon and Norah Gibbons, *Report of the Independent Child Death Review Group* (Department of Children and Youth Affairs, 2012).

This Audit outlined a number of areas of concern including a lack of formal child protection training within An Garda Síochána, failings in inter-agency co-operation, and insufficient access to out-of-hours services.[70] Subsequent to the publication of the audit, as discussed above, the Minister for Children and Youth Affairs published an Implementation Plan for Tusla Actions arising from the recommendations.[71] The Minister also subsequently announced her intention to open specialist child support centres where children would be able disclose abuse to teams of Gardaí, social workers, health professionals and lawyers working together.[72] Currently, the lack of inter-agency co-operation means that different agencies deal with children independently. This new system, if put in place, would allow for multidisciplinary teams to provide support to children in the same place.

The current lack of co-ordination between child protection agencies is a recurring feature in reports on the child protection system. This issue was highlighted again in "Molly's case", an investigation conducted by the Ombudsman for Children's Office (OCO) into the supports provided by Tusla and the HSE for a child with a disability in the care of the State.[73] "Molly" (not her real name) is a teenager with Down Syndrome and severe autism, who has spent her life in foster care. Molly is completely dependent on her foster carers in all areas of her care, including feeding, toileting, bathing, and dressing. Molly's foster carer made a complaint to the OCO about the level of supports and services being provided to Molly by Tusla and the HSE. In the course of the investigation, the OCO found that there was a lack of co-ordination between the two agencies which meant that services and supports provided by both organisations were insufficient. The report emphasised that the findings were not confined to Molly's case; it found that, as a general matter, insufficient supports are available to children with a diagnosed disability in the care of the State. In this regard, one of the recommendations made by the OCO was for Tusla and the HSE to review the supports and services being offered to the approximately 471 children with a moderate or severe disability in foster care in

---

[70] Geoffrey Shannon, *Audit of the exercise by An Garda Síochána of the provisions of Section 12 of the Child Care Act 1991* (2017).

[71] Department of Children and Youth Affairs, *Implementation Plan for Tusla Actions arising from Dr. Shannon's audit of the application of section 12 by An Garda Síochána* (June 2017).

[72] Harry McGee, "Zappone to open specialist child support centres" *Irish Times* (Dublin, 28 December 2017).

[73] Ombudsman for Children's Office, *Molly's* case: How Tusla and the HSE provided and coordinated supports for a child with a disability in the care of the State (OCO, 2018).

the State within 12 months. The OCO also recommended that the provision and co-ordination of supports and services to children with a diagnosed moderate to severe disability in foster care should be addressed by the State through legislative, regulatory, policy and/or budgetary means.

Children First

Children First: National Guidance for the Protection and Welfare of Children ("*Children First*") was first published in 1999 and was revised most recently in 2017.[74] This guidance is designed to assist people to recognise where a child is being abused or neglected, and to report reasonable concerns about abuse or neglect to Tusla. The guidance operates alongside the Children First Act 2015, which imposes specific statutory obligations on individuals and organisations working with children and young people to report child protection concerns. The most recent revision of the guidance incorporates details of these statutory obligations. The guidance sets out non-statutory best practice which operates alongside the statutory obligations in the 2015 Act.

Chapter two of the *Children First* guidance describes the four main types of abuse that may be experienced by children and how such abuse may be recognised. The four categories are: neglect, emotional abuse, physical abuse and sexual abuse. Child neglect is described as the most frequently reported category of abuse, and is extremely harmful to the development and well-being of children. Section 2 of the Children First Act 2015 defines neglect as "in relation to a child, to deprive the child of adequate food, warmth, clothing, hygiene, supervision, safety or medical care."[75] This definition is expanded upon in the *Children First* guidance, which explains that neglect occurs when:

> "a child does not receive adequate care or supervision to the extent that the child is harmed physically or developmentally. It is generally defined in terms of an omission of care, where a child's health, development or welfare is impaired by being deprived of food, clothing, warmth, hygiene, medical care, intellectual stimulation or supervision and safety."[76]

---

[74] Department of Children and Youth Affairs, *Children First: National Guidance for the Protection and Welfare of Children* (2017).

[75] Children First Act 2015, s 2.

[76] Department of Children and Youth Affairs, *Children First: National Guidance for the Protection and Welfare of Children* (2017), pp 7–8.

Examples of neglect include situations where:

- Children are left alone without adequate care and supervision;
- Malnourishment, lacking food, unsuitable food or erratic feeding;
- Lack of adequate clothing;
- Inattention to basic hygiene;
- Persistent failure to attend school;
- Abandonment or desertion.[77]

Emotional abuse is defined as "the systematic emotional or psychological ill-treatment of a child as part of the overall relationship between a caregiver and a child."[78] Occasional difficulties between the adult and child are not categorised as emotional abuse. Instead, the abuse occurs "when a child's basic need for attention, affection, approval, consistency and security are not met, due to incapacity or indifference from their parent or caregiver."[79]

Examples of emotional abuse include situations where there is:

- Rejection;
- Lack of comfort and love;
- Lack of attachment;
- Continuous lack of praise and encouragement;
- Persistent criticism, sarcasm, hostility or blaming of the child;
- Bullying;
- Extreme overprotectiveness;
- Inappropriate non-physical punishment (e.g. locking child in bedroom);
- Ongoing family conflicts and family violence.[80]

The guidance notes that there might not be any physical signs of emotional abuse unless it occurs alongside another form of abuse. Emotional abuse can be identified through the child's actions or emotions such as insecure attachment, unhappiness, low self-

---

[77] Department of Children and Youth Affairs, *Children First: National Guidance for the Protection and Welfare of Children* (2017), p 8.

[78] Department of Children and Youth Affairs, *Children First: National Guidance for the Protection and Welfare of Children* (2017), p 8.

[79] Department of Children and Youth Affairs, *Children First: National Guidance for the Protection and Welfare of Children* (2017), p 8.

[80] Department of Children and Youth Affairs, *Children First: National Guidance for the Protection and Welfare of Children* (2017), p 9.

esteem, educational and developmental underachievement, risk-taking and aggressive behaviour.

Physical abuse is defined as:

"when someone deliberately hurts a child physically or puts them at risk of being physically hurt. It may occur as a single incident or as a pattern of incidents. A reasonable concern exists where the child's health and/or development is, may be, or has been damaged as a result of suspected physical abuse."[81]

Physical abuse can include:

- Physical punishment;
- Beating, slapping, hitting or kicking;
- Use of excessive force in handling;
- Suffocation;
- Female genital mutilation.[82]

Sexual abuse is defined as occurring:

"when a child is used by another person for his or her gratification or arousal, or for that of others. It includes the child being involved in sexual acts (masturbation, fondling, oral or penetrative sex) or exposing the child to sexual activity directly or through pornography."[83]

This definition accompanies a statutory definition of sexual abuse in s 2 of the 2015 Act, as amended by s 55 of the Criminal Law (Sexual Offences) Act 2017.

Examples of child sexual abuse include:

- Any sexual act intentionally performed in the presence of a child;
- An invitation to sexual touching or intentional touching or molesting of a child's body;
- Masturbation in the presence of a child or the involvement of a child in an act of masturbation;

[81] Department of Children and Youth Affairs, *Children First: National Guidance for the Protection and Welfare of Children* (2017), p 9.
[82] Department of Children and Youth Affairs, *Children First: National Guidance for the Protection and Welfare of Children* (2017), p 9.
[83] Department of Children and Youth Affairs, *Children First: National Guidance for the Protection and Welfare of Children* (2017), p 10.

- Sexual intercourse with a child, whether oral, vaginal or anal;
- Exposing a child to inappropriate or abusive material through information and communication technology;
- Consensual sexual activity involving an adult and an underage person.[84]

Any person with reasonable grounds for concern that a child may have been, is being, or is at risk of being abused or neglected under any of the headings above is required to report this concern to Tusla following the procedures set out in the guidance. Pursuant to the Children First Act 2015, "mandated persons" have a statutory obligation to report these concerns to Tusla. The list of mandated persons is set out in Sch 2 of the 2015 Act and includes professionals working with children in the education, health, justice, youth and childcare sectors. Under s 14(1) of the 2015 Act, where a mandated person knows, believes or has reasonable grounds to suspect, on the basis of information that he or she has received, acquired or becomes aware of in the course of his or her employment or profession as such a mandated person, that a child has been harmed, is being harmed, or is at risk of being harmed, he or she is required to report that information to Tusla as soon as practicable.[85] Section 14(2) of the 2015 Act also places obligations on mandated persons to report any disclosures of harm made by a child to them.[86] "Harm" is defined in s 2 of the Act as "(a) assault, ill-treatment or neglect of the child in a manner that seriously affects or is likely to seriously affect the child's health, development or welfare, or (b) sexual abuse of the child."[87] The threshold of harm for each category of abuse at which mandated persons have a legal obligation to report concerns is as follows:

Neglect: the person knows, believes or has reasonable grounds to suspect that a child's needs have been, are, or are at risk of being neglected to the point where the child's health, development or welfare have been or are being seriously affected, or are likely to be seriously affected.

Emotional abuse: the person knows, believes or has reasonable grounds to suspect that a child has been, is being, or is at risk of being ill-treated to the point where the child's health, development

---

[84] Department of Children and Youth Affairs, *Children First: National Guidance for the Protection and Welfare of Children* (2017), p 10.
[85] Children First Act 2015, s 14(1).
[86] Children First Act 2015, s 14(2).
[87] Children First Act 2015, s 2.

or welfare have been or are being seriously affected, or are likely to be seriously affected.

Physical abuse: the person knows, believes or has reasonable grounds to suspect that a child has been, is being, or is at risk of being assaulted and that as a result the child's health, development or welfare have been or are being seriously affected, or are likely to be seriously affected.

Sexual abuse: the person knows, believes or has reasonable grounds to suspect that a child has been, is being, or is at risk of being sexually abused. All sexual abuse is deemed to seriously affect a child's health, welfare or development, and so all concerns about sexual abuse must be reported to Tusla.[88]

Should a mandated person fail to report a concern to Tusla, they may be subject disciplinary proceedings or to criminal prosecution under the Criminal Justice (Withholding of Information on Offences against Children and Vulnerable Persons) Act 2012. Under the 2012 Act, it is a criminal offence to withhold information about a serious offence, including a sexual offence, against a person under 18 years or a vulnerable person.

The Children First Act 2015 also imposes obligations on relevant organisations to keep children safe from harm. They are required to carry out a risk assessment to identify whether a child or young person could be harmed while receiving services, and to develop a Child Safeguarding Statement that outlines the policies and procedures that are in place to manage the risks that have been identified.[89] The services that are subject to this obligation are set out in Sch 1 of the 2015 Act. All provisions of the Children First Act 2015 were commenced as of 11 December 2017. All relevant services were required to have Child Safeguarding Statements in place within three months of that commencement date.

Garda Vetting

The *Children First* guidance also makes reference to Garda vetting. Garda vetting is the process whereby An Garda Síochána provide information on an individual to a prospective employer following a request to do so. This information will include any previous convictions acquired by the person. The National Vetting Bureau

---

[88] *Children First: National Guidance for the Protection and Welfare of Children* (2017), pp 20–22.
[89] Children First Act 2015, s 11.

(Children and Vulnerable Persons) Act 2012 places the vetting process on a statutory footing and makes it a statutory requirement for all relevant organisations conducting "relevant work" with children and vulnerable persons to vet employees and volunteers prior to their commencing work. The 2012 Act was commenced on 29 April 2016.

Under s 12 of the 2012 Act, "relevant organisations" are prohibited from employing or otherwise engaging any person in "relevant work or activities" or arranging for the placement of an individual to do such work or activities, unless the organisation first receives a vetting disclosure from the National Vetting Bureau in respect of that person.[90] Breach of this prohibition is a criminal offence punishable summarily or on conviction on indictment to a fine not exceeding €10,000 or imprisonment for a term not exceeding five years or both.[91]

The vetting requirements apply to both new and existing employees. New employees must be vetted before commencing employment/volunteering activities while any existing employees who were employed by the organisation prior to the commencement of the legislation were required to undertake retrospective vetting before 31 December 2017.[92] Employees and volunteers are also subject to "re-vetting" after a specified period where they engage in work or activities covered by the 2012 Act.[93]

The term "relevant organisation" is defined in s 2 of the 2012 Act to mean a person (including a body corporate or an unincorporated body of persons) that employs, enters into a contract of services with, or permits any person to undertake relevant work or activities, or is a provider of courses of education or training, including internship schemes, for persons and, as part of such education or training or scheme, places or makes arrangements for the placement of any person in work experience or activities where a necessary part of the placement involves participation in relevant work or activities. Relevant work or activities are those that relate to children or to vulnerable persons. These are defined separately in Pts 1 and 2 of Sch 1, although the definitions are broadly the same for both categories.

There are some exceptions to the vetting requirements. The 2012

---

[90] National Vetting Bureau (Children and Vulnerable Persons) Act 2012, s 12.
[91] National Vetting Bureau (Children and Vulnerable Persons) Act 2012, s 27.
[92] National Vetting Bureau (Children and Vulnerable Persons) Act 2012, s 21.
[93] National Vetting Bureau (Children and Vulnerable Persons) Act 2012, s 20.

Act does not apply to any relevant work or activity undertaken in the course of a family relationship or personal relationship or where persons assist with activities or events occasionally and on a voluntary basis.[94] This recognises the occasional but necessary involvement or assistance of parents or other persons in school, sporting or community activities. However, the 2012 Act will apply where the occasional voluntary involvement includes coaching, mentoring, counselling, teaching or training of the children or vulnerable persons.[95] Therefore, a volunteer will have to be vetted before engaging in the coaching, mentoring, counselling, teaching or training of the children or vulnerable persons even where this is a once-off event.

Whether or not a certain activity is one that is covered by the 2012 Act will be for the relevant organisation to decide. A defence will apply to a relevant organisation which did not know or could not reasonably have expected to know that the work or activity in question constituted relevant work or activities.[96]

Vetting is undertaken by each relevant organisation. This means that an individual may be required to undergo vetting multiple times where they take up different roles. For example, if the person requires vetting for employment purposes but they also take on a volunteering role with a vetting requirement, they must be vetted twice. Although e-vetting[97] has reduced the processing time involved, the requirement for multiple vetting may be regarded as creating a strain on resources and could create an administrative backlog in the relevant organisation. To alleviate this, the Children's Rights Alliance has recommended that a "passport-style system for Garda vetting should be introduced so that it becomes person rather than service-focused."[98]

The 2012 Act is part of a suite of legislation that is designed to strengthen the protection of children and vulnerable persons in Ireland. The other relevant legislation is the Criminal Justice (Spent Convictions and Certain Disclosures) Act 2016 and the Criminal

---

[94] National Vetting Bureau (Children and Vulnerable Persons) Act 2012, s 3.
[95] National Vetting Bureau (Children and Vulnerable Persons) Act 2012, s 3(c).
[96] National Vetting Bureau (Children and Vulnerable Persons) Act 2012, s 8.
[97] E-vetting facilities were launched in 2016 to reduce processing times for vetting applications. Most online applications are now processed within five working days. Children's Rights Alliance, *Report Card 2018* (Children's Rights Alliance, 2018), p 80.
[98] Children's Rights Alliance, *Report Card 2018* (Children's Rights Alliance, 2018), p 80.

Justice (Withholding of Information on Offences against Children and Vulnerable Persons) Act 2012, discussed above.

Corporal Punishment

Children experience violence and abuse in many forms and in many settings. The home should be a safe haven against such abuse but, for many children, the home is where violence occurs in the form of physical punishment inflicted by parents and other care givers. Data from UNICEF shows that, globally, three-quarters of children aged two to four years (close to 300 million children) are regularly subjected to violent discipline (physical punishment and/ or psychological aggression) at home, and around six in 10 children (250 million children) are subjected to physical punishment.[99] Many children are also indirectly affected by violence in the home where a parent or carer experiences domestic violence.

Corporal punishment is the most widespread form of violence against children. The term "corporal punishment" is used to describe the physical punishment endured by children by way of discipline. The Committee on the Rights of the Child defines this form of punishment as "any punishment in which physical force is used and intended to cause some degree of pain or discomfort, however light."[100] Smacking, slapping, and spanking are included in this definition, as is forced ingestion (for example, washing a child's mouth with soap). Article 37 of the UNCRC requires States to ensure that "no child shall be subjected to torture or other cruel, inhuman or degrading treatment or punishment."[101] In addition, Art 19 UNCRC places an obligation on States to

> "take all appropriate legislative, administrative, social and educational measures to protect the child from all forms of physical or mental violence … while in the care of parent(s), legal guardian(s) or any other person who has the care of the child."[102]

According to the Committee on the Rights of the Child, all forms of corporal punishment are covered by this provision and therefore

---

[99] UNICEF, *A Familiar Face: Violence in the lives of children and adolescents* (UNICEF 2017).

[100] Committee on Rights of the Child, *General Comment No 8 on the Right to Protection from Corporal Punishment and other Cruel or Degrading forms of Punishment* CRC/C/GC8/2006, para 11.

[101] United Nations Convention on the Rights of the Child, Art 37.

[102] United Nations Convention on the Rights of the Child, Art 19.

States must take appropriate measures to eliminate them and to prohibit all forms of physical and degrading punishment against children.[103]

Many other international bodies have stated that the use of corporal punishment is inconsistent with human rights standards. For example, the European Committee of Social Rights (ECSR) has stated that corporal punishment is not in accordance with human rights standards as defined under the European Social Charter. According to the ECSR, Art 17 of the Charter requires a prohibition in legislation against any form of violence against children, whether at school, in other institutions, in their home or elsewhere. As far back as 2004, the Council of Europe's Parliamentary Assembly adopted a Recommendation calling for a Europe-wide ban on corporal punishment of children.[104]

A number of cases have also come before the European Court of Human Rights (ECtHR) concerning the corporal punishment of children. The ECtHR has found that, depending on the severity of the punishment, it can amount to inhuman or degrading treatment or punishment contrary to Art 3 of the European Convention on Human Rights (ECHR). For example, in *Tyrer v United Kingdom*,[105] the ECtHR found a violation of Art 3 ECHR in circumstances where a 15-year old boy had been set the punishment of birching (beating with twigs from a birch tree inflicted onto bare skin). The punishment was found to be degrading (though it did not amount to torture or inhuman treatment) and the Court held that it involved a level of humiliation or debasement in excess of the usual element of humiliation involved in a conviction for a crime. It did not matter that the punishment had taken place in private and resulted in no lasting injury. The Court held that the birching was degrading punishment and therefore there was a violation of Art 3 ECHR.

In *A v United Kingdom*,[106] a nine-year old boy had been beaten on more than one occasion with a garden cane by his step-father, resulting in bruising and wounds. The step-father was charged with assault occasioning actual bodily harm but was acquitted as the UK law provided for a defence of reasonable chastisement. The

---

[103] Committee on Rights of the Child, *General Comment No 8 on the Right to Protection from Corporal Punishment and other Cruel or Degrading forms of Punishment* CRC/C/GC8/2006, para 18.

[104] Parliamentary Assembly of the Council of Europe, *Europe-wide ban on corporal punishment of children. Recommendation 1666 (2004).* Adopted 23 June 2004.

[105] *Tyrer v United Kingdom*, App no 5856/72 (ECtHR, 25 April 1978).

[106] *A v United Kingdom*, App no 100/1997/884/1096 (ECtHR, 23 September 1998).

ECtHR found that the punishment reached the level of severity prohibited by Art 3 ECHR. It held that the UK law did not provide adequate protection to the child against treatment or punishment contrary to Art 3. Thus, a violation was found.

By contrast, in *Costello-Roberts v United Kingdom*,[107] no violation of Art 3 ECHR was found. In this case, a seven-year old boy was subjected to the punishment of "slippering" by the headmaster of his private boarding school. The punishment involved the child being hit three times over his clothes with a rubber-soled shoe. The Court held that the punishment in this case was not degrading and did not reach the level of severity required as per *Tyrer*. Although no violation was found, an important aspect of *Costello-Roberts* was the Court's finding that the State could be held responsible for the actions of its servants or agents and could therefore be held responsible for disciplinary practices in both public and private schools.

The cases above demonstrate that corporal punishment must attain a certain level of severity before it will come within the ambit of Art 3 ECHR. However, the case law makes it clear that such punishment is often harmful, humiliating and debasing and runs the risk of violating the ECHR. The case law also raises question marks about the compatibility of a defence of "reasonable chastisement" with the ECHR.

Ireland introduced a complete prohibition on the use of corporal punishment against children in 2015. Prior to this, a defence of "reasonable chastisement" had existed in statute and at common law for parents or carers who used physical force against their children. The defence also applied in foster care, residential care and certain childminding settings.[108] The statutory defence was provided for under s 37 of the Children Act 1908. This set out that provisions within that Act preventing cruelty to children would not be construed to "take away or affect the right of any parent, teacher or other person having the lawful control or charge of a child or young person to administer punishment to such child or young person."[109] The Children Act 1908 was repealed in its entirety by the Children Act 2001 and thus the statutory defence of "reasonable chastisement" was abolished. However, the defence also existed at common law.

---

[107] *Costello-Roberts v United Kingdom*, App no 13134/87 (ECtHR, 25 March 1993).
[108] *Association for the Protection of All Children (APPROACH) Ltd v Ireland*, Complaint No 93/2013, Resolution CM/ResChS(2015)9. It should, however, be noted that the National Standards for Foster Care 2003 stated that corporal punishment should not be used.
[109] Children Act 1908, s 37.

Therefore, until the enactment of s 28 of the Children First Act 2015, which inserted a new s 24A into the Non-Fatal Offences Against the Person Act 1997 to abolish the common law defence, parents could lawfully subject their children to physical punishment. Prior to the enactment of the Children First Act 2015, Ireland's failure to prohibit corporal punishment was found to be in breach of Art 17 of the European Social Charter[110]; it was the subject of recommendations made by the United Nations during the Universal Periodic Review[111]; and the Committee on the Rights of the Child had called on Ireland to prohibit corporal punishment completely.[112] The abolishment of the common law defence of reasonable chastisement is thus an encouraging, but long overdue, development that brings Ireland in line with its international obligations.

Of course, it could be argued that the prohibition on corporal punishment interferes with the ability of parents to educate their children in the way that they think best. However, this is tenuous argument in the face of the wealth of research that shows that corporal punishment is associated with negative outcomes for children. There is also evidence to suggest that physical punishment such as slapping is ineffective in changing a child's behaviour.[113] Furthermore, the abolishment of the defence of reasonable chastisement does not prevent parents from disciplining their children. It simply means that, rather than using force to do so, they must engage in positive, non-violent forms of discipline.

Although the complete prohibition of corporal punishment is a relatively recent development in Ireland, it should be noted that the physical punishment of children in settings outside of the home has been outlawed for a longer period. For example, s 24 of the Non-Fatal Offences against the Person Act 1997 removed teacher's immunity from criminal prosecution for the physical punishment of children and reg 8 of the Child Care (Pre-School Services) Regulations 1996 prohibited the use of corporal punishment in pre-school settings.

---

[110] *Association for the Protection of All Children (APPROACH) Ltd v Ireland,* Complaint No. 93/2013, Resolution CM/ResChS(2015)9.

[111] United Nations General Assembly, *Report of the Working Group on the Universal Periodic Review: Ireland* A/HRC/19/9 (21 December 2011).

[112] Committee on the Rights of the Child, *Concluding observations: Ireland* (September 2006).

[113] Global Initiative to End All Corporal Punishment of Children, *Corporal punishment of children: summary of research on its impact and associations* (June, 2016).

Overview

As noted throughout this chapter, a number of criticisms have been made of Ireland's child protection system over the years. In 2018, the Children's Rights Alliance Report Card gave Ireland a Grade B for child protection and an overall Grade B- for Rights in the Family Environment and Alternative Care.[114] These grades represented significant improvement from 2017 when a Grade C was awarded for child protection and a D+ for Rights in the Family Environment and Alternative Care. The 2018 Report Card notes that this improved Grade is attributable in part to the implementation of Child Safeguarding Statements as part of the Children First Act 2015 and the fast turnaround time for e-vetting. However, there are still areas for improvement. For example, the Report Card recommends that vetting requirements should be reviewed and consideration given to the introduction of a passport-style system for vetting that would reduce multiple vetting applications made by one person. The Report Card also makes a number of recommendations in respect of the reform of the guardian ad litem service and measures that allow the child's voice to be heard in child care and other child protection proceedings. The latter recommendations are discussed in Chapter 7 of this book.

---

[114] Children's Rights Alliance, *Report Card 2018* (Children's Rights Alliance, 2018).

REPRESENTATION AND PARTICIPATION

Introduction

The representation and participation of children in legal proceedings that affect them is a vital component of child-friendly proceedings. The child is the individual who will be most affected by the decision and it is therefore important that appropriate procedures are adopted. The child has an important contribution to make and, arguably, will provide the best insight into the nuances of the situation at hand. As such, his or her views must be heard and taken into account in the decision-making process.

Article 12 of the United Nations Convention on the Rights of the Child (UNCRC) supports the representation and participation of children by providing that the child should be given a voice in legal proceedings. Article 12 UNCRC requires that the child should be supported in expressing his or her views and that those views should be taken seriously. However, it is arguable that participation alone is not enough. Adults must do more than simply apply the mechanics that allow children to be heard; the adults also have to listen. In other words, judges and other decision makers must adopt a children's rights *perspective*—a mindset shift for some—when hearing cases concerning children. A children's rights perspective requires recognition of the child's status as a rights holder and ensures that the child's voice is heard and considered in decision-making.

This chapter outlines the mechanisms that exist under Irish law that allow children to participate and have their voice heard in legal proceedings. It also examines Ireland's obligations in this area under the UNCRC, in particular under Art 12 UNCRC. Unfortunately, child-friendly procedures and perspectives are sometimes lacking in legal proceedings. As Stalford, Hollingsworth and Gilmore note, there is still a tendency to "side-line" children in court proceedings. It is rare that children are able to bring proceedings on their own, without adult assistance, and as a result cases tend to adopt an adult perspective.[1] These and other difficulties that arise in maximising the representation and participation of children in legal proceedings are addressed throughout the chapter.

Article 12 UNCRC

Article 12(1) UNCRC provides that

---

[1]   Helen Stalford, Kathryn Hollingsworth and Stephen Gilmore, *Rewriting Children's Rights Judgments: From Academic Vision to New Practice* (Hart Publishing, London, 2017), p 33.

> "States Parties shall assure to the child who is capable of forming his or her own views the right to express those views freely in all matters affecting the child, the views of the child being given due weight in accordance with the age and maturity of the child."[2]

As was discussed in Chapter 2, Article 12 UNCRC is one of the four guiding or general principles of the UNCRC and is regarded as one of the fundamental values of the Convention. It is variously referred to as "the voice of the child", "the right to be heard" and the "right to participate." Whatever title is given to Art 12, it is clear that it forms part of the participatory rights of the child. As the Committee on the Rights of the Child explains

> "The concept of participation emphasizes that including children should not only be a momentary act, but the starting point for an intense exchange between children and adults on the development of policies, programmes and measures in all relevant contexts of children's lives."[3]

Thus, it is not enough to simply listen to the child; the child's views must be taken seriously and must be genuinely considered in decision-making, policy-making and preparation of laws.

Article 12 imposes a clear legal obligation on States parties to facilitate the right of the child to freely express his or her views and to accord those views due weight, according to the child's age and maturity. The Article entails a two-step process: (i) the child has the right to express a view (or not to express a view if that is what the child wants), and (ii) the child has the right to have their view given due weight. The first part of the Article applies to any child who is "capable" of expressing his or her views. The UNCRC does not set a minimum age in this regard, nor are States parties encouraged to set their own. Instead, States must assess the capacity of each individual child on an individual basis and States are encouraged to begin with presumption in favour of the child having capacity.[4] This reflects the fact that, in reality, *any* child can express a view; the UNCRC does not require that this is an intelligible view or that is expressed in words. Therefore, even very young children can express themselves, and should be allowed to do so, whether that

---

[2]   United Nations Convention on the Rights of the Child, Art 12(1).
[3]   *Committee on the Rights of the Child, General Comment No 12 (2009) The right of the child to be heard (1 July 2009)* CRC/C/GC/12, para 13.
[4]   *Committee on the Rights of the Child, General Comment No 12 (2009) The right of the child to be heard (1 July 2009)* CRC/C/GC/12, para 20.

is through their body language, play, drawing, or other non-verbal forms of communication.

Once the child has expressed his or her views, the second part of Art 12(1) requires that those views must be "given due weight in accordance with the age and maturity of the child." In this regard, State Parties should assess the age and maturity of the child on a case-by-case basis. Children's levels of understanding are not uniformly linked to their biological age and so it is not appropriate to set an age limit to determine the weight to be afforded to the child's views. The "maturity" of the child, for the purpose of Art 12, refers to his or her ability to understand the implications of the matter in question.[5]

After the child has expressed his or her views, and those views have been considered, it is important that the decision maker explains to the child how his or her views were taken into account in the decision-making process. This follow-up action is an important component of Art 12. As the Committee explains, "[t]he feedback is a guarantee that the views of the child are not only heard as a formality, but are taken seriously."[6]

Notwithstanding the admirable aims of Art 12 UNCRC, it must be noted that the wording of the Article leaves a lot of discretion to the decision maker to decide how much weight to afford to the child's views. Thus, it is essential that adults are provided with support to help them to develop the skills required to facilitate children's participation effectively, and overall to ensure that they are able to listen to children and that this process is not merely a tokenistic gesture.[7]

Lundy Model of Participation

A well-known model of child participation is the "Lundy Model", which was developed by Professor Laura Lundy. This model conceptualises the key features of Art 12 UNCRC. The aim of this model of participation is to focus decision-makers on the distinct,

---

[5]   *Committee on the Rights of the Child, General Comment No 12 (2009) The right of the child to be heard (1 July 2009)* CRC/C/GC/12, paras 28 – 31.

[6]   *Committee on the Rights of the Child, General Comment No 12 (2009) The right of the child to be heard (1 July 2009)* CRC/C/GC/12, para 45.

[7]   *Committee on the Rights of the Child, General Comment No 12 (2009) The right of the child to be heard (1 July 2009)* CRC/C/GC/12, paras 132 and 134.

yet inter-related, elements of Art 12 UNCRC.[8] Lundy identifies four main elements to conceptualise Art 12:

- Space: Children must be given the opportunity to express a view;
- Voice: Children must be facilitated to express their views;
- Audience: The view must be listened to;
- Influence: The view must be acted upon, as appropriate.[9]

The Lundy Model emphasises that the four elements are inter-related. Thus, there is a significant degree of overlap between: (a) space and voice, and (b) audience and influence. The Lundy Model of Participation is endorsed in the Department of Children and Youth Affairs' *National Strategy on Children and Young People's Participation in Decision-Making, 2015–2020.* The goal of this strategy is to ensure that children and young people have a voice in the areas covered under the five national outcome areas set out in *Better Outcomes, Brighter Futures: The National Policy Framework for Children and Young People, 2014–2020.* As part of the development of the *National Strategy on Children and Young People's Participation in Decision-Making, 2015–2020,* Professor Lundy, in consultation with a sub-group, developed a checklist for participation. The aim of the checklist is to help organisations working with children and young people comply with Art 12 UNCRC and to ensure that "children have the space to express their views; their voice is enabled; they have an audience for their views; and their views will have influence."[10] The checklist is as follows:

1. Space

HOW: Provide a safe and inclusive space for children to express their views.

- Have children's views been actively sought?
- Was there a safe space in which children can express themselves freely?
- Have steps been taken to ensure that all children can take part?

---

[8] Laura Lundy, "'Voice' is not enough: conceptualising Article 12 of the United Nations Convention on the Rights of the Child." (2007) 33 *British Educational Research Journal* 927.

[9] Laura Lundy, "'Voice' is not enough: conceptualising Article 12 of the United Nations Convention on the Rights of the Child." (2007) 33 *British Educational Research Journal* 927 at 933.

[10] Department of Children and Youth Affairs, *National Strategy on Children and Young People's Participation in Decision-Making, 2015–2020,* p 22.

2. Voice

HOW: Provide appropriate information and facilitate the expression of children's views.

- Have children been given the information they need to form a view?
- Do children know that they do not have to take part?
- Have children been given a range of options as to how they might choose to express themselves?

3. Audience

HOW: Ensure that children's views are communicated to someone with the responsibility to listen.

- Is there a process for communicating children's views?
- Do children know who their views are being communicated to?
- Does that person/body have the power to make decisions?

4. Influence

HOW: Ensure that children's views are taken seriously and acted upon, where appropriate.

- Were the children's views considered by those with the power to effect change?
- Are there procedures in place that ensure that the children's views have been taken seriously?
- Have the children and young people been provided with feedback explaining the reasons for decisions taken?[11]

The National Strategy also adopts the principles of participation set out in the 2012 *Council of Europe Recommendation on participation in decision-making of children and young people under the age of 18.*[12] These principles include the following:

- There is no age limit on the right of the child or young person to express her or his views;

---

[11] Department of Children and Youth Affairs, *National Strategy on Children and Young People's Participation in Decision-Making, 2015–2020,* p 22.
[12] Council of Europe (2012) *Recommendation CM/Rec(2012)2 of the Committee of Ministers to Member States on the participation of children and young people under the age of 18* (Adopted by the Committee of Ministers on 28 March 2012 at the 1138th meeting of the Ministers' Deputies).

- The right of children and young people to participate applies without discrimination on any grounds;
- Consideration needs to be given to the evolving capacities of children and young people;
- Particular efforts should be made to enable participation of more vulnerable children and young people;
- Parents and carers play a fundamental role in affirming and nurturing the child's right to participate, from birth onwards;
- In order to be able to participate meaningfully and genuinely, children and young people should be provided with all relevant information and offered adequate support for self-advocacy appropriate to their age and circumstances;
- Participation must be understood as a process and not a once-off event;
- Children and young people who exercise their right to freely express their views must be protected from harm;
- Children and young people should always be fully informed of the scope of their participation, including the limitations on their involvement, the expected and actual outcomes of their participation, and how their views were ultimately considered;
- All processes in which children and young people are heard should be transparent and informative, voluntary, respectful, relevant to children's lives, in child-friendly environments, inclusive (non-discriminatory), supported by training, safe and sensitive to risk, and accountable.[13]

The National Strategy outlines a number of legal and policy reforms that are required to implement the model of participation contained therein. This includes reference to Art 42A of the Irish Constitution and to reform of the guardian ad litem service, both of which are discussed below.

Hearing the Voice of the Child

Under Art 12(2) UNCRC, the child has the right to be heard "either directly, or through a representative or appropriate body."[14] Therefore, States Parties must put mechanisms in place that allow for the child to be heard. Wherever possible, the child must be

---

[13] Department of Children and Youth Affairs, *National Strategy on Children and Young People's Participation in Decision-Making, 2015–2020,* p 23.
[14] United Nations Convention on the Rights of the Child, Art 12(2).

given the opportunity to be heard directly in any proceedings.[15] This might not always be possible, however, and in such cases, the child should have the opportunity to express his or her views indirectly through a representative. This section considers the provisions of Irish law that facilitate the child's right to be heard in public law proceedings and in cases where the child is a witness in legal proceedings. Hearing the voice of the child in private family law disputes is discussed in the context of guardianship, custody and access in Chapter 4. Before turning to consider the legislative provisions that apply in public law proceedings, it is necessary to consider Art 42A of the Irish Constitution.

1. Article 42A of the Irish Constitution

As was noted in Chapter 2, Art 42A of the Irish Constitution expressly recognises the rights of the child. As part of this, Art 42A.4.2° provides that:

> "Provision shall be made by law for securing, as far as practicable, that in all proceedings [brought by the State, as guardian of the common good, for the purpose of preventing the safety and welfare of any child from being prejudicially affected, or concerning the adoption, guardianship or custody of, or access to, any child] in respect of any child who is capable of forming his or her own views, the views of the child shall be ascertained and given due weight having regard to the age and maturity of the child."[16]

This provision does not give children a constitutional right to have their voices heard but it creates a constitutional obligation for legislation to be put in place to allow children to express their views in the matters referred to, that is both in child care (public law) proceedings and adoption, guardianship, custody or access (private law) proceedings. The language that is adopted in Art 42A.4.2° is comparable to that in Art 12 UNCRC and it creates a similar two-part process for the subsequent legislation: (i) the child who is capable of expressing his or her views must be listened to and (ii) the views of the child must be given due weight in accordance with age and maturity. It is notable, however, that while Art 12 UNCRC applies "in all matters affecting the child", Art 42A.4.2° is confined to child care proceedings and cases concerning adoption, guardianship, custody or access.

---

[15] *Committee on the Rights of the Child, General Comment No 12 (2009) The right of the child to be heard* (1 July 2009) CRC/C/GC/12, para 35.
[16] Bunreacht na hÉireann, Art 42A.4.2°.

Various pieces of legislation require the Irish courts to consider the views of the child. For example, s 25 of the Guardianship of Infants Act 1964, as inserted by s 11 of the Children's Act 1997, provides that in any case concerning the best interests of the child, "the court shall, as it thinks appropriate and practicable having regard to the age and understanding of the child, take into account the child's wishes in the matter."[17] The views of the child are now also a factor to be considered as part of the best interests checklist under s 31(2) of the Guardianship of Infants Act 1964, as inserted by s 63 of the Children and Family Relationships Act 2015. Under s 32 of the Guardianship of Infants Act 1964,[18] the court has a number of options available to it to facilitate this task. For example, the court may procure an expert report on any question affecting the welfare of the child and/or it may appoint an expert to determine and convey the child's views. These provisions apply in guardianship, custody and access proceedings and are considered in detail in Chapter 4.

This section focuses on the voice of the child in public law proceedings, in particular child care proceedings where the child may be represented by a guardian ad litem or a legal representative. The special procedures that apply where child witnesses give evidence in court are also examined.

2. Guardian Ad Litem

Section 26 of the Child Care Act 1991 provides for the appointment of a guardian ad litem (GAL) in child care proceedings. A GAL is a person who helps the child to have their views heard and considered in certain types of legal proceedings. The GAL also provides the court with an independent assessment of the child's interests. Thus, the appointment of the GAL helps to give effect to Art 12 UNCRC by facilitating the voice of the child and by allowing the child to have their views heard through a representative.

Under s 26 of the Child Care Act 1991, the GAL is appointed by the court and can only be appointed where the child is not a party to the proceedings and where the court is satisfied that the appointment is in the interests of the child and in the interests of justice.[19] As noted in Chapter 4, s 28 of the Guardianship of Infants

---

[17] Guardianship of Infants Act 1964, s 25, inserted by Children's Act 1997, s 11.
[18] Guardianship of Infants Act 1964, s 32, inserted by Children and Family Relationships Act 2015, s 63.
[19] Child Care Act 1991, s 26(1), amended by Child Care (Amendment) Act 2011, s 13(a).

Act 1964, as inserted by s 11 of the Children Act 1997, provides for the appointment of a GAL in private law proceedings concerning guardianship, custody and access. However, s 28 was never commenced and so it is not possible for a GAL to be appointed in private law proceedings. As such, this section will discuss the appointment and function of GALs in public law proceedings only.

At present, the GAL system is largely unregulated. The Child Care Act 1991 does not define the role and function of the GAL, nor does it establish any eligibility criteria for people who act as GALs.[20] Thus, the very important task of facilitating the voice of the child might be left to an individual who many not have any professional qualifications or practical experience in doing so. This apparent lacuna in Irish law would appear to run contrary to the advice of the Committee on the Rights of the Child, which has noted that individuals representing children "must have sufficient knowledge and understanding of the various aspects of the decision-making process and experience in working with children."[21] No such requirement is imposed on individuals who act as GALs in Ireland, though in practice the GAL will typically have professional expertise in working with children.[22]

There is also inconsistency in the appointment of GALs in child care proceedings. In the 1,272 cases analysed by the Child Care Law Reporting Project between 2012 and 2015, GALs were appointed in approximately 53 percent of child care cases.[23] In 2004, a review of the GAL system by Capita Consulting found that GALs were appointed in approximately 60 percent of cases.[24] This suggests that in between 40 to 47 percent of child care cases, the views and best interests of the child are not independently represented by a GAL. The inconsistency in the appointment of GALs is explained by the lack of guidance available to judges to consider when the appointment of a GAL is required: the only criteria to consider are whether the appointment is "necessary in the interests of the child

---

[20] It should be noted that s 13(c) of the Child Care (Amendment) Act 2011 amends s 26 of the Child Care Act 1991 to provide that the role of the GAL is to "promote the best interests of the child concerned and convey the views of that child to the court." However, at the time of writing, s 13(c) of the Child Care (Amendment) Act 2011 has not been commenced.

[21] *Committee on the Rights of the Child, General Comment No 12 (2009) The right of the child to be heard* (1 July 2009) CRC/C/GC/12, para 36.

[22] See: Barnardos, "Guardian ad Litem–What We Do" < https://www.barnardos. ie/what-we-do/our-services/specialist-services/guardian-ad-litem.html>

[23] Carol Coulter, *Child Care Law Reporting Project, Final Report* (November 2015), p 14.

[24] Capita Consulting Ireland, *Review of the Guardian ad Litem Service* (March 2004).

and in the interests of justice."[25] As a result, considerable discretion is left to the individual judge such that there is "significant disparity in appointment between court districts within the State."[26]

The General Scheme of the Child Care (Amendment) Bill 2017 proposes to overhaul and reform the current GAL system. If enacted, the Bill will address many of the difficulties noted above. Head 3 of the General Scheme proposes that a national guardian ad litem service will be established. This service will be responsible for providing GALs to the courts and will support the professional practice and development of GALs and monitor their performance.[27] The Bill also seeks to define the role and function of GALs and the qualifications and experience required to act as such. Head 5 provides that the function of the GAL is to enhance the decision-making capacity of the court by: (a) informing the court of the child's views, and (b) advising the court on what is in the child's best interests in the proceedings before the court having considered the views of the child. Head 5 also sets out a list of requirements that the GAL must adhere to in exercising his or her functions. Among other things, the GAL must promote and facilitate the child's right to a voice and right to have his or her views considered in the proceedings; regard the best interests of the child as the paramount consideration; ascertain the views of the child and inform the court of same; provide the court with any information, including opinion, in relation to the views and best interests of the child; and provide a written report and recommend to the court a course of action that, in the professional opinion and experience of the GAL, would be in the best interests of the child.

Head 6 proposes to establish the independence of the GAL and provides that the GAL will not be a party to the proceedings. Essentially, the GAL would work "for the court to enhance its decision-making capacity as a special type of expert witness."[28] The disadvantage of conferring such a status on the GAL is that it restricts his or her role. Currently, there is nothing to prevent a GAL from obtaining legal representation and, in some cases, this

---

footnotes[25] Child Care Act 1991, s 26(1), amended by Child Care (Amendment) Act 2011, s 13(a).

[26] Children's Rights Alliance, *Report Card 2018* (Children's Rights Alliance, 2018), p 74.

[27] Minister for Children and Youth Affairs, *General scheme of Child Care (Amendment) Bill 2017–Guardian ad litem arrangements Pre-legislative Scrutiny by the Joint Oireachtas Committee for Children and Youth Affairs. Opening statement of Minister for Children and Youth Affairs* (5 April 2017).

[28] Explanatory note accompanying Head 6 of the General Scheme of the Child Care (Amendment) Bill 2017.

has proven vital to allow the GAL to vigorously defend the rights of the child. If Head 6 of the General Scheme is enacted, the GAL would not be able to make applications to the court on the child's behalf nor would they be able to cross-examine experts on their findings. These functions are currently within the remit of the GAL's role. Thus, the General Scheme would restrict the role of the GAL and, arguably, weaken their status and impact as the child's representative. For this reason, the Children's Rights Alliance has recommended that the GAL should be given legal standing in proceedings to represent the child.[29]

Head 7 of the General Scheme proposes to set out minimum qualifications for GALs. It provides that a GAL must have a professional qualification in social work or psychology, be registered with the Health and Social Care Professionals Council, have a minimum of five years postgraduate experience in child welfare and child protection and have undergone vetting.

The General Scheme also proposes that there will be a presumption in favour of the appointment of a GAL in all child care proceedings and where the court decides not to appoint a GAL, the court will be required to give the reasoning behind its decision. The Explanatory Note accompanying Head 8 of the General Scheme explains that

> "The intention is that the appointment of a Guardian ad litem will be the norm in District and Circuit Court proceedings unless the court having considered particular matters as provided for under this subhead declines to make the appointment."[30]

Thus, there will be a presumption in favour of appointment, but the District and Circuit Court will still have discretion whether or not to appoint the GAL. The same discretion would not apply in High Court proceedings involving children in need of special care or protection—in these cases, High Court "will" order the appointment of a GAL.[31]

It is clear from the above that the General Scheme of the Child Care (Amendment) Bill 2017 proposes to introduce significant changes to the GAL system, but the suitability of some of the proposals

---

[29] Children's Rights Alliance, *Report Card 2018* (Children's Rights Alliance, 2018), p 76.
[30] Explanatory note accompanying Head 8 of the General Scheme of the Child Care (Amendment) Bill 2017.
[31] General Scheme of the Child Care (Amendment) Bill 2017, Head 8(1).

could certainly be questioned. It is also notable that the Bill remains focused on public law proceedings and there is no express provision for the appointment of a GAL in private family law disputes.

3. Legal Representation

Section 25 of the Child Care Act 1991 provides that a child may be joined as a party to child care proceedings where "having regard to the age, understanding and wishes of the child and the circumstances of the case … it is necessary in the interests of the child and in the interests of justice to do so."[32] Where the child is made a party to the proceedings, the court may appoint a solicitor to represent the child and may direct the solicitor on his/her duties in the case. Thus, the child may be separately represented and the costs of such representation will be paid by Tusla.[33] However, even where the child is made a party and separately represented, the child may be physically excluded from the proceedings as per s 30 of the 1991 Act.[34]

Currently, where a child is made a party to the proceedings and a GAL was previously appointed for the child, s 26(4) of the 1991 Act provides that the appointment of the GAL must cease.[35] At present, therefore, it is not possible for the child to be represented by both a solicitor and a GAL. This is unfortunate as the two professionals play very different roles in the child's representation. The solicitor's role is to provide independent legal representation and advice to the child, but the solicitor does not present the court with an independent assessment of the child's interests. The latter role is the function of the GAL. The General Scheme of the Child Care (Amendment) Bill 2017 proposes to alter the current position by providing that where a child becomes a party to the proceedings, the court "may determine that the appointment of the Guardian ad litem may continue or cease, as it may consider appropriate."[36] If enacted, this provision would allow the child to benefit from representation by both professionals and, arguably, would enhance the best interests of the child by allowing for

---

32 Child Care Act 1991, s 25(1), amended by Child Care (Amendment) Act 2011, s 12(a) and (b).
33 Child Care Act 1991, s 25(4), amended by Child and Family Agency Act 2013, s 97 and Sch 2. It should be noted that, under s 25(5) of the 1991 Act, Tusla may apply to the court for an order directing any other party to the proceedings in question to pay any costs or expenses of the child's separate legal representation.
34 Child Care Act 1991, s 25(3) and s 30.
35 Child Care Act 1991, s 26(4).
36 General Scheme of the Child Care (Amendment) Bill 2017, Head 8(12).

independent representation of his or her legal interests, separate to the independent assessment of his or her best interests. The continuation of the appointment of the GAL would, however, be at the discretion of the court.

There is no specific provision in Irish law allowing for a child to be added as a party to private family law proceedings concerning guardianship, custody or access. In civil cases, where the plaintiff is a child, the child must sue through a "next friend" who will normally be a parent of the child. In this situation, the adult is legally represented and will instruct the lawyer on the child's behalf. Where civil proceedings are commenced against a child, the proceedings will be defended by a guardian ad litem.

Solicitors are encouraged to only accept instructions from a child where they have appropriate training to so. The solicitor must also ensure that the child is competent to give instructions and must take steps to explain matters to the child in a clear and understandable manner.[37]

4. Special Protections for Children in Court

(a) In Camera Proceedings

When children are involved in legal proceedings, public or private, special procedures are in place to protect them. A prime example of this is the *in camera* rule. The *in camera* rule operates such that any case concerning a child is heard in private and members of the public are excluded from the proceedings. The rule helps to maintain the privacy and anonymity of the child. The rule does not mean that reporting on the case is prohibited: it is permissible to publish reports of child and family law cases so long as the report does not identify any party. As such, the decisions in such cases can be published and made available.[38] A more recent development has been the introduction of provisions that allow members of the media to report on family and child care proceedings in the courts. Again, these reports are subject to the preservation of the anonymity of the parties and must not include any information likely to identify the parties to the proceedings or any children to whom the proceedings relate. The courts also retain a discretion

---

[37] Law Society of Ireland, *Code of Practice: Family Law in Ireland* (4th edn, Law Society of Ireland, 2017), pp 18–19.
[38] Child Care Act 1991, s 29(5), amended by Child Care (Amendment) Act 2007, s 3.

to exclude members of the media and to impose restrictions on reporting where necessary.[39]

In family law proceedings and child care cases, the court will also "be as informal as is practicable and consistent with the administration of justice."[40] The usual dress code for judges and barristers (wigs and gowns) is dispensed with and proceedings are as informal as possible to accommodate the parties. The aim is to make court a less daunting experience for those involved in family law or child care cases. Child care cases are also heard at a different place or at different times or on different days from those at or on which the ordinary sittings of the Court are held.[41]

(b) Child Witnesses and Child Victims

As noted in Chapter 2, Ireland has not yet ratified the Optional Protocol to the UN Convention on the Rights of the Child on the Sale of Children, Child Prostitution and Child Pornography (OPSC). Article 8 of OPSC provides that States Parties shall adopt appropriate measures to protect the rights and interests of child victims at all stages of the criminal justice process. Among other things, the special procedures referred to include:

- adapting procedures to recognise the special needs of child victims including their special needs as witnesses;
- allowing the views, needs and concerns of child victims to be presented and considered in proceedings;
- protecting, as appropriate, the privacy and identity of child victims.

Although Ireland has not ratified OPSC, special provisions are in place to protect children who give evidence in legal proceedings, discussed below. It should also be noted that the Criminal Justice (Victims of Crime) Act 2017 transposes the EU Directive on the rights of victims of crime[42] into Irish law. The 2017 Act contains further provisions to protect child victims as does the Criminal Law (Sexual Offences) Act 2017.

---

[39] Child Care Act 1991, s 29(5A), inserted by Courts and Civil Law (Miscellaneous Provisions) Act 2013, s 8.
[40] Judicial Separation and Family Law Reform Act 1989, s 33; Child Care Act 1991, s 29.
[41] Child Care Act 1991, s 29(3).
[42] *European Council Directive 2012/29/EU of the European Parliament and of the Council establishing minimum standards on the rights, support and protection of victims of crime* [2012] OJ L315/57.

i. Evidence by Video-Link

In certain cases, children are permitted to give evidence to the court by audio-visual link. In criminal cases, s 13 of the Criminal Evidence Act 1992 provides that any person under the age of 18 years may give evidence through a live television link, unless the court sees good reason to the contrary. This section applies to criminal cases involving allegations of a sexual offence, an offence involving violence or the threat of violence to a person, certain offences under the the Child Trafficking and Pornography Act 1998, certain offences under the Criminal Law (Human Trafficking) Act 2008 or an offence involving aiding or abetting in any of these offences.[43]

The constitutionality of s 13 of the Criminal Evidence Act 1992 was challenged in *Donnelly v Ireland*.[44] In this case, the plaintiff was charged with a sexual offence against a child. During the trial, the child testified by way of a live video link pursuant to s 13. The plaintiff was convicted and sentenced to five years imprisonment. The plaintiff instituted proceedings challenging the constitutionality of s 13 on the grounds that it interfered with his right to a fair trial, in particular his constitutional right to physically confront his accuser in open court. This claim was dismissed by both the High Court and Supreme Court. The Supreme Court noted that the purpose of s 13 is to minimise the likelihood of trauma experienced by young people through giving evidence in open court.[45] The Court noted that a witness giving evidence via video link would be required to do so under oath and would be cross-examined through the video link. In this way, the accused has "ample opportunity to assess the reliability of such testimony."[46] As such, the Supreme Court held that the requirements of fair procedures are satisfied and the accused person's right to a fair trial is adequately protected and vindicated where a witness gives evidence through a live video link. The Court further held that the right to a fair trial does not include a right to physical confrontation with the accuser.[47]

It is also possible for a video-recording of a statement made by a child to be admitted as evidence of any fact stated therein during a trial involving any of the offences above. However, the court may exclude any such recording where it is in the interests of justice to exclude it. In considering whether the exclusion is in the interests

---

[43] Criminal Evidence Act 1992, s 13, amended by Criminal Justice (Victims of Crime) Act 2017, s 30.
[44] *Donnelly v Ireland* [1998] 1 IR 321.
[45] *Donnelly v Ireland* [1998] 1 IR 321 at 356.
[46] *Donnelly v Ireland* [1998] 1 IR 321 at 357.
[47] *Donnelly v Ireland* [1998] 1 IR 321 at 357–358.

of justice, the court will consider all of the circumstances, including any risk that admission of the recording would result in unfairness to the accused. Where the video-recording is allowed, the child must be available for cross-examination at trial.[48]

It should also be noted that s 23 of the Children Act 1997 provides that hearsay evidence is admissible in certain cases concerning children. For the purpose of this provision, hearsay evidence refers to any out-of-court statements made by the child. Such statements may be admissible where the child is unable to give evidence by reason of age or where it would not be in the interest of the welfare of the child to give evidence by video link. The evidence will not be admitted where the admission of the statement would not be in the interests of justice.[49] Where the hearsay evidence is admitted, the court will consider what weight is to be attached to the statement, taking into account "all the circumstances from which any inference can reasonably be drawn as to its accuracy or otherwise."[50]

Children may give evidence via video link in civil proceedings pursuant to s 21 of the Children Act 1997.

ii. Evidence Through an Intermediary

Section 14 of the Criminal Evidence Act 1992 provides for the appointment of an intermediary to assist a child witness who gives evidence via live video link. The Court may appoint the intermediary where, having regard to the age or mental condition of the witness, it is satisfied that the interests of justice require that questions put to the witness first go through the intermediary. The questions put to the witness through the intermediary will either be in the words used by the questioner or the meaning of the questions being asked may be conveyed to the witness in a way that is appropriate to his or her age and mental condition.[51]

iii. Evidence from Behind a Screen

There is also provision for a child to give evidence in court, but from behind a screen. Section 14A of the Criminal Evidence Act 1992, as inserted by s 36 of the Criminal Law (Sexual Offences) Act 2017, provides that in the same categories of cases listed above, "the court may, if satisfied that the interests of justice so require, direct

---

48 Criminal Evidence Act 1992, s 16, as amended.
49 Children Act 1997, s 23(2).
50 Children Act 1997, s 24.
51 Criminal Evidence Act 1992, s 14(2).

that evidence be given from behind a screen or other similar device so as to prevent the witness from seeing the accused."[52] Where the screen is used, the witness will be able to see, and will be seen by, the judge and jury, legal representatives, and any interpreter or intermediary. The witness will not be able to see the accused, but the accused will be able to see and hear the witness. This provision is intended to minimise further trauma to the child caused by giving evidence in the presence of the accused in court. It is still problematic, however, as it requires the child to be present in the same room as the accused. It has been argued that the live video link is a preferable method of allowing the child to give evidence and the screen should only be used where the child has expressly opted out of using the video link and expresses a wish to give evidence in court.[53]

Infrastructural Supports: Complaints Procedures

As was discussed above, in order to vindicate the child's right to be heard, the child must be given opportunities to express him or herself and should be encouraged to express his or her views where possible. These requirements are not confined to legal proceedings. Therefore, infrastructural supports must be put in place to facilitate the right of the child to be heard. An example of such a support that exists at international level is the UNCRC Complaints Procedure, while at national level children can bring complaints to the Ombudsman for Children.

1. UNCRC Complaints Procedure

Ireland signed and ratified the UNCRC's Third Optional Protocol on a Communications Procedure (the "Protocol") in 2014. The Protocol sets out an international complaints procedure for children's rights violations whereby children from States that have ratified the Protocol are able to bring complaints about violations of their UNCRC rights directly to the Committee on the Rights of the Child if they have not found a solution at national level. Complaints may be made with respect to rights contained in the UNCRC, or in either of the first two Protocols (the Optional Protocol to the UNCRC on the Involvement of Children in Armed Conflict (OPAC) and the Optional Protocol to the UNCRC on the Sale of Children, Child Prostitution and Child Pornography (OPSC)).

---

[52] Criminal Evidence Act 1992, s 14A inserted by Criminal Law (Sexual Offences) Act 2017, s 36.

[53] Geoffrey Shannon, *Ninth Report of the Special Rapporteur on Child Protection* (2016), p 28.

A number of criteria must be met before a complaint will be admissible. Among other things, the applicant must first exhaust their domestic remedies; the complaint cannot be anonymous; the alleged violation cannot have occurred before the Protocol came into force (unless the complaint concerns an ongoing violation); and the Committee will not consider a matter that it has already adjudicated on. Where the Committee finds that a violation of a child's rights has occurred, pursuant to Art 11 of the Optional Protocol, the State is required to prepare a written response including information on any action taken and envisaged in the light of the views and recommendations of the Committee. Ireland's ratification of the Third Optional Protocol strengthens the voice of the child in Ireland by allowing individual children to submit complaints regarding violations of their rights under the UNCRC. However, it should be noted that the requirement for the applicant to have exhausted domestic remedies will limit the number of cases that come before the Committee.

2. Ombudsman for Children

In order to give effect to the right to be heard, the Committee on the Rights of the Child has noted that

> "Children should have the possibility of addressing an ombudsman or a person of a comparable role in all children's institutions, inter alia, in schools and day-care centres, in order to voice their complaints. Children should know who these persons are and how to access them."[54]

In Ireland, the Ombudsman for Children's Office (OCO) was established in 2004 under the Ombudsman for Children Act 2002. This Office is independent of the Government and is answerable to the Oireachtas. The role of the OCO is to promote the rights and welfare of children and young people; to investigate complaints by, or on behalf of, children and young people about the actions of public organisations; to provide advice to the Government on matters affecting children and young people; to encourage public organisations to work in child-centred ways; and to carry out research.

The Ombudsman for Children Act 2002 sets out the framework for the complaints mechanisms. Anyone can make a complaint to the OCO about a service provided by a public body within the

---

[54] *Committee on the Rights of the Child, General Comment No 12 (2009) The right of the child to be heard (1 July 2009)* CRC/C/GC/12, para 46.

Republic of Ireland. Children can complain directly to the OCO but most complaints are made by parents on the child's behalf. Professionals working with children can also submit complaints on the child's behalf. When a complaint is received, the OCO will conduct a preliminary examination to see if the complaint can be resolved in a relatively informal manner. If resolution is not possible at the preliminary stage, the OCO will issue to the public body a proposal to investigate, notifying it of potential areas of investigation. Finally, the OCO will investigate the matter fully. At the conclusion of the investigation, the OCO will issue its decision and, if necessary, will set out recommendations for the public body to rectify the situation. The OCO frequently runs workshops and other initiatives for children and young people to make them aware of the services offered by OCO and of their rights.[55]

Beyond Participation: Child-Friendly Judgments

As discussed above, child-friendly procedures are those that maximise children's participation by allowing the child's voice to be heard in legal proceedings and other areas that affect them. Increasingly, however, it is argued that child-friendly procedures alone are not enough. Where legal proceedings are taken concerning a child, the judgment itself must be child-friendly. This means that child-friendly procedures must be adopted, the narrative of the judgment should centralise the child's perspective and voice, and children should be acknowledged as one of the audiences for the judgment through the use of child-appropriate language. Stalford, Hollingsworth and Gilmore, co-ordinators of the Children's Rights Judgment Project, regard these features as pre-requisites for a child-friendly judgment.[56]

The narrative of the judgment refers to the story-telling aspect of judicial decision-making: judges tell a story through facts, structure and language and ultimately "it is through this storytelling method that judges seek to convince their audience that they have made the right decision."[57] A child-friendly judgment should centralise the experience of the child through the narrative. One way that Stalford, Hollingsworth and Gilmore believe this can be achieved is by giving

---

[55] See: <https://www.oco.ie/>.
[56] Helen Stalford, Kathryn Hollingsworth and Stephen Gilmore, Rewriting *Children's Rights Judgments: From Academic Vision to New Practice* (Hart Publishing, London, 2017), pp 53–54.
[57] Helen Stalford, Kathryn Hollingsworth and Stephen Gilmore, Rewriting *Children's Rights Judgments: From Academic Vision to New Practice* (Hart Publishing, London, 2017), p 79.

the child a pseudonym in the judgment, rather than referring to the child as an initial as is usually the case. This approach helps to remind the reader of the impact that this judgment will have on a *real* child, and that they are not a theoretical or abstract being to be considered.[58] Children should also be recognised as an audience for the judgment. The child may seek access to the court report later in life, but the judgment should also be written in such a way as to allow the child to understand the outcome during childhood.[59]

A notable example of a recent child-friendly approach to decision-making can be seen in the English judgment of Mr Justice Peter Jackson in *Re A: Letter to a Young Person*.[60] In many ways, this judgment is exceptional and it is suggested that the same approach could not be adopted in every case due to the requirements of the doctrine of precedent in common law jurisdictions and the need to adopt formal, precise language so as to facilitate the doctrine of stare decisis.[61] Nonetheless, it provides a good example of a child-friendly approach in action. The judgment is written in the form of a letter to a 14-year old boy who was the subject of a private family law case. The judge refers to the boy as Sam, though that is not his real name. The boy's father wished for him to move to a Scandinavian country, and the boy said that he wanted to go, but the mother opposed this. The original application was made by Sam himself (after Sam had instructed his own solicitor) but was later taken over by the father. With the consent of Sam and his parents, Mr Justice Peter Jackson's judgment was published in the original letter format. Selected passages are set out below:

> "13 July 2017
>
> Dear Sam,
>
> It was a pleasure to meet you on Monday and I hope your camp this week went well.

---

[58] Helen Stalford, Kathryn Hollingsworth and Stephen Gilmore, Rewriting *Children's Rights Judgments: From Academic Vision to New Practice* (Hart Publishing, London, 2017), p 81.

[59] Helen Stalford, Kathryn Hollingsworth and Stephen Gilmore, Rewriting *Children's Rights Judgments: From Academic Vision to New Practice* (Hart Publishing, London, 2017), p 82.

[60] *Re A: Letter to a Young Person* [2017] EWFC 48.

[61] This difficulty would arguably be exacerbated rather than mitigated if the court was to produce two judgments: one "standard" judgment and one "child-friendly" judgment. Helen Stalford, Kathryn Hollingsworth and Stephen Gilmore, Rewriting *Children's Rights Judgments: From Academic Vision to New Practice* (Hart Publishing, London, 2017), p 83.

This case is about you and your future, so I am writing this letter as a way of giving my decision to you and to your parents.

When a case like this comes before the court, the judge has to apply the law as found in the Children Act 1989, and particularly in Section 1. You may have looked at this already, but if you Google it, you will see that when making my decision, your welfare is my paramount consideration – more important than anything else. If you look at s.1(3), there is also a list of factors I have to consider, to make sure that everything is taken into account.

....

Here are the main matters that I take into account:

1. Your stated views. You told me that you have long wanted to live in Scandinavia and that you could see yourself living there with your dad. If that doesn't happen, you want to go back to having week on/week off. It worked in the past and you enjoyed it. You feel that your father helps you more with your education. If your dad goes to Scandinavia without you, you would be extremely unhappy. Your mum and Paul are very against you seeing more of your dad.

....

3. I was impressed with the way you gave evidence. You are of an age where your views carry a lot of weight with me, and I consider them in the light of your understanding of what has made things as they are. As to that, I don't think anyone of your age in your situation could understand it better than you do, but nor could they fully understand the influences that you are under and the effect that has on you.

....

7. Sam, the evidence shows that you are doing well in life at the moment. You have your school, your friends, your music, and two homes. You've lived in England all your life. All your friends and most of your family are here. I have to consider the effect of any change in the arrangements and any harm that might come from it. In any case where parents don't agree about a move overseas, the parent wanting to move has at least to show that they have a realistic plan. That plan can then be

compared with other plans to see which is best. That has not been possible here. ...

....

Sam, I realise that this order is not the one that you said you wanted me to make, but I am confident that it is the right order for you in the long run. Whatever each of your parents might think about it, I hope they have the dignity not to impose their views on you, so that you can work things out for yourself. I know that as you get older, you will do this increasingly and I hope that you will come to see why I have made these decisions. I wish you every success with your future and if you want to reply to this letter, I know that your solicitor will make sure that your reply reaches me.

Kind regards
Mr Justice Peter Jackson"[62]

In this judgment, Jackson J is cognisant of the narrative and audience of the decision throughout. He also adopts child-friendly procedures: Sam was able to express his views during the trial and he expressed the view that he wanted to go and live with his father. In the end, Jackson J found that this would not be in Sam's best interests and therefore does not reach the conclusion that Sam said he wanted. The judge takes steps to explain his reasoning to Sam in this regard—he notes that Sam expressed his views in an impressive manner and that his views were taken seriously and given much weight but ultimately the judge felt that Sam's expressed views were formed out of loyalty to his father and that it would not be in Sam's best interests to move to Scandinavia due to the lack of any clear plan in relation to the move. There is a lot to be admired in the judgment and it is to be hoped that more judges will adopt a similar style in their judicial narrative—even if this is confined to one paragraph directed at the child in accessible, child-friendly language.

Overview

Child-friendly procedures are those that maximise the representation and participation of children in legal proceedings. This chapter has examined the provisions that exist in Irish law to maximise children's participation. It has been argued that procedures alone

---

[62] *Re A: Letter to a Young Person* [2017] EWFC 48.

are not enough. In many cases, a child-friendly perspective is required to ensure that participation is meaningful. This requires adults to understand and acknowledge the right of the child to participate as well as the benefits of allowing children to have a voice in matters that affect them. There has been a move towards child-friendly judgments that adopt child-friendly procedures, narrative and are cognisant of the tone and language required. This form of judgment epitomises the child-friendly perspective and it acknowledges that the child is the individual most affected by the decision and therefore should be fully represented both during the proceedings and in the resulting judgment.

EDUCATION

Introduction

The topic of education involves consideration of many aspects of children's rights. It is necessary to not only examine children's rights *to* education, but also children's rights *in* education. The issues arising range from questions of access, non-discrimination and participation through to liability for bullying and absenteeism. These issues encompass aspects of constitutional law, the law of torts, employment law and criminal law among others. Within all of this, although the focus of the discussion is on the rights of children, it is important to also consider the rights of parents (as parents are typically recognised as the primary educators of their children) as well as the rights of others in the school community, such as teachers and school patrons.

A variety of legal sources impact upon the provision of education in Ireland. These include the United Nations Convention on the Rights of the Child (UNCRC), the European Convention on Human Rights (ECHR), the Irish Constitution, and various pieces of legislation. These sources will be examined in this chapter to provide an overview of Ireland's education laws and to understand the challenges that these laws create for children's rights in the Irish education system. The chapter also discusses the issue of bullying in schools, school admissions and freedom of religion in the context of education.

An International Right

1. United Nations Convention on the Rights of the Child

The right to education is an internationally recognised human right and was among the first specific rights of the child recognised by the international community as part of the UN Declaration of the Rights of the Child 1959.[1] The right to education is now recognised as an international right of the child in Arts 28 and 29 of the UNCRC. Article 28 UNCRC provides that:

> "1. States Parties recognize the right of the child to education, and with a view to achieving this right progressively and on the basis of equal opportunity, they shall, in particular:

---

[1] Principle 7 of the UN Declaration of the Rights of the Child 1959 provides, among other things, that the child is entitled to receive education; that this should be free and compulsory at the elementary stages; and that the best interests of the child should be the guiding principle of those responsible for the child's education and guidance; and that that responsibility lies in the first place with the child's parents.

(a) Make primary education compulsory and available free to all;

(b) Encourage the development of different forms of secondary education, including general and vocational education, make them available and accessible to every child, and take appropriate measures such as the introduction of free education and offering financial assistance in case of need;

(c) Make higher education accessible to all on the basis of capacity by every appropriate means;

(d) Make educational and vocational information and guidance available and accessible to all children;

(e) Take measures to encourage regular attendance at schools and the reduction of drop-out rates.

2. States Parties shall take all appropriate measures to ensure that school discipline is administered in a manner consistent with the child's human dignity and in conformity with the present Convention.

3. States Parties shall promote and encourage international cooperation in matters relating to education, in particular with a view to contributing to the elimination of ignorance and illiteracy throughout the world and facilitating access to scientific and technical knowledge and modern teaching methods. In this regard, particular account shall be taken of the needs of developing countries."[2]

Article 29 UNCRC provides that:

"1. States Parties agree that the education of the child shall be directed to:

(a) The development of the child's personality, talents and mental and physical abilities to their fullest potential;

(b) The development of respect for human rights and fundamental freedoms, and for the principles enshrined in the Charter of the United Nations;

(c) The development of respect for the child's parents, his or her own cultural identity, language and values, for the national values of the country in which the child is living, the country from which he or she may originate, and for civilizations different from his or her own;

(d) The preparation of the child for responsible life in a free society, in the spirit of understanding, peace, tolerance,

---

[2]   United Nations Convention on the Rights of the Child, Art 28.

equality of sexes, and friendship among all peoples, ethnic, national and religious groups and persons of indigenous origin;

(e) The development of respect for the natural environment.

2. No part of the present article or article 28 shall be construed so as to interfere with the liberty of individuals and bodies to establish and direct educational institutions, subject always to the observance of the principle set forth in paragraph 1 of the present article and to the requirements that the education given in such institutions shall conform to such minimum standards as may be laid down by the State."[3]

Thus, Art 28 establishes the child's right to education and imposes specific obligations on States Parties to facilitate this right and to ensure that the right can be realised by all children. Article 29 establishes standards for the substance and aims of the education provided. Article 29 does not address or dictate the academic content of education, but requires that education is provided in a manner that facilitates the holistic development of the full potential of the child; fosters respect for human rights; promotes the child's sense of identity and integration in society; and enhances respect for the environment. Thus, Art 29 ensures that education is "child-centred, child-friendly and empowering."[4] The Article goes beyond the provision of formal schooling and emphasises that education should be designed to foster children's personalities, talents and abilities so as to facilitate their participation in a free society. The Committee on the Rights of the Child (the "Committee") has explained that education should not be confined to literacy and numeracy, but should encompass

"life skills such as the ability to make well-balanced decisions; to resolve conflicts in a non violent manner; and to develop a healthy lifestyle, good social relationships and responsibility, critical thinking, creative talents, and other abilities which give children the tools needed to pursue their options in life."[5]

The values promoted by Art 29 underline the interconnected nature of the UNCRC's provisions, as the values echo those in the other provisions of the UNCRC, including the four guiding principles

[3] United Nations Convention on the Rights of the Child, Art 29.
[4] Committee on the Rights of the Child, *General Comment 1 (2001): The Aims of Education* CRC/GC/2001/1, para 2.
[5] Committee on the Rights of the Child, *General Comment 1 (2001): The Aims of Education* CRC/GC/2001/1, para 9.

of non-discrimination (Art 2), the best interests of the child (Art 3), the right to life, survival and development (Art 6), and the right to be heard (Art 12). The values enshrined in Art 29 also relate to those in Art 5 (respect for the responsibilities, rights and duties of parents), Art 8 (preservation of identity), Art 14 (freedom of thought, conscience and religion), Art 30 (protection of cultural rights) and many other provisions of the UNCRC.

There is a clear advantage in promoting these values to children at an early stage. Doing so ensures that future generations are educated in human rights standards and will be more likely to apply these standards in society to avoid human rights abuses. For example, the emphasis on non-discrimination and cultural understanding in Art 29 seeks to reduce prejudice and racism among children and aims to promote an ethos of acceptance which is then carried into adulthood. In this way, the Committee believes that appropriate education can provide a "reliable and enduring antidote" to intolerance amongst future generations.[6] Equally, the Committee notes that educators must be trained to promote the principles reflected in Art 29(1) because:

> "The relevant values cannot be effectively integrated into, and thus be rendered consistent with, a broader curriculum unless those who are expected to transmit, promote, teach and, as far as possible, exemplify the values have themselves been convinced of their importance."[7]

The school itself must also promote the values of Art 29 and thus prevent bullying and exclusionary practices that would run contrary to the principles articulated in the Article.

There are various other specific references to education in the UNCRC. For example, Art 23 requires States to ensure that disabled children have effective access to and receive "education, training, health care services, rehabilitation services, preparation for employment and recreation opportunities" to allow them to achieve the fullest possible social integration and individual development; Art 24 requires States Parties to ensure that children have access to education on topics relating to child health and nutrition including environmental sanitation and the prevention of accidents; and Art 32 protects the child from performing any

---

[6] Committee on the Rights of the Child, *General Comment 1 (2001): The Aims of Education* CRC/GC/2001/1, para 11.

[7] Committee on the Rights of the Child, *General Comment 1 (2001): The Aims of Education* CRC/GC/2001/1, para 18.

work that is likely to interfere with his or her education, or to be harmful to the child's health or physical, mental, spiritual, moral or social development. In addition to these specific obligations (as well as those rights that are integrated into Art 29 set out above), the State must also be cognisant of related areas that are relevant to the provision of education, such as Art 19 which protects the child from all forms of physical or mental violence, injury or abuse, including bullying. Hence, the provision of education involves consideration of an array of rights protected by the UNCRC. These rights must be considered in a holistic manner to ensure that the provision of education protects and enhances the child's rights. It is clear, therefore, that States parties obligations in education go far beyond a textual analysis of Arts 28 and 29 UNCRC.

2. European Convention on Human Rights

Article 2 of Protocol No 1 to the European Convention on Human Rights (ECHR) provides that:

> "No person shall be denied the right to education. In the exercise of any functions which it assumes in relation to education and to teaching, the State shall respect the right of parents to ensure such education and teaching in conformity with their own religious and philosophical convictions."[8]

The first sentence of this Article protects the right to education, while the second sentence guarantees the right of parents to have their children educated in conformity with their religious and philosophical convictions. It is notable, however, that the wording of the first sentence does not create a positive right to access education, nor does it impose a positive obligation on States to provide education. It is instead a negative formulation of the right that prevents the State from impeding access to education facilities that already exist. Thus, it cannot be used to argue that the State must establish or subsidise a particular type of education facility. The Article merely guarantees that access to existing resources cannot be denied; that there is a right of access to educational institutions already existing at a given time. For example, in the *Belgian Linguistic Case*, the European Court of Human Rights (ECtHR) held that the right to education does not encompass a right to education in one's own language.[9] In this

---

[8] European Convention on Human Rights, Protocol No 1, Art 2.

[9] *"In the case relating to certain aspects of the laws on the use of languages in education in Belgium" v Belgium*, App nos 1474/62; 1677/62; 1691/62; 1769/63; 1994/63; 2126/64 (ECtHR, 23 July 1968).

case, the applicants were French-speaking nationals of Belgium who wanted their children to be educated in the French language. This was not possible under the relevant law. Although the ECtHR found that Art 2 of Protocol No 1 does not create a right to be educated in a particular language, it held that the measures in this case amounted to a violation of Art 14 ECHR (the principle of non-discrimination), taken in conjunction with Art 2 of Protocol No 1 because the French-speaking children were prevented from having access to French-language schools based on their parents' residence, whereas Dutch-speaking children living in French-speaking areas were allowed to be educated in Dutch-speaking schools. It is clear therefore that there cannot be discrimination in the application of the right to education.

In *McIntyre v United Kingdom*,[10] the applicant suffered from muscular dystrophy and required a lift to be installed at her school but her request was rejected. She complained (through her mother as next friend) that she was discriminated against by virtue of her disability, contrary to Art 14 ECHR, as she was denied full enjoyment of her right to education as contained in Art 2 of Protocol No 1 of the Convention. She did not have the same access to all classes attended by other students (as she could not access certain rooms) and therefore argued that she did not have full access to the national curriculum. The European Commission of Human Rights rejected this complaint on the basis that, although the applicant did not have access to the full national curriculum, she received an adequate education and so it could not find that the Local Education Authority's refusal to install a lift deprived the applicant of her right to education. The Local Education Authority was entitled to provide the educational facilities in a manner that was consistent with a practical and efficient use of resources and public funds.

Although Art 2 of Protocol No 1 is primarily a negative obligation, it may also give rise to positive obligations to ensure respect for the right to education in the context of educational institutions that the State has chosen to establish or authorise[11] and the State cannot delegate its obligations in this regard. For example, in *O'Keeffe v Ireland*,[12] a case concerning the failure by the Irish State to protect the applicant from sexual abuse by a teacher in her primary school, the ECtHR held that the State has a positive obligation to protect pupils in both State and private schools from ill-treatment.

---

[10] *McIntyre v United Kingdom*, App no 29046/95 (ECtHR, 21 October 1998).
[11] The Article applies to both public and private schools.
[12] *O'Keeffe v Ireland*, App no 35810/09 (ECtHR, 28 January 2014).

Under Art 2 of Protocol No 1, it is legitimate for the State to impose certain restrictions on the right to education, once those restrictions are proportionate and pursue a legitimate aim. As noted above, the State may not discriminate in its provision of education. However, it is legitimate for the State to impose disciplinary measures on students, which may include suspension or expulsion from a particular school for misbehaviour,[13] and the State may impose conditions on access to education such as admissions criteria or require students to undertake entrance examinations to gain entry to an educational institution.[14]

Article 2 of Protocol No 1 also requires the State to uphold the rights of parents to have their religious and philosophical convictions respected in the provision of education. The term "parents" does not just refer to the mother and father of a child, but may encompass the wider family. For example, in *Lee v United Kingdom*,[15] the applicant complained on behalf of his grandchildren that they were deprived of their right to education contrary to Art 2 of Protocol No 1 as he and his family had been refused permission to remain on his own land. This complaint was admissible but ultimately, the ECtHR held that the applicant had failed to substantiate his complaints that his grandchildren had been denied the right to education as a result of the planning measures complained of.

In *Kjeldsen, Busk Madsen and Pedersen v Denmark*,[16] the ECtHR noted that the second sentence of Art 2 of Protocol No 1 does not prevent schools from teaching or imparting knowledge about religious or philosophical matters or from integrating such material into the curriculum. The ECtHR clarified that:

> "The second sentence of Article 2 (P1-2) implies ... that the State, in fulfilling the functions assumed by it in regard to education and teaching, must take care that information or knowledge included in the curriculum is conveyed in an objective, critical and pluralistic manner. The State is forbidden to pursue an aim of indoctrination that might be considered as not respecting parents' religious and philosophical convictions. That is the limit that must not be exceeded."[17]

---

[13] *Whitman v United Kingdom*, App no 13477/87 (ECtHR, 4 October 1989).

[14] *Tarantino v Italy*, App nos 25851/09, 29284/09 and 64090/09 (ECtHR, 9 September 2013).

[15] *Lee v United Kingdom*, App no 25289/94 (ECtHR, 18 January 2001).

[16] *Kjeldsen, Busk Madsen and Pedersen v Denmark*, App nos 5095/71; 5920/72; 5926/72, (ECtHR, 7 December 1976).

[17] *Kjeldsen, Busk Madsen and Pedersen v Denmark*, App nos 5095/71; 5920/72; 5926/72, (ECtHR, 7 December 1976), para 53.

In this case, the applicants complained that integrated, and hence compulsory, sex education in State schools was contrary to their beliefs as Christian parents and amounted to a violation of the second sentence of Art 2 of Protocol No 1. The Government argued that the applicants were not obliged to send their children to the State school; the law permitted parents to educate their children, or to have them educated, at home or to send them to private institutions that were substantially subsidised by the State. The ECtHR noted, however, that the second sentence of Art 2 applied to "all functions" of the State in providing education and therefore extended to both State and private education. The ECtHR held that the provision of sex education served the public interest by educating children on important matters such as pregnancy, abortion and STIs. Furthermore, the ECtHR found that the provision of such education did not affect the right of parents to enlighten and advise their children, in line with the parents' own religious or philosophical convictions. As such, there was no violation of the second sentence of Art 2 of Protocol No 1.

In *Campbell and Cosans v United Kingdom*,[18] the applicants did not wish to send their children to State schools in Scotland where corporal punishment was used as a disciplinary measure, but there was no alternative school available to them. The ECtHR found that the corporal punishment in question did not violate the children's rights under Art 3 ECHR (freedom from torture and inhuman or degrading treatment or punishment), but held that the school's failure to act on the parents' opposition to the use of corporal punishment failed to respect their convictions and was thus contrary to the second sentence of Art 2 of Protocol No 1.

In some cases, the religious and philosophical convictions of the parents might require that children are exempted from certain classes. In the case of *Folgerø v Norway*, for example, a refusal to grant a full exemption to children enrolled at a State primary school from attending "Christianity, religion and philosophy" classes was found to give rise to a violation of Art 2 of Protocol No 1.[19] The obligation to respect the religious and philosophical convictions of the parents does not, however, preclude the presence of crucifixes in State-school classrooms.[20] Similarly, it is not a violation of either sentence of Art 2 of Protocol No 1 for schools to refuse access to

---

[18] *Campbell and Cosans v United Kingdom*, App nos 7511/76; 7743/76, (ECtHR, 25 February 1982).

[19] *Folgerø v Norway*, App no 15472/02, (ECtHR, 29 June 2007).

[20] *Lautsi v Italy*, App no 30814/06, (ECtHR, 18 March 2011).

students wearing religious clothing or symbols provided that the restriction is foreseeable and proportionate.[21]

The Irish Legal Framework

1. The Irish Constitution

Article 42 of the Irish Constitution is entitled "Education". This Article provides that:

> "1 The State acknowledges that the primary and natural educator of the child is the Family and guarantees to respect the inalienable right and duty of parents to provide, according to their means, for the religious and moral, intellectual, physical and social education of their children.
>
> 2 Parents shall be free to provide this education in their homes or in private schools or in schools recognised or established by the State.
>
> 3 1° The State shall not oblige parents in violation of their conscience and lawful preference to send their children to schools established by the State, or to any particular type of school designated by the State.
>
> 2° The State shall, however, as guardian of the common good, require in view of actual conditions that the children receive a certain minimum education, moral, intellectual and social.
>
> 4 The State shall provide for free primary education and shall endeavour to supplement and give reasonable aid to private and corporate educational initiative, and, when the public good requires it, provide other educational facilities or institutions with due regard, however, for the rights of parents, especially in the matter of religious and moral formation."[22]

This Article establishes that parents are the primary and natural educators of their children, while the role of the State is a subsidiary one. Notably, the Article does not create a right to education for children. Instead, education is expressed in adult-centred terms as being the right and duty of parents. Parents have the right to educate their children however and wherever they wish and they cannot be compelled to send their children to a particular school.

---

[21] *Köse v Turkey*, App no 26625/02, (ECtHR, 24 January 2006).
[22] Bunreacht na hÉireann, Art 42.

The State plays a secondary role in the provision of education, although it has still has certain duties. It must ensure that children receive a certain minimum education, provide for free primary education, endeavour to supplement and give reasonable aid to private and corporate educational initiatives and, when the common good requires it, provide other educational facilities or institutions but always "with due regard" for the rights of parents.

Although the right to education is primarily expressed as a right of the parents, Art 42 is not devoid of children's rights. The duty on the State to provide for primary education has been found to give rise to a corresponding right for children to access this free primary education.[23] In addition, the courts have found that the "natural rights" of the child include

> "the right to be fed and to live, to be reared and *educated*, to have the opportunity of working and of realising his or her full personality and dignity as a human being. These rights of the child ... must equally be protected and vindicated by the State."[24]

The concept of education has been defined broadly by the Irish courts. In *Ryan v Attorney General*, Ó Dálaigh CJ defined education as "the teaching and training of a child to make the best possible use of his inherent and potential capacities, physical, mental and moral."[25] In *O'Shiel v Minister for Education*, Laffoy J noted that primary education is "the first stage or level in time of that process."[26]

(a) Primary Education

The leading case on the right to primary education under Art 42.4 is *Crowley v Ireland*.[27] In this case, a dispute arose between the Irish National Teachers Organisation (INTO) and a school manager, which led to the closure through strike action of three national schools in the Drimoleague parish in Co Cork. This closure left approximately 180 children without schooling for a considerable period of time as INTO sent a circular to all of their members in the areas adjoining Drimoleague directing them not to enrol pupils from Drimoleague. Ultimately, the Minister for Education provided

---

[23] *Crowley v Ireland* [1980] IR 102 at 122.
[24] *G v An Bord Uchtála* [1980] IR 32 at 55–56 [emphasis added].
[25] *Ryan v The Attorney General* [1965] IR 294 at 350.
[26] *O'Shiel v Minister for Education* [1999] 2 IR 321 at 327.
[27] *Crowley v Ireland* [1980] IR 102.

transport for these pupils to access schools in other districts. The children, who were plaintiffs in the case suing through their parents, claimed that the closure of the schools infringed their constitutional right to free primary education. The Supreme Court noted that Art 42.4 does not impose a duty on the State to "provide", but to "provide for" free primary education. O'Higgins CJ explained that this duty required the State to "to see that machinery exists under which and in accordance with which such education is in fact provided."[28] In this light, the Supreme Court could not find that there had been a breach of the constitutional duty to provide for free primary education. The State had provided the machinery but, as Kenny J noted, "[t]he State cannot by laws compel teachers to teach when they do not wish to do so, though it may and should protect their right to teach when they wish to do so and others want to prevent them."[29] Thus, the State did not fail to discharge the duty imposed on it by the Constitution to provide for free primary education.

The case of *Crowley v Ireland* underlines the fact that the Constitution does not contain any express right to education. It demonstrates that once the State has made arrangements for the provision of free primary education, it is absolved of any further duty to ensure that the education is actually delivered. As Kenny J explained, "the State is under no obligation to educate."[30]

In keeping with the broad definition of education, the courts have found that the obligation on the State to provide for free primary education extends beyond scholastic education where this is necessary to meet the needs of children. In *O'Donoghue v Minister for Health*, O'Hanlon J held that the duty to provide for free primary education

> "involves giving each child such advice, instruction and teaching as will enable him or her to make the best possible use of his or her inherent and potential capacities, physical, mental and moral, however limited these capacities may be."[31]

The learned judge noted that the aim of education is to allow the child to achieve "the fullest possible social integration and individual development."[32] For children with disabilities, the judge

---

[28]   *Crowley v Ireland* [1980] IR 102 at 122.
[29]   *Crowley v Ireland* [1980] IR 102 at 130.
[30]   *Crowley v Ireland* [1980] IR 102 at 126.
[31]   *O'Donoghue v Minister for Health* [1996] 2 IR 20 at 65.
[32]   *O'Donoghue v Minister for Health* [1996] 2 IR 20 at 24.

noted that "a completely different programme of education has to be adopted and a completely different rate of progress has to be taken for granted," than would be regarded as appropriate for other children.[33]

In *O'Donoghue v Minister for Health*, the mother of a physically and mentally disabled child had sought to enrol him as a student at the Cope Foundation, a voluntary organisation in receipt of State funds that provides full-time educational facilities to children with both physical and mental disabilities. There were no places available and so the mother was placed on a waitlist and arranged for the child to be educated privately at her own expense. The child, suing through his mother, brought an application to the High Court seeking an order of mandamus compelling the Minister for Health and the Minister for Education to provide the child with free primary education. The respondents argued that that the child was "ineducable" and that the education that the State was obliged to provide under Art 42.4 was education of a scholastic nature, which could be of no benefit to the child. In the High Court, O'Hanlon J held that the State had failed to provide for the child's free primary education and thus had deprived him of his constitutional rights under Art 42 of the Constitution. The judge found that the obligation to provide for free primary education required the State to give

> "each child such advice, instruction and teaching as will enable him or her to make the best possible use of his or her inherent and potential capacities, physical, mental and moral, however limited these capacities may be."[34]

The judge also noted that research on the education of children with disabilities shows that such children can positively benefit from formal education and from integration in the school environment. Accordingly, there was a constitutional obligation on the State to provide for free primary education for disabled children in as full and positive a manner as it provides for all other children in the community.[35]

The definition of education adopted by O'Hanlon J in *O'Donoghue* is in keeping with the broad understanding of education in Art 29 UNCRC. As was seen above, that Article focuses on education as part of the holistic development of all children. Therefore,

---

[33] *O'Donoghue v Minister for Health* [1996] 2 IR 20 at 65.
[34] *O'Donoghue v Minister for Health* [1996] 2 IR 20 at 65.
[35] *O'Donoghue v Minister for Health* [1996] 2 IR 20 at 66.

education should not only be scholastic but should encompass broader attributes and proficiencies, as was noted by O'Hanlon J.

The approach adopted in *O'Donoghue v Minister for Health*, was subsequently endorsed by McGuinness J in *Comerford v Minister for Education*, where she held that "the right to free primary education extends to every child, although the education provided must vary in accordance with the child's abilities and needs."[36] In this case, the applicant was an 11-year old child who had been diagnosed with "attention deficit disorder" (ADD) and was in the care of the Eastern Health Board pursuant to an interim care order at the date of the proceedings. At the time of his diagnosis of ADD, the consultant psychiatrist recommended that the child would "benefit strongly from being placed in a consistent, caring, structured setting where he would be able to get a one-to-one [sic] at personal level and would be in a very small classroom with a high teacher/pupil ratio."[37] Despite a number of efforts, a suitable placement had not been possible. McGuinness J found that there was "no doubt on the evidence that the applicant has not been provided with education of a type from which he could truly benefit"[38] and held that the State had failed in its constitutional duty to provide for a suitable primary education for the child.

In *Sinnott v Minister for Education*,[39] a claim was brought to the High Court alleging that the State had failed in its constitutional duty to provide primary education for the first plaintiff (Jamie Sinnott), a 23 year old man with severe mental and physical disabilities. The plaintiff sought an injunction directing the State to provide for free education for the first plaintiff appropriate to his needs for as long as he was capable of benefiting from same. The High Court granted the injunction on the basis that Art 42.4 of the Constitution imposes a constitutional obligation on the State to provide for free, basic, elementary education for all children. The High Court held that there is no age limit on a citizen's right to primary education because the obligation to provide free primary education is based on need, not age. Therefore, the obligation on the State to provide for such education could apply to a person over the age of 18 years. The High Court also found that the State had violated the constitutional rights of the plaintiff's mother and awarded damages to her.

---

[36] *Comerford v Minister for Education* [1997] 2 ILRM 134 at 143.
[37] *Comerford v Minister for Education* [1997] 2 ILRM 134 at 140.
[38] *Comerford v Minister for Education* [1997] 2 ILRM 134 at 146.
[39] *Sinnott v Minister for Education* [2001] 2 IR 545.

The State agreed to pay the damages awarded and to provide for the plaintiff's education, but appealed to the Supreme Court regarding the issue of whether the State has a constitutional obligation under Art 42 to provide for the plaintiff's education beyond the age of 18 years. The Supreme Court held that the duty to provide for free primary education under Art 42.4 of the Constitution was owed to children and not to adults. Therefore, the State had breached the first plaintiff's constitutional rights by not providing adequate education up to the age of 18 years, but his right to education ended at that point.

The approach of the Irish courts in the cases above appears to largely conform with the principles expressed in Art 29 UNCRC. These principles emphasise that the provision of education should be directed at the child's personal development and integration and participation in society. Furthermore, the interpretation of the right to free primary education, for the most part, respects the requirements of Art 23 UNCRC, which requires States to ensure that disabled children have effective access to and receive education. However, the *Sinnott* case makes it clear that the State's duty to provide for free primary education ends at 18 years. The education of children with special educational needs is addressed in the Education for Persons with Special Educational Needs Act 2004, which will be discussed later in this chapter.

As discussed above, Art 42.4 of the Irish Constitution imposes a duty on the State to provide for free primary education. It does not impose a duty on the State to provide for free post-primary education. Instead, Art 42.4 simply requires that the State "supplement and give reasonable aid to private and corporate educational initiative, and, when the public good requires it, provide other educational facilities or institutions." The wording of this Article implies that there is no constitutional duty on the State to provide for free post-primary education but simply to supplement it. As such, it would seem that young people have no corresponding constitutional right to free post-primary education. That said, as discussed later in this chapter, the Minister for Education is under a legislative duty to ensure that an appropriate level and quality of education is provided to "each person resident in the State."[40]

(b) The Rights of Parents

Article 42.1 of the Constitution provides that parents are the

---

[40] Education Act 1998, s 7(1)(a).

primary and natural educators of their children and that they have an inalienable right and duty to provide for their children's education. In the case of *Burke and O'Reilly v Burke and Quail*,[41] a direction in a will was declared void because it conflicted with the parents' rights under Art 42. In this case, a child had been left property on trust with a direction that income generated by the property was to be used to maintain and educate the child and to bring him up as a Roman Catholic. The will directed that the choice of Roman Catholic school was to be left to the absolute discretion of the trustees (who were unrelated to the child). Gavan Duffy P held that this direction was invalid as it conflicted with the right and duty of the child's parents to make decisions as to his education. Similarly, in *Re Blake*[42] a testator bequeathed a legacy to trustees in trust to apply the income towards the maintenance and education of the children of his daughter provided that they were brought up in the Roman Catholic faith. Dixon J held that the conditions in the will were void as they restricted the right and duty of the parents to provide for the education of their children.

Articles 42.2 and 42.3.1° of the Constitution establish that parents can choose where and how their children will be educated. Parental choice is not, however, absolute and cannot be used to demand that the State funds a particular system of education. In the case of *O'Shiel v Minister for Education*,[43] a group of parents had set up their own primary school based on Steiner principles.[44] They sought funding from the State for this school but funding was refused as the school did not meet the requirements for recognition set by the Department of Education. The parents claimed that this refusal violated the children's right to free primary education under Art 42 of the Constitution. In the High Court, the State argued that it had already discharged its constitutional obligation to provide for free primary education by funding 15 denominational schools within a 12-mile radius of the plaintiffs' school, all of which operated open access enrolment. Laffoy J noted that Art 42

> "underpins the freedom of choice of parents in relation to the education of their children by expressly prohibiting the State obliging parents to send their children to schools established by the State or to any particular type of school

---

[41] *Burke and O'Reilly v Burke and Quail* [1951] IR 216.
[42] *Re Blake* [1955] IR 89.
[43] *O'Shiel v Minister for Education* [1999] 2 IR 321.
[44] The Waldorf Steiner pedagogy of education regards the artistic activity and the development of the imagination as integral to learning.

designated by the State in violation of their conscience and lawful preference."[45]

According to the learned judge, "it would pervert the clear intent of the Constitution" to interpret the obligation to provide for free primary education "as merely obliging the State to fund a single system of education which is on offer to parents on a 'take it or leave it' basis." This would amount to clear disregard for the guarantee of parental choice. Similarly, to accept the State's argument that it had discharged its duty by providing other schools in the locality, "would render meaningless the guarantee of parental freedom of choice"[46]

At the same time, the judge found that the guarantee of parental choice did not mean that the State had to give financial assistance to parents to establish their own preferred system of primary education; the State was entitled to adopt reasonable criteria to distribute public funding. Consequently, Laffoy J found that the correct constitutional position was somewhere between the arguments advanced by the State (that it had discharged its obligation to provide for free primary education) and the arguments of the plaintiffs (that they were entitled to State funding). Hence,

> "Fulfilment of the State's constitutional obligation under Article 42.4 must take account of the parental freedom of choice guaranteed by Article 42, but it must be based on arrangements which have a rational foundation and prescribe proper criteria for eligibility which accord with the purpose of Article 42 and of the provisions of the Constitution generally."[47]

Ultimately, on the particular facts of the case, the High Court held that the refusal of funding for the plaintiffs' school did not amount to a violation of Art 42.4 of the Constitution. Thus, parental choice in education is not unlimited.

(c) A Certain Minimum Education

Under Art 42.2.2° of the Constitution, the State has a power and a duty to intervene in the education of children "as guardian of the common good" to ensure that children "receive a certain minimum

---

[45] *O'Shiel v Minister for Education* [1999] 2 IR 321 at 345.
[46] *O'Shiel v Minister for Education* [1999] 2 IR 321 at 347.
[47] *O'Shiel v Minister for Education* [1999] 2 IR 321 at 348.

education, moral, intellectual and social."[48] The extent of this power and duty of intervention was considered by the Supreme Court in *In Re Art 26 of the Constitution and The School Attendance Bill, 1942*.[49] In this case, the Supreme Court was asked to consider the constitutionality of s 4(1) of the School Attendance Bill 1942 which provided that

> "[a] child shall not be deemed for the purposes of this Act to be receiving suitable education in a manner other than by attending a national school, a suitable school, or a recognised school unless such education and the manner in which such child is receiving it, have been certified under this section by the Minister to be suitable."

Thus, where a child was not attending school, for example where he or she was educated at home, the child would not be deemed to be receiving suitable education unless that education, and the manner in which the child was receiving education, was certified as suitable by the Minister for Education. The difficulty was that, under Art 42, the right and duty of educating children is vested in parents and the State can only intervene in limited circumstances under Art 42.2.2° to ensure that the children receive a certain minimum education. The Supreme Court noted that the phrase "a certain minimum education" is not defined by the Constitution and thus the Oireachtas had the power to define it in legislation. In respect of the impugned provision, the Court noted that there would necessarily be a delay between the start of the child's education and the issue of a certificate by the Minister in accordance with the section. This was because a period of time would have to elapse before it would be possible to evaluate the quality of the education that the child was receiving. This fact rendered the section unconstitutional since

> "the parent would be in default in respect of the period intervening between the time when the child attained the age of six years and the time when the certificate is actually given, and might be subjected in respect of such default to penalties."[50]

The parent would be in default due to the very nature of the test. In addition, the Supreme Court noted that:

---

[48] Bunreacht na hÉireann, Art 42.2.2°.
[49] *In Re Art 26 of the Constitution and The School Attendance Bill, 1942* [1943] IR 334.
[50] *In Re Art 26 of the Constitution and The School Attendance Bill, 1942* [1943] IR 334 at 346.

> "Under sub-s. 1 not only the education, but also the manner in which such child is receiving it must be certified by the Minister. We do not consider that this is warranted by the Constitution. The State is entitled to require that children shall receive a certain minimum education. So long as parents supply this general standard of education we are of opinion that the manner in which it is being given and received is entirely a matter for the parents and is not a matter in respect of which the State under the Constitution is entitled to interfere."[51]

In *DPP v Best*,[52] the Supreme Court further clarified the definition of "a certain minimum education" as set out in Art 42.2.2° of the Constitution. In this case, a mother had been issued a warning notice under s 17 of the School Attendance Act 1926 for failing to send her children to school without reasonable excuse and was subsequently charged with an offence before the District Court. Within one week of receiving this notice, the mother informed An Garda Síochána that she was educating her children at home and that this constituted a reasonable excuse within the terms of the relevant Act. The District Court found that the education received by the children in the home had shortcomings and did not amount to suitable elementary education of general application, that is, education of the standard of the primary school curriculum of the State. The legislation did not, however, define the meaning of "suitable elementary education." The District Court stated a case for the opinion of the High Court on the relevant definition of "suitable elementary education" and whether the mother could be prosecuted in the absence of a statutory definition. The High Court determination was subsequently appealed to the Supreme Court.

The Supreme Court held that the absence of a statutory definition of "suitable elementary education" did not prevent the District Court from convicting a parent of failing to provide it. Further, it was held that, although it was within the competence of the Oireachtas to define what was meant by "certain minimum education" in legislation, it was not required to do so.[53] The Court also commented on the nature of the phrase "suitable elementary education." Denham J noted that the evaluation of "suitable elementary education" must not exceed "a certain minimum education, moral,

---

[51] *In Re Art 26 of the Constitution and The School Attendance Bill, 1942* [1943] IR 334 at 346.
[52] *DPP v Best* [2000] 2 IR 17.
[53] *DPP v Best* [2000] 2 IR 17 at 60.

intellectual and social" as this is the threshold set by Art 42.2.2° of the Constitution. It was noted that the phrase referred to

> "a minimum standard of elementary education of a general character but should have regard to the intellectual and other capacities of the child. It is not necessarily equivalent to the primary school curriculum. It is a minimum education, moral, intellectual and social which must be considered in light of factors, including those previously reviewed, such as the time the issue is determined, the family, the parents, their means, the child, the geographical situation, the actual circumstances and the common good."[54]

Similarly, Murphy J opined that the phrase "certain minimum education" referred to a "a very basic standard" of education. The judge stated that:

> "The underlying objective is to provide young people with a basic education so that they can communicate orally and in writing within society and record, organise and deal with ordinary social and business matters involving communication, enumeration and arithmetic. The common good also requires that children should be encouraged to develop a sense of responsibility and the capacity to live within a civilised society."[55]

Thus, the phrase "certain minimum education" must be decided in light of the actual conditions arising in a particular case. It is a mandatory minimum standard and does not set a high threshold for the provision of education but it must be conducive to the child achieving intellectual and social development.[56]

The concept of "a certain minimum education" is now addressed in the Education (Welfare) Act 2000 (the "2000 Act"). Section 14 of the 2000 Act provides that parents may educate their children in places other than recognised schools, for example through home-schooling. Where the child is not educated in a recognised school, the parents must register the child with the Educational Welfare Services of the Child and Family Agency (EWS) and EWS, in turn, must assess the provision of education to ensure that the child

---

[54] *DPP v Best* [2000] 2 IR 17 at 50.
[55] *DPP v Best* [2000] 2 IR 17 at 70.
[56] *DPP v Best* [2000] 2 IR 17 at 49–50.

receives "a certain minimum education."[57] If EWS is satisfied that the child is receiving a certain minimum education, the child may be included on the register.

Pursuant to s 16 of the 2000 Act, the *Guidelines on the Assessment of Education in Places Other Than Recognised Schools*[58] provide a working definition of "a certain minimum education" and set down guidance on how this may be assessed for the purpose of the 2000 Act. The guidelines do not establish a strict definition of "a certain minimum education" but identify some broad characteristics of a certain minimum education derived from the provisions of the Constitution, the interpretation of the requirement by the Supreme Court in various cases, and the requirements of the 2000 Act. The guidelines suggest that a certain minimum education should:

- be suited to the age, ability, aptitude and personality of the child;
- be responsive to the child's individual needs, take cognisance of the areas of learning that are of interest to the child, and ensure that his/her personal potential is enhanced and not suppressed;
- address the immediate and prospective needs of the child, in the context of the cultural, economic and social environment;
- provide a reasonably balanced range of learning experiences, so that no one aspect of the child's learning is emphasised to the exclusion of others;
- develop the personal and social skills of the child and prepare him/her for the responsibilities of citizenship;
- contribute to the moral development of the child;
- ensure the development of basic skills so as to prepare the child to participate in society and everyday life;[59]
- provide opportunities for the child to develop his/her intellectual capacities and understanding.[60]

Where a parent chooses to educate his or her child in a place other than a recognised school and he or she has applied to EWS to have the child concerned registered, EWS will assess the education to

---

[57] Education (Welfare) Act 2000, s 14(4), as amended by Child and Family Agency Act 2013, s 97 and Sch 2.

[58] Department of Education and Science, *Guidelines on the Assessment of Education in Places Other Than Recognised Schools* (September 2003).

[59] "Basic skills" include language, literacy and numeracy skills, without which a child would be placed at a serious disadvantage.

[60] Department of Education and Science, *Guidelines on the Assessment of Education in Places Other Than Recognised Schools* (September 2003), p 19.

ensure that it meets this working definition of "a certain minimum education." This will include assessment of:

"(a)   the education that is being provided, or that it is proposed will be provided, to the child,

(b)   the materials used, or that it is proposed will be used, in the provision of such education, and

(c)   the time spent, or that it is proposed will be spent, in the provision of such education."[61]

(d) Religious Freedom

Article 42.4 of the Irish Constitution imposes a duty on the State to "provide for" free primary education and in providing for same, the State must have due regard for the rights of parents, "especially in the matter of religious and moral formation."[62] In the context of religious education, it is also necessary to have regard to Art 44.2.4° of the Constitution which provides that:

"Legislation providing State aid for schools shall not discriminate between schools under the management of different religious denominations, nor be such as to affect prejudicially the right of any child to attend a school receiving public money without attending religious instruction at that school."[63]

This Article allows for State funding of denominational schools and makes provision for children attending such schools to opt-out of religious education. The right to opt-out of religious education is given further effect by s 30(2)(e) of the Education Act 1998, which provides that a child can opt out of any subject, not just religious education, that "is contrary to the conscience of the parent of the student."[64] However, although children can opt out of timetabled classes concerned with religious education, the religious ethos of the school cannot be supressed and, in many cases, this ethos will be woven into all aspects of the school day. In *Campaign to Separate Church and State Ltd v Minister for Education*, the Supreme Court noted that:

"The Constitution ... distinguishes between religious 'education' and religious 'instruction' — the former being

---

[61]   Education (Welfare) Act 2000, s 14(5).
[62]   Bunreacht na hÉireann, Art 42.4.
[63]   Bunreacht na hÉireann, Art 44.2.4°.
[64]   Education Act 1998, s 30(2)(e).

the much wider term. A child who attends a school run by a religious denomination different from his own may have a constitutional right not to attend religious instruction at that school but the Constitution cannot protect him from being influenced, to some degree, by the religious 'ethos' of the school. A religious denomination is not obliged to change the general atmosphere of its school merely to accommodate a child of a different religious persuasion who wishes to attend that school."[65]

Consequently, a child cannot avoid informal religious instruction when attending a denominational school and might, for example, be exposed to aspects of religious teaching as part of a secular subject. It should also be noted that the Constitution does not prescribe a method to facilitate children who opt-out of religious education. It is unclear therefore whether such children are entitled to leave the classroom or whether it is sufficient that they stay in class but not participate. Until 2018, this question was left to the discretion of each individual school. As a result, many schools required that children who had opted out of religious classes had to remain in the classroom while the subject was being taught. In many cases, this was necessary because religion was tabled as a "core" subject, meaning that there was no alternative class available and it was deemed too expensive to supervise the child elsewhere.[66] A circular issued by the Department of Education and Skills in 2018 has put an end to this practice in publicly-funded schools. Now, State schools must offer an alternative subject(s) for children who choose not to attend religious instruction. These new rules require that children who opt-out of religious classes are given access to tuition in other subjects in other rooms, thereby effectively securing the right to opt out.[67]

2. Legislation

The statutory framework for the Irish education system is established by three main Acts: the Education Act 1998, the Education (Welfare) Act 2000, and the Education for Persons with

---

[65] *Campaign to Separate Church and State Ltd v Minister for Education* [1998] 2 ILRM 81 at 101.

[66] See: Ronan McGreevy, "Parents suing over teaching of religion being unreasonable, says school board" *The Irish Times* (Dublin, 9 September 2011); Peter McGuire and Gráinne Faller, "Forced into faith: 'We are second-class citizens in the education system'" *The Irish Times* (Dublin, 8 May 2017).

[67] Department of Education and Skills, *Religious instruction and worship in certain second level schools in the context of Article 44.2.4 of the Constitution of Ireland and Section 30 of the Education Act 1998* (Circular Letter 0013/2018).

Special Educational Needs Act 2004. These Acts regulate a number of areas including the functions of the Minister for Education, school attendance, school admissions, school inspections and special needs education.

(a) Education Act 1998

The Education Act 1998 (the "1998 Act") was the first substantive piece of legislation dealing with education in Ireland. Section 6 sets out the objectives of the 1998 Act and imposes duties on persons involved in educational matters. The objectives of the 1998 Act include, among other things:

- giving practical effect to the constitutional rights of children, including children who have a disability or who have other special educational needs, as they relate to education;
- providing an appropriate quality of education, subject to available resources;
- promoting equality of access to and participation in education;
- promoting opportunities for adult learners;
- promoting the right of parents to send their children to a school of the parents' choice;
- promoting best practice in teaching methods and developing the skills and competences of teachers;
- promoting effective liaison and consultation between schools and centres for education, patrons, teachers, parents, the communities served by schools, local authorities, Tusla, persons or groups of persons who have a special interest in, or experience of, the education of students with special educational needs and the Minister;
- contributing to the realisation of national educational policies and objectives;
- promoting greater use of the Irish language at school and in the community;
- contributing to the maintenance of Irish as the primary community language in Gaeltacht areas;
- promoting the language and cultural needs of students;
- enhancing the accountability and transparency of the education system.[68]

The functions of the school are set out in s 9 of the 1998 Act and

---

[68] Education Act 1998, s 6, amended by Child and Family Agency Act 2013, s 97 and Sch 2.

there is much overlap between those functions and the objectives set out in s 6. For example, schools must use their resources to ensure that the educational needs of all students are provided for; ensure that the education provided meets the requirements of the national education policy; promote the development of the Irish language; and establish systems for accountability and transparency.[69]

Section 9(d) provides that the school shall "promote the moral, spiritual, social and personal development of students and provide health education for them, in consultation with their parents, having regard to the characteristic spirit of the school."[70] There are echoes here of Art 29 UNCRC which requires that the education of the child should be directed at the child's personal development and integration in society. A difference is that, in the Irish legislation, this education is to be provided in consultation with the parents and with regard to the "characteristic spirit" of the school. The "characteristic spirit" of the school refers to "the cultural, educational, moral, religious, social, linguistic and spiritual values and traditions" which inform the objectives and conduct of the school.[71] This proviso is unsurprising in the context of an Irish school system which is largely denominational in nature and is therefore protective of the religious ethos of individual schools. In Ireland, approximately 90 percent of primary schools are Catholic denominational schools, six percent are run by other religious denominations, and the remainder are made up of non-denominational and multi-denominational primary schools.[72] Hence, the majority of primary schools in Ireland are run in accordance with the values and traditions of the Catholic Church.

Section 9(m) of the 1998 Act provides that schools must establish and maintain an admissions policy which provides for maximum accessibility to the school. The Board of Management is responsible for the admissions policy. It is required to publish the policy and ensure that

> "principles of equality and the right of parents to send their children to a school of the parents' choice are respected and such directions as may be made from time to time by the Minister, having regard to the characteristic spirit of the

---

[69] Education Act 1998, s 9.
[70] Education Act 1998, s 9(d).
[71] Education Act 1998, s 15(2)(b).
[72] Oireachtas Library and Research Service, "Choosing segregation? The implications of school choice" *Spotlight* (No 1 of 2015), p 6.

school and the constitutional rights of all persons concerned, are complied with."[73]

Where parents apply to enrol their children in a particular school, the child will be admitted as long as places are available. Unfortunately, many schools are oversubscribed and so some pupils will not obtain a place in the school of their first choice due to the admissions policy of that school. For this reason, school admissions policies have come under increasing scrutiny in recent years. School admissions are discussed in detail later in the chapter.

Section 7 of the 1998 Act establishes the functions of the Minister for Education. Among the Minister's functions is the duty to ensure that that there is made available to each person resident in the State, including a person with a disability or who has other special educational needs, support services and a level and quality of education appropriate to meeting the needs and abilities of that person.[74] This section gives legislative effect to Art 42.4 of the Constitution, which imposes a duty on the State to provide for free primary education. Notably, while Art 42.4 only imposes a duty on the State to provide for free primary education, s 7 of the 1998 Act applies equally to primary and post-primary schools.

(b) Education (Welfare) Act 2000

The Education (Welfare) Act 2000 (the "2000 Act") was introduced to create a system of compulsory education for children up to the age of 16 years. It provides a system for monitoring school attendance and for addressing absenteeism, in addition to ensuring that the education provided meets the standard of "a certain minimum education" discussed earlier. Tusla has responsibility for ensuring that children attend a recognised school or otherwise receive a certain minimum education.[75] This function is undertaken by the Educational Welfare Services (EWS) of Tusla.[76]

i. School Attendance

Under s 17 of the 2000 Act, parents are required to send their children to recognised schools (or to register them for assessment

---

[73] Education Act 1998, s 15(2)(d).
[74] Education Act 1998, s 7(1)(a).
[75] Education (Welfare) Act 2000, s 10, as amended by Child and Family Agency Act 2013, s 72.
[76] Previously, the National Educational Welfare Board (NEWB) undertook this function. The Child and Family Agency Act 2013 transferred the functions of NEWB to Tusla.

as receiving education elsewhere), subject to limited exceptions.[77] For the purpose of the 2000 Act, a child is defined as being between 6 and 16 years of age, but includes a child who has not completed three years of post-primary education, whichever occurs later, up to the age of 18 years.[78] The 2000 Act also puts in place procedures to address absenteeism. Where a child is absent from school during part of a school day, or longer, the parent is required to notify the principal of the school.[79] The principal, in turn, must keep a register of attendance. If the student is absent for more than 20 days, or if in the opinion of the principal, the student is not attending regularly, the principal must notify an educational welfare officer (EWO) who will subsequently consult with the student and his or her parents with the aim of achieving the continued education of the child and his or her full participation in school.[80] Under s 22, the school must adopt a proactive strategy to reduce absenteeism. It must devise a "statement of strategy" to be used to reward students who have a good school attendance record; identify, at an early stage, students who are at risk of developing school attendance problems; establish closer contacts with the families of students who are at risk of poor attendance; foster and promote contact with other schools and bodies providing youth work programmes with a view to developing programmes of activities designed to encourage the full participation of students in the life of the school.[81]

Under s 25, notice can be served on a parent who is failing or neglecting to cause his or her child to attend a recognised school. Should the parent fail to comply with this notice, they will be guilty of a criminal offence and liable to a fine or to imprisonment if convicted.[82]

ii. School Discipline

Section 23 of the 2000 Act requires that the school puts in place a code of behaviour for its students. Before registering a child as a student, the school must provide the parents of the child with a copy of the code of behaviour. The code must specify:

> "(a) the standards of behaviour that shall be observed by each student attending the school;

---

[77] Education (Welfare) Act 2000, s 17.
[78] Education (Welfare) Act 2000, s 2.
[79] Education (Welfare) Act 2000, s 18.
[80] Education (Welfare) Act 2000, s 21.
[81] Education (Welfare) Act 2000, s 22.
[82] Education (Welfare) Act 2000, s 25(4).

(b) the measures that may be taken when a student fails or refuses to observe those standards;

(c) the procedures to be followed before a student may be suspended or expelled from the school concerned;

(d) the grounds for removing a suspension imposed in relation to a student; and

(e) the procedures to be followed relating to notification of a child's absence from school."[83]

Where a student does not comply with the code of practice, he or she may be expelled from, or suspended by, the school in accordance with the procedures set out in the code. "Suspension" refers to the situation where the student is required to absent himself/herself from the school for a specified period of school days, while "expulsion" refers to the situation where a student is permanently excluded from a particular school.[84]

Before a student is expelled from a school, the school must notify the educational welfare officer (EWO) of the reasons for the expulsion. The EWO must then take all reasonable efforts to ensure that provision is made for the continued education of the student to whom the notification relates. The student may not be expelled from the school within 20 days of notifying the EWO, although he or she could be suspended during this period.[85]

The guidance document *Developing a Code of Behaviour: Guidelines for Schools* provides advice for schools in relation to developing a school code of behaviour.[86] The guidelines emphasise that the school must apply fair procedures when proposing to suspend or expel a student. The student has the right to be heard and the right to impartiality in the investigation and decision-making process.[87] The procedures for suspension and expulsion must be clearly set out in the code of practice. The decision to suspend a student must be based on serious factors such as:

• the student's behaviour has had a seriously detrimental effect on the education of other students;

---

[83] Education (Welfare) Act 2000, s 23(2).

[84] National Educational Welfare Board, *Developing a Code of Behaviour: Guidelines for Schools* (May 2008), pp 70 and 80.

[85] Education (Welfare) Act 2000, s 24.

[86] National Educational Welfare Board, *Developing a Code of Behaviour: Guidelines for Schools* (May 2008).

[87] National Educational Welfare Board, *Developing a Code of Behaviour: Guidelines for Schools* (May 2008), p 67.

- the student's continued presence in the school at this time constitutes a threat to safety;
- the student is responsible for serious damage to property.[88]

The suspension must be proportionate to the behaviour that is causing concern and should normally be preceded by other interventions, for example peer mediation, restorative justice approaches or family conferencing. The school must also have a plan in place to allow for the successful re-integration of the student into the school following the suspension "to avoid the possibility that suspension starts or amplifies a cycle of academic failure."[89] The student's emotions and non-academic needs must be addressed in the re-integration plan.

Expulsion must also be a proportionate response to the student's behaviour and should only be considered in the most extreme cases, such as where:

- the student's behaviour is a persistent cause of significant disruption to the learning of others or to the teaching process;
- the student's continued presence in the school constitutes a real and significant threat to safety;
- the student is responsible for serious damage to property.[90]

The school must take steps to try to avoid the expulsion, such as meeting with parents and the student to try to find ways of helping the student to change their behaviour, ensuring that all other possible options have been tried, and seeking the assistance of support agencies such as Child and Adolescent Mental Health Services.[91] The school must have exhausted all alternative options before turning to expulsion.

(c) Education for Persons with Special Educational Needs Act 2004

The Education for Persons with Special Educational Needs Act

---

[88] National Educational Welfare Board, *Developing a Code of Behaviour: Guidelines for Schools* (May 2008), p 71.
[89] National Educational Welfare Board, *Developing a Code of Behaviour: Guidelines for Schools* (May 2008), p 77.
[90] National Educational Welfare Board, *Developing a Code of Behaviour: Guidelines for Schools* (May 2008), p 81.
[91] National Educational Welfare Board, *Developing a Code of Behaviour: Guidelines for Schools* (May 2008), p 80.

2004 (the "2004 Act") provides a framework to ensure that people with special educational needs have the same right to avail of, and benefit from, appropriate education as their peers. It aims to assist children with special educational needs to leave school with the skills necessary to participate, to the level of their capacity, in an inclusive way in the social and economic activities of society and to live independent and fulfilled lives.[92] It should be noted, however, that many provisions of this legislation have yet to be commenced.

For the purpose of the 2004 Act, special educational needs refer to

> "a restriction in the capacity of the person to participate in and benefit from education on account of an enduring physical, sensory, mental health or learning disability, or any other condition which results in a person learning differently from a person without that condition."[93]

Section 2 of the Act provides that a child with special educational needs shall be educated in an inclusive environment with children who do not have such needs unless the nature or degree of the child's needs is such that to do so would be inconsistent with the best interests of the child or the effective provision of education for other children.[94]

In line with the principle of integration, as set out in s 2 of the 2004 Act, children with special educational needs may be educated

- in special schools;
- in special classes attached to ordinary schools;
- in integrated settings in mainstream classes.

The type of education that is provided will depend on an assessment of the child's individual education needs. The 2004 Act makes provision for this and for identifying and providing the services that the child requires in order to be able to participate in, and benefit from, education.[95] The school attended by a student with special educational needs must also create an education plan which sets out how the educational needs of that student will be met by the school,[96] and must periodically review that plan at least once a year.[97]

---

[92] Education for Persons with Special Educational Needs Act 2004, Long Title.
[93] Education for Persons with Special Educational Needs Act 2004, s 1.
[94] Education for Persons with Special Educational Needs Act 2004, s 2.
[95] Education for Persons with Special Educational Needs Act 2004, ss 4–7.
[96] Education for Persons with Special Educational Needs Act 2004, s 3.
[97] Education for Persons with Special Educational Needs Act 2004, s 11.

The National Council for Special Needs Education (NCSE) has responsibility for ensuring that special needs education is carried out effectively in Ireland. Its aim is to improve the delivery of education services to persons with special educational needs arising from disabilities.[98] NCSE provides services through a national network of Special Educational Needs Organisers (SENOs) who provide resources to support children with special educational needs.[99] Each SENO has responsibility for specific schools (primary, secondary and special schools) within their area. The role of the SENO is to ensure that a child with special educational needs receives the supports they are entitled to. When a school reviews its education plan concerning a particular child with special educational needs, the outcome must be reported to the parents and to the SENO.[100]

Bullying in Schools

School should be a safe space for children to foster their personal development and academic competence. For some students, however, school does not provide a tranquil escape into education. Unfortunately, and despite the best efforts of schools, the educational setting remains a breeding ground for bullying behaviour. As such, it is incumbent on schools to have appropriate procedures in place to protect children from the harmful effects of bullying.

In accordance with the Education (Welfare) Act 2000 all schools must have an up-to-date anti-bullying policy set out in their code of behaviour. The Board of Management of a school must have policies to prevent or address bullying and harassment and these policies should be set out in the code of practice.[101] Positive school culture plays an important role in tackling bullying behaviour and any policy that aims to reduce bullying must adopt a school-wide approach in order for it to be effective. In this approach, bullying is the responsibility of the whole school, including management, staff, pupils and parents.

The Department of Education and Skills published *Anti-Bullying Procedures for Primary and Post-Primary Schools* in September 2013.[102]

---

[98] Education for Persons with Special Educational Needs Act 2004, s 20.
[99] Education for Persons with Special Educational Needs Act 2004, s 26.
[100] Education for Persons with Special Educational Needs Act 2004, s 11(2).
[101] Education (Welfare) Act 2000, s 23.
[102] Department of Education and Skills, *Anti-Bullying Procedures for Primary and Post-Primary Schools* (September 2013).

The purpose of these procedures is to give direction and guidance to schools in preventing and tackling school-based bullying. The procedures define bullying as "unwanted negative behaviour, verbal, psychological or physical conducted, by an individual or group against another person (or persons) and which is repeated over time."[103] This definition includes:

- deliberate exclusion, malicious gossip and other forms of relational bullying;
- cyber-bullying; and
- identity-based bullying such as homophobic bullying, racist bullying, bullying based on a person's membership of the Traveller community and bullying of those with disabilities or special educational needs.[104]

The procedures note that an effective anti-bullying policy must include

"prevention and awareness raising measures across all aspects of bullying and involves strategies to engage pupils in addressing problems when they arise. In particular, such strategies need to build empathy, respect and resilience in pupils."[105]

The procedures establish an anti-bullying policy template that must be used by all schools, primary and post-primary. Certain aspects of the template are mandatory while others allow flexibility to enable each individual school to tailor their anti-bullying policy to their own needs and to the needs of their students. The template requires that schools develop education and prevention measures to address all forms of bullying behaviour. The school's anti-bullying policy must also set out the school's procedures for investigating and dealing with bullying and the school's procedures for the formal recording of bullying behaviour. In addition to adopting an official anti-bullying policy, the school is under a duty to implement it—the policy cannot gather dust on the shelf.

In the case of physical injury resulting from bullying or unruliness at school, the school may be liable in negligence if it is found to have breached its duty of care towards the student in question.

---

[103] Department of Education and Skills, *Anti-Bullying Procedures for Primary and Post-Primary Schools* (September 2013), p 8.
[104] Department of Education and Skills, *Anti-Bullying Procedures for Primary and Post-Primary Schools* (September 2013), p 8.
[105] Department of Education and Skills, *Anti-Bullying Procedures for Primary and Post-Primary Schools* (September 2013), p 25.

This issue was addressed by the High Court in the case of *Mulvey (A Minor) v McDonagh*.[106] In this case, a student claimed damages for personal injuries suffered by her from an assault by a fellow pupil at school when she was aged 4 years. She claimed that the school had been negligent in failing to monitor the conduct of the pupils. She alleged that she had been bullied since the previous October, and that numerous complaints had been made to the school. The High Court found that the duty of care required by a school was that of

> "a prudent parent exercising reasonable care and … that must be taken in the context of a prudent parent behaving reasonably with a class of 28 four year olds having their first experience of mingling socially with other children."[107]

In the particular circumstances of the case, the school was found not to have breached this duty of care towards the student.

In *Murphy v County Wexford VEC*,[108] a student suffered a severe injury when he was struck in the eye by a chocolate bar thrown by another pupil while at school. Although a teacher had been assigned to supervise the room in which the incident occurred, the area was unsupervised at the time. In the Supreme Court, McCracken J noted that school authorities owe a duty of care to their students to take reasonable care to ensure that they do not suffer injury. To do this, the judge was satisfied that some degree of supervision is required and that the extent of the supervision would depend on a number of factors including

> "the age of the pupils involved, the location of the places where the pupils congregate, the number of pupils which may be present at any one time and the general propensity of pupils at that particular school to act dangerously."[109]

In the instant case, the school had a history of serious disciplinary problems and, as a result, had introduced a supervision rota system. Ultimately, it was held that the particular circumstances of the case imposed a duty of care on the school to provide supervision at lunch time in accordance with its rota system and that the failure to do so constituted negligence.

---

[106] *Mulvey (A Minor) v McDonagh* [2004] 1 IR 497.
[107] *Mulvey (A Minor) v McDonagh* [2004] 1 IR 497 at para 33.
[108] *Murphy v County Wexford VEC* [2004] 4 IR 202.
[109] *Murphy v County Wexford VEC* [2004] 4 IR 202 at para 27.

In *Maher (A Minor) v Presentation School Mullingar*,[110] a student had suffered a severe injury to his eye when he was struck by a pencil which had been shot towards him by another pupil using a rubber band. The plaintiff's claim for negligence was dismissed by the High Court. Here, the High Court endorsed the duty of care set out in *Murphy v County Wexford VEC* and the fact that the extent of supervision of students will depend on a number of factors. In the instant case, the High Court was satisfied that the standard of supervision was satisfactory and that the only way to provide additional insurance against incidents occurring would be

> "to search each child's person and schoolbag upon arrival and that is an unreasonable burden and one not required in my opinion in discharge of the duty of care owed by the school to its pupils."[111]

According to the High Court, a school "is expected to be no more and no less vigilant of those in its care than a prudent parent would be in his or her own home."[112] The High Court held that

> "simply because an injury takes place in a school does not mean that the school management or any individual teacher has been negligent. Negligence must be established and in this case I find no such evidence."[113]

The incident was found to have occurred "out of the blue" and not to have been reasonably foreseeable.

These cases underline the importance of providing appropriate levels of supervision in schools to protect children from injury. Although some of the cases mentioned are not strictly about bullying *per se*, they highlight the fact that a failure to address bullying behaviour may render the school liable for negligence. The cases also emphasise the need for appropriate anti-bullying policies in schools to protect children where the harm suffered is as a result of repeated, unwanted negative behaviour. A whole school approach is needed to tackle bullying.

School Admissions Policies

School admissions policies have come under increasing scrutiny

---

[110] *Maher (A Minor) v Presentation School Mullingar* [2004] 4 IR 211.
[111] *Maher (A Minor) v Presentation School Mullingar* [2004] 4 IR 211 at para 29.
[112] *Maher (A Minor) v Presentation School Mullingar* [2004] 4 IR 211 at para 29.
[113] *Maher (A Minor) v Presentation School Mullingar* [2004] 4 IR 211 at para 32.

in recent years as certain provisions of Irish law have effectively allowed schools to discriminate against particular children in their admissions process. As was noted earlier, the Education Act 1998 requires school admissions policies to provide for maximum accessibility to the school, but also to uphold the school's "characteristic spirit."[114] In addition, s 7(3)(c) of the Equal Status Act 2000 provides that where the school promotes certain religious values, it is not discrimination if the school

> "admits persons of a particular religious denomination in preference to others or it refuses to admit as a student a person who is not of that denomination and, in the case of a refusal, it is proved that the refusal is essential to maintain the ethos of the school."[115]

In other words, where a religious school is over-subscribed, it is permitted to refuse to admit a student on the basis of his or her religion. This restriction has been labelled the "baptism barrier",[116] as it allows Ireland's predominately Catholic schools to refuse to admit a student who has not been baptised according to the Catholic faith in order to protect the religious ethos of the school.[117] As discussed below, the Education (Admission to Schools) Bill 2016 proposes to remove the role of religion in school admissions for virtually all primary schools and so the "baptism barrier" may be removed from Irish law in the near future.

Religion is not the only barrier to admission at particular schools; various other practices are adopted by some schools that have the effect of limiting accessibility to that school. For example, it is currently permissible for schools to reserve places for the children of past pupils of the school, thereby excluding other children where the school is oversubscribed. Other schools ask parents to make a voluntary financial contribution to the school when seeking to have their child admitted. This means that the children of parents

---

114 Education Act 1998, s 15(2)(d).
115 Equal Status Act 2000, s 7(3)(c).
116 See, for example: Tim O'Brien, "Baptism barrier: there may be other ways, says Catholic Primate" *The Irish Times* (Dublin, 7 January 2018); David Graham, "Time for schools to face up to the change in Irish society" *Irish Examiner* (Cork, 2 February 2018).
117 *In re Article 26 and the Employment Equality Bill, 1996* [1997] 2 IR 321 at 358, Hamilton CJ held (in the context of religious discrimination in the employment of teachers) that "it is constitutionally permissible to make distinctions or discriminations on grounds of religious profession belief or status insofar—but only insofar—as this may be necessary to give life and reality to the guarantee of the free profession and practice of religion contained in the Constitution."

without the financial means to make such a contribution will be at a disadvantage.

In *Stokes v CBS High School Clonmel*,[118] a mother who was a member of the Travelling Community brought a case against CBS High School Clonmel claiming that the school's inclusion of a "parental rule" in its admissions policy was indirectly discriminatory against members of the Travelling Community. The school's admissions policy gave preferential access to applicants:

- whose parents are seeking to submit their son to a Roman Catholic education in accordance with the mission statement and Christian ethos of the school;
- who already has a brother who attended or is in attendance at the school, or is the child of a past pupil, or has close family ties with the school;
- who attended for his primary school education at one of the schools listed in Schedule Two, being a school within the locality or demographic area of the school.

Where the school was oversubscribed in a particular year, a lottery was carried out to allocate places to those who did not meet the above three criteria. The father of the child in question in the instant case had not attended the school and so the child did not meet the three admissions criteria. The child was also unsuccessful in securing a place at the school on the basis of the admissions lottery but was placed fourth on the waiting list.

The mother argued that the admissions policy was indirectly discriminatory against members of the Travelling Community. She argued that her son had less of a chance of having a father who went to the school as many members of the Travelling Community did not traditionally attend second level education. The Equality Tribunal found in favour of the applicant and ordered the school to offer a place to the child and to review its admissions policy to ensure that it did not indirectly discriminate against pupils in the future. The school appealed the decision to the Circuit Court, which found in favour of the school. The mother appealed to the case to the High Court and subsequently to the Supreme Court.

The Supreme Court noted that, under s 3(1)(c) of the Equal Status Act 2000, discrimination occurs where

"an apparently neutral provision puts a person referred to in

[118] *Stokes v CBS High School Clonmel* [2015] IESC 13.

any paragraph of s 3(2) at a particular disadvantage compared with other persons, unless the provision is objectively justified by a legitimate aim and the means of achieving that aim are appropriate and necessary."[119]

Members of the Travelling Community are specified in s 3(2)(i). Thus, in order for discrimination to be established, the Court noted that it had to be shown that the admissions policy placed the student, as a member of the Travelling Community, at a "particular disadvantage" when compared to persons who are not members of the Travelling Community.[120] In considering the meaning of this phrase, the Supreme Court noted that "particular disadvantage" does not arise at a general level. As such, the fact that the admissions policy generally disadvantaged persons who did not have a father who went to secondary school was "neither here nor there."[121] The Supreme Court found that the central question to be addressed was "[h]as it been shown that a member of the Travelling Community is at a disadvantage compared with a non-Traveller as a result of the measure under challenge?"[122] Statistical information was required to answer this question but the Court was not satisfied that sufficient reliable data was available for this purpose. As a result, the Supreme Court held that "particular disadvantage" could not be proven and it upheld the decision of the High Court and dismissed the appeal.

In its Concluding Observations on Ireland's combined third and fourth periodic reports, the Committee on the Rights of the Child expressed concern in relation to restrictive school admissions policies in Ireland. The Committee recommended that Ireland should amend the existing legislative framework, including the Equal Status Act 2000, to eliminate all such discrimination in school admissions.[123] The current system, in particular the "baptism barrier" negatively impacts on children of minority religions or no religion in Ireland. In many cases, the child's constitutional right to access free primary education under Art 42.4 (as well as his or her right to religious freedom under Art 44.2.1°) of the Constitution cannot be realised, as he or she can be refused a place at the local State primary school where he or she does not conform to the religious ethos of that school. The rights of parents under Art 42.1 to determine the religious education of their children may also

---

[119] Equal Status Act 2000, s 3(1)(c).
[120] *Stokes v CBS High School Clonmel* [2015] IESC 13 at para 2.4.
[121] *Stokes v CBS High School Clonmel* [2015] IESC 13 at para 8.2.
[122] *Stokes v CBS High School Clonmel* [2015] IESC 13 at para 11.3.
[123] Committee on the Rights of the Child, *Concluding observations on the combined third and fourth periodic reports of Ireland* (1 March 2016), p 13.

be impeded as they may feel pressure to baptise their children in a particular religion simply to ensure that the child can secure a place at the local school.[124]

The Education (Admission to Schools) Bill 2016 (the "2016 Bill") proposes to address a range of issues concerning school admissions. The overall objective of the 2016 Bill is to provide a new framework for school enrolment that is designed to ensure that every child is treated fairly and that the way in which schools decide on applications for admission is structured, fair and transparent. The 2016 Bill, if enacted, would require the school to include a statement in its admissions policy that it will not discriminate against any child seeking to be admitted to that school on a number of grounds including gender, family status, religion, sexual orientation and race. The restrictions on gender-based discrimination would not apply to single-sex schools.

The 2016 Bill, as amended at Report Stage, seeks to amend s 7(3)(c) of the Equal Status Act 2000 so as to prohibit State-funded primary schools from giving preference to applicants of a particular religion or denomination in cases where the school is oversubscribed. There is an exception for primary schools where the ethos reflects that of a minority religion.[125] In this case, the school could give preference to an applicant of that minority religion. The objective of this exception is to ensure that children of minority religions are able to find a place in schools aligned to their religious beliefs. However, the school would not be *required* to give preference to children of the minority faith; the school could still admit a child of a different faith in accordance with the admissions policy of the school.

There is no exception in the Bill for denominational schools that adhere to the majority Catholic religion. If the Bill is enacted, these schools would be prohibited from refusing admission to an applicant on the basis of his or her religion. The exception would not apply here because Catholic primary schools make up 2,802 of the total of 3,123 primary schools (90 percent) in the State. As such, a child of Catholic faith would not be prevented from accessing a primary school under Catholic patronage as a result of the proposed provisions since the majority of primary schools in the state currently provide for Catholic religious instruction.

---

[124] Sheils McNamee, "'Like most of my friends, I baptised my children so they could go to school': The anger of Ireland's non-religious parents", *The Journal. ie* (Dublin, 16 May 2016).
[125] For the purpose of the Bill, a minority religion is one whose membership is not in excess of 10 percent of the population of Ireland.

Some groups have claimed that a complete prohibition on schools giving preference to children on the basis of religion would be unconstitutional. For example, in 2018, the Catholic Primary Schools Management Association argued that such a move would conflict with the constitutional protections for parents and religious schools, as parents may be prevented from sending their children to the school of their choosing contrary to Art 42 of the Constitution. Concerns have also been raised in respect of the constitutionality of provisions that restrict the ability of religious denominations to manage their own affairs in line with Art 44.2.5° of the Constitution.[126]

O'Mahony, Daly and Kenny argue that it would not be unconstitutional to prohibit *publicly-funded* denominational schools from giving preference to children based on religion because religious denominations would not be prevented from operating discriminatory admissions policies in *private* religious institutions.[127] In this way, the denominational school could uphold its religious ethos, but it could not demand State funding in doing so. This argument is in line with the reasoning of the *O'Shiel* case, discussed above, where it was held that conditions can be attached to State funding of schools. According to O'Mahony, Daly and Kenny,

> "[m]aking funding conditional on a non-discriminatory admissions policy cannot be argued to be an infringement on a constitutional right to be provided with public funding for denominational schools, since no such positive right exists."[128]

It is encouraging that the Education (Admission to Schools) Bill 2016 proposes to remove the role of religion in school admissions. The current "baptism barrier" creates a significant impediment to the education of children who do not adhere to the majority religion and raises serious questions about the fairness of the system. The proposed amendments, if enacted, would improve the position of children of minority religions or no religion and would level the playing field between these children and the children of Catholic faith in terms of school admissions.

The Report Stage amendments to the 2016 Bill also propose to

---

[126] Carl O'Brien, "Catholic groups warn of legal action over 'Baptism barrier' removal" *Irish Times* (Dublin, 3 January 2018).
[127] Conor O'Mahony, Eoin Daly and David Kenny, *Opinion on the Constitutionality of Reforming s.7(3)(c) of the Equal Status Act 2000* (EQUATE, 2016), p 7.
[128] Conor O'Mahony, Eoin Daly and David Kenny, *Opinion on the Constitutionality of Reforming s.7(3)(c) of the Equal Status Act 2000* (EQUATE, 2016), p 8.

allow schools that provide an education through the medium of Irish to give priority to Irish speaking children. This amendment recognises that there are only a small number of schools, in particular secondary schools, that provide an education though the medium of Irish. The amendment is intended to enable students who have attained a level of proficiency in the Irish language to continue their education through the medium of Irish.

The 2016 Bill also includes provisions in respect of selection criteria for school admissions. The 2016 Bill provides that where a school is oversubscribed, it would be free to decide its own selection criteria but it would be prohibited from taking into account certain factors including:

- a student's prior attendance at a specified category of pre-school;
- the payment of fees or contributions to the school;
- the occupation, financial status, academic ability, skills or aptitude of a student's parents;
- a student's connection to the school by virtue of a member of his or her family attending or having previously attended the school.

The above would not, however, prevent the school from devising selection criteria based on a student's connection to the school by virtue of (i) having a sibling that is attending/previously attended the school or (ii) having a parent or grandparent who previously attended the school, so long as these selection criteria are used to fill not more than 25 percent of the available places at the school.[129]

It is clear from the above that the Education (Admission to Schools) Bill 2016 addresses a range of issues. If enacted, it will significantly reform the system of school admissions in Ireland and will create a fairer and more balanced school admission process for all pupils.

Overview

The provision of education in Ireland is largely dictated by the Constitution. Although there are echoes of Arts 28 and 29 UNCRC in the Irish legal framework, it is clear that the Irish framework remains focused on the rights of parents. In Ireland, the topic of education also raises issues concerning religious freedom due to the

---

[129] Education (Admission to Schools) Bill 2016, as amended in the Select Committee on Education and Skills, s 8.

very high number of denominational schools in the country. The landscape of the education system means that children of a minority religion or no religion sometimes struggle to gain admission to their local school and the ability of children to secure their constitutional right to opt out of religious education is not always realised. A circular issued by the Department of Education and Skills in 2018 has addressed the right to opt-out of religious education in State schools and the Education (Admission to Schools) Bill 2016 proposes to address a range of issues concerning school admissions. As such, it is likely that there will be further changes in this area in years to come.

CHAPTER 9

CONSIDERATIONS FOR THE FUTURE

"Our vision is to make Ireland the best small country in the
world in which to grow up and raise a family, and where
the rights of all children and young people are respected,
protected and fulfilled; where their voices are heard and where
they are supported to realise their maximum potential now
and in the future."[1]

In *Better Outcomes, Brighter Futures: The National Policy Framework
for Children & Young People 2014–2020*, the Irish Government set
itself a sizeable objective, outlined in the quotation above. It is
an impressive commitment, and Irish law, policy and practice
is certainly making progress, but it is arguable whether the title
of "the best small country in the world in which to grow up and
raise a family" can be applied at this time. This book has charted
significant legal developments that have occurred in the areas of
children's rights, parentage, parental responsibilities, adoption,
child protection, participation, and education. However, each
chapter has also outlined areas for potential future reform.
Arguably, these issues need to be addressed before Ireland can be
labelled the "the best small country in the world in which to grow
up and raise a family."

In Chapter 2 of this book, it was noted that Ireland has yet to ratify
the Optional Protocol to the Convention on the Rights of the Child
on the sale of children, child prostitution and child pornography
(OPSC). This Optional Protocol requires that States Parties designate
a specified list of acts and activities as criminal offences in their
legal systems. This list includes sexual exploitation of the child;
engagement of the child in forced labour; improperly inducing
consent; and any involvement in the production, distribution or
possession of child sexual abuse images.[2] The Optional Protocol
also requires that appropriate measures are put in place to protect
the rights and interests of child victims, for example, when
giving evidence as witnesses; in respect of the timing, progress
and disposition of cases; and in relation to provision of support
services.[3] In *Better Outcomes, Brighter Futures: The National Policy
Framework for Children and Young People 2014–2020*, the Government
made commitments to support all efforts to protect children from
sexual abuse, exploitation and trafficking[4] and to provide support

---

[1] *Better Outcomes, Brighter Futures: The National Policy Framework for Children &
    Young People 2014-2020* (Stationery Office, 2014), p 4.
[2] Optional Protocol to the Convention on the Rights of the Child on the sale of
    children, child prostitution and child pornography, Art 3(1).
[3] Optional Protocol to the Convention on the Rights of the Child on the sale of
    children, child prostitution and child pornography, Art 8.
[4] *Better Outcomes, Brighter Futures: The National Policy Framework for Children and*

services for victims of crime.[5] The Government has worked towards these commitments since *Better Outcomes, Brighter Futures* was first published. For example, the Criminal Justice (Victims of Crime) Act 2017 and the Criminal Law (Sexual Offences) Act 2017 contain provisions that are designed to protect children from sexual abuse and introduce safeguards and protections for child victims. The enactment of these Acts has also brought Irish law broadly into compliance with OPSC. It is to be hoped, therefore, that ratification will occur as a matter of priority.

Chapter 3 of this book addressed the topic of parentage. In that chapter, it was noted that a major shortcoming in the current law is the fact that the provisions of the Children and Family Relationships Act 2015 that relate to donor-assisted human reproduction (DAHR) have yet to be commenced. This means that the provisions do not yet have any legal effect and so parentage continues to be determined by recourse to the traditional laws.[6] Another major lacuna in this area is the absence of any specific legislation to address the allocation of parentage in cases of surrogacy. The Assisted Reproduction Bill 2017 was approved for drafting on 3 October 2017 and it proposes to address the area of surrogacy, along with other aspects of reproduction. In Chapter 3, it was argued that the model of parentage proposed in the 2017 Bill does not adequately address the interests of all stakeholders in the surrogacy process. Instead, it was argued that a pre-conception model of parentage should be introduced. Nonetheless, whatever its ultimate form, the 2017 Bill will be subject to much debate in the near future and will likely result in legislative changes in this area in due course.

In Chapter 4, it was suggested that consideration should be given to the Law Reform Commission's recommendation that the terms "guardianship", "custody" and "access" be amended. Although this change in wording would not alter the scope of each role, it may encourage a more child-centred approach to the care of children. Given that the current definition of guardianship seems to prioritise the rights of the adult *over* the child, rather than

---

Young People 2014–2020 (Stationery Office, 2014), Commitments 3.13, 3.14, and 3.15.

[5] *Better Outcomes, Brighter Futures: The National Policy Framework for Children and Young People 2014–2020* (Stationery Office, 2014), Commitment 3.10.

[6] It should be noted that, once the provisions are commenced, it will be possible to apply to court to retrospectively allocate parentage in the case of children born following the use of a DAHR procedure at any time prior to the coming into force of the legislation. See: Children and Family Relationships Act 2015, ss 21 and 22.

the responsibilities of the adult *towards* the child, the change in language may prove particularly beneficial in the Irish context to remind the guardian of his or her responsibilities. Chapter 4 also examined the current procedures for hearing the voice of the child in guardianship, custody and access proceedings and identified some shortcomings in this area. For example, it was noted that provisions to allow for the appointment of a guardian ad litem in proceedings concerning guardianship, custody and access were never commenced.[7] In addition, where an expert is appointed to facilitate the expression of the child's views in legal proceedings, the fees and expenses of the expert must be paid by the parties to the proceedings.[8] These issues need to be addressed to ensure that the child's views can be heard and considered in legal proceedings concerning guardianship, custody and access and to adequately give effect to the obligations created by Art 42A.4.2° of the Irish Constitution.

Chapter 5 documented recent changes to Irish adoption law. It was noted that further reforms have been tabled in the Adoption (Information and Tracing) Bill 2016. This Bill proposes to provide for a scheme whereby adoption information, including the information required to obtain a birth certificate, may be provided to an adopted person in certain circumstances and subject to conditions. These provisions will be subject to debate in the not-too-distant future and the legislature will be forced to consider whether the current proposals adequately balance and vindicate the right to identity of the adopted person with the right to privacy of the birth parents. The Minister for Children will also publish her report on open adoption by November 2019. As such, that area of adoption law is likely also to be subject to discussion and scrutiny in the coming months and years.

Chapter 6 highlighted a number of failings in Ireland's child protection system. It was noted throughout that Chapter that there is currently a lack of co-ordination between child protection services[9]; foster care services often fall short of what is required[10]; and there are issues concerning the current system for Garda

---

[7] Guardianship of Infants Act 1964, s 28, inserted by Children Act 1997, s 11.

[8] Guardianship of Infants Act 1964, s 32(9), inserted by Children and Family Relationships Act 2015, s 63; Family Law Act 1995, s 47(4).

[9] Geoffrey Shannon, *Audit of the exercise by An Garda Síochána of the provisions of Section 12 of the Child Care Act 1991* (2017).

[10] HIQA, *Statutory foster care service inspection report. Mid-West Region* (13 March – 16 March 2017); Ombudsman for Children's Office, *Molly's* case: How Tusla and the HSE provided and coordinated supports for a child with a disability in the care of the State* (OCO, 2018).

vetting. Given that children in care are among the most vulnerable in the State, these and others matters noted in the chapter must be addressed as a matter of urgency.

Chapter 7 addressed the provisions of Irish law that concern the representation and participation of children in legal proceedings. Among other things, the chapter examined the suitability of proposals to reform the guardian ad litem (GAL) service set out in the General Scheme of the Child Care (Amendment) Bill 2017. This Bill proposes to introduce significant changes to the GAL system and the provisions will be subject to scrutiny going forward. This chapter also examined the concept of the child-friendly judgment. It is to be hoped that this form of judicial decision-making will become more common in the coming years to ensure that children are central to the narrative of decision-making and that they are recognised as one of the audiences for legal judgments.

A myriad of issues pertaining to the future of Ireland's laws concerning education were discussed in Chapter 8. The chapter discussed proposed future changes in this area, such as proposed reforms to school admissions policies contained in the Education (Admission to Schools) Bill 2016. The role of religion in school admission policies is currently subject to considerable debate in Ireland as some schools are accused of instituting a "baptism barrier" to admission. The 2016 Bill proposes to remove the role of religion in school admissions and to do so before the 2019/20 academic year. It is likely that this will continue to be an area of debate for some time to come.

There are clearly issues that need to be addressed throughout the child law system in order to fully protect children and to ensure that their best interests are secured. It is encouraging that proposals for reform have been put forward to tackle many pressing issues. If and when future reforms are forthcoming, action is required and any subsequent legislation must be commenced without delay. Far too many enacted provisions in different areas of child law languish uncommenced on the statute books. It is to be hoped that outstanding areas will be addressed without delay to ensure that the whole child law system operates cohesively to fully vindicate all of the rights of Irish children. Perhaps then the title of "best small country in the world in which to grow up" can be revisited.

United Nations Convention on
    the Rights of the Child
    (UNCRC)—*contd.*
ECtHR and 15
education, right to 207-11
General Comments 27-8
general/guiding principles 17-22
generally 3, 13, 14, 15-28, 43-4
Ireland
    implementation in 25-7
    ratification in 3, 15, 25
minimum standards 3, 15-16, 22
monitoring implementation of 25-7
non-discrimination 17-18
Optional Protocols 22-5, 249-50
parents, role of 13
participation rights 16
periodic reports 25
protecting children from harm 147
protection rights 16
provision rights 16
right to life, survival and
    development 20-1
sale of children 23-4, 249-50
State, role of 13
    Article 4 16-17

Unmarried fathers
    guardianship and *see*
        Guardianship
Unmarried parents
    subsequent marriage of 39-40
    succession rights of child 30, 31-2

Video link
    evidence by 195-6
Violence
    corporal punishment 174-8
    household violence 80
    right to freedom from 20-1, 211
Voting age 26

War *see* Armed conflict
Welfare of the child
    best interests of the child and 78-9
    custody and 37-8
    moral welfare 79
    presumption in favour of marital
        family 36-40
    religious welfare 79